THIS LAND IS MY LAND

A **GRAPHIC HISTORY**
of **BIG DREAMS,**
MICRONATIONS,
and Other
SELF-MADE STATES

By **Andy Warner**
and
Sofie Louise Dam

CHRONICLE BOOKS
SAN FRANCISCO

Library of Congress Cataloging-in-Publication Data available.

ISBN: 978-1-4521-7018-3

Manufactured in China.

MIX
Paper from responsible sources
FSC™ C136333

Artwork and design by Sofie Louise Dam.

10 9 8 7 6 5 4 3 2 1

Chronicle Books LLC
680 Second Street
San Francisco, California 94107
www.chroniclebooks.com

Andy

For Will & Ollie & the dream of a better world

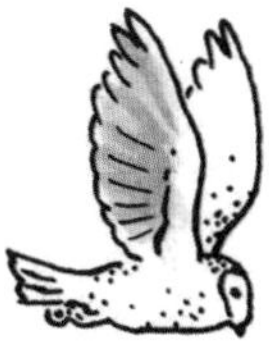

Sofie

For my parents

INTRODUCTION

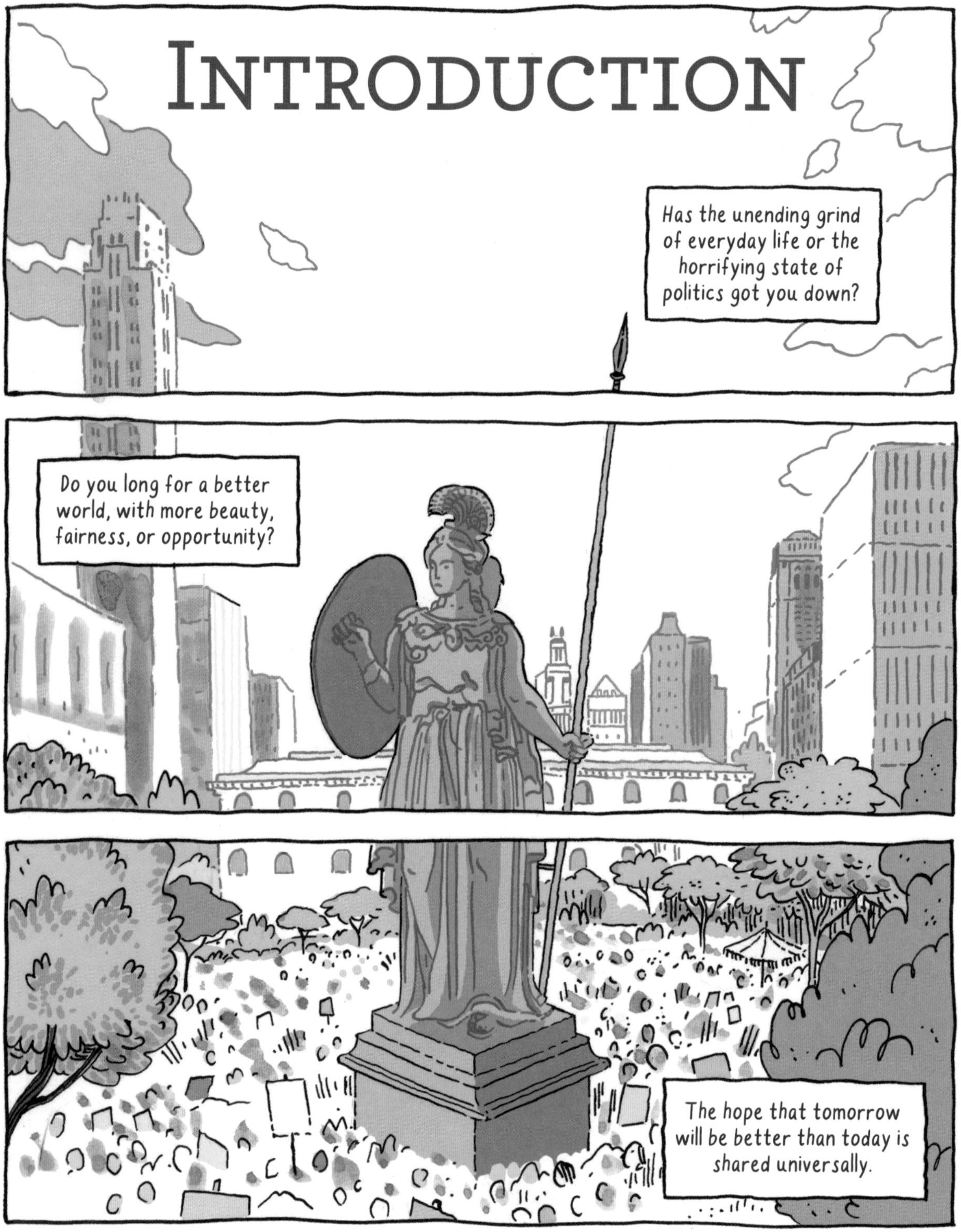
Has the unending grind of everyday life or the horrifying state of politics got you down?
Do you long for a better world, with more beauty, fairness, or opportunity?
The hope that tomorrow will be better than today is shared universally.

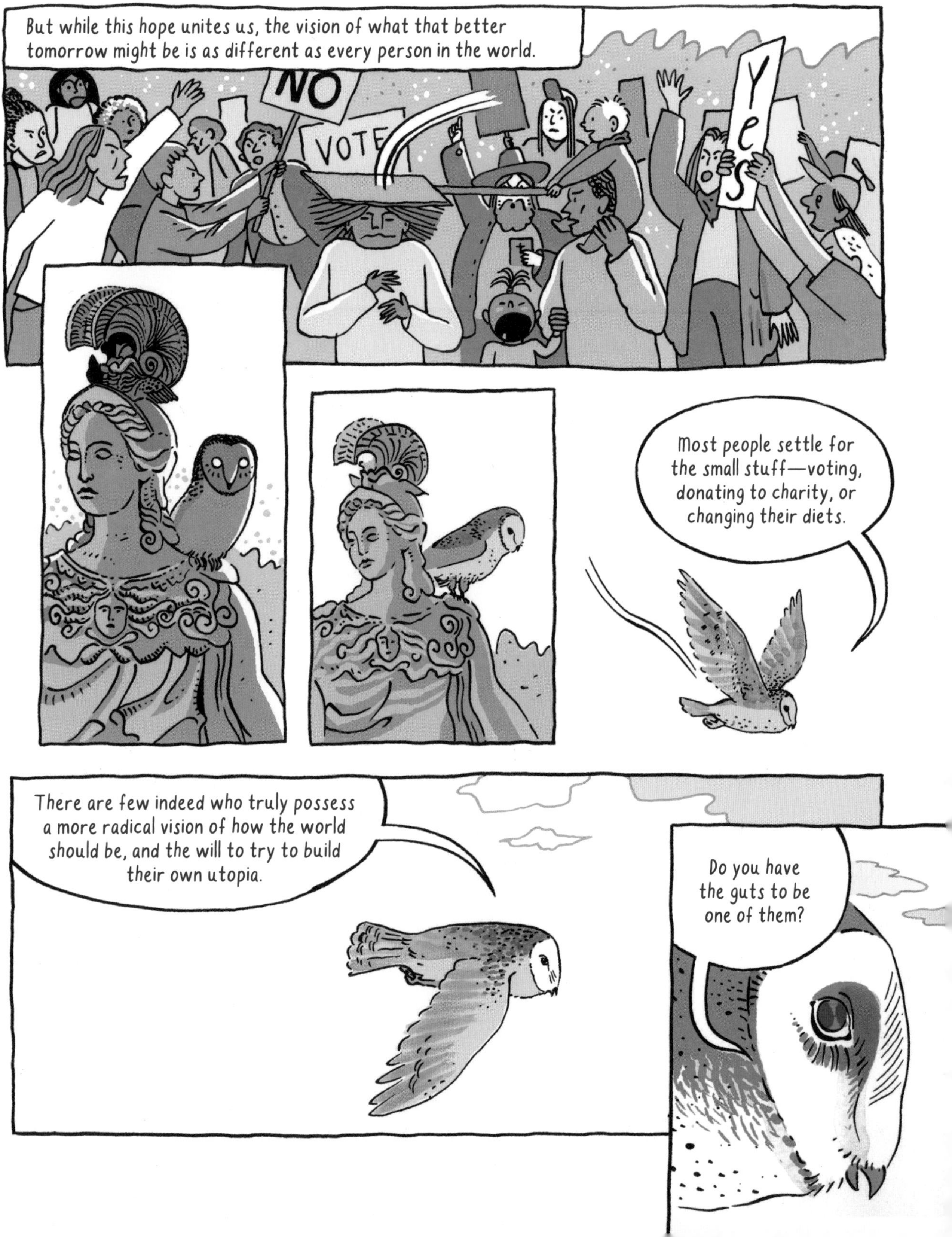

But while this hope unites us, the vision of what that better tomorrow might be is as different as every person in the world.
NO
VOTE
YES
Most people settle for the small stuff—voting, donating to charity, or changing their diets.
There are few indeed who truly possess a more radical vision of how the world should be, and the will to try to build their own utopia.
Do you have the guts to be one of them?

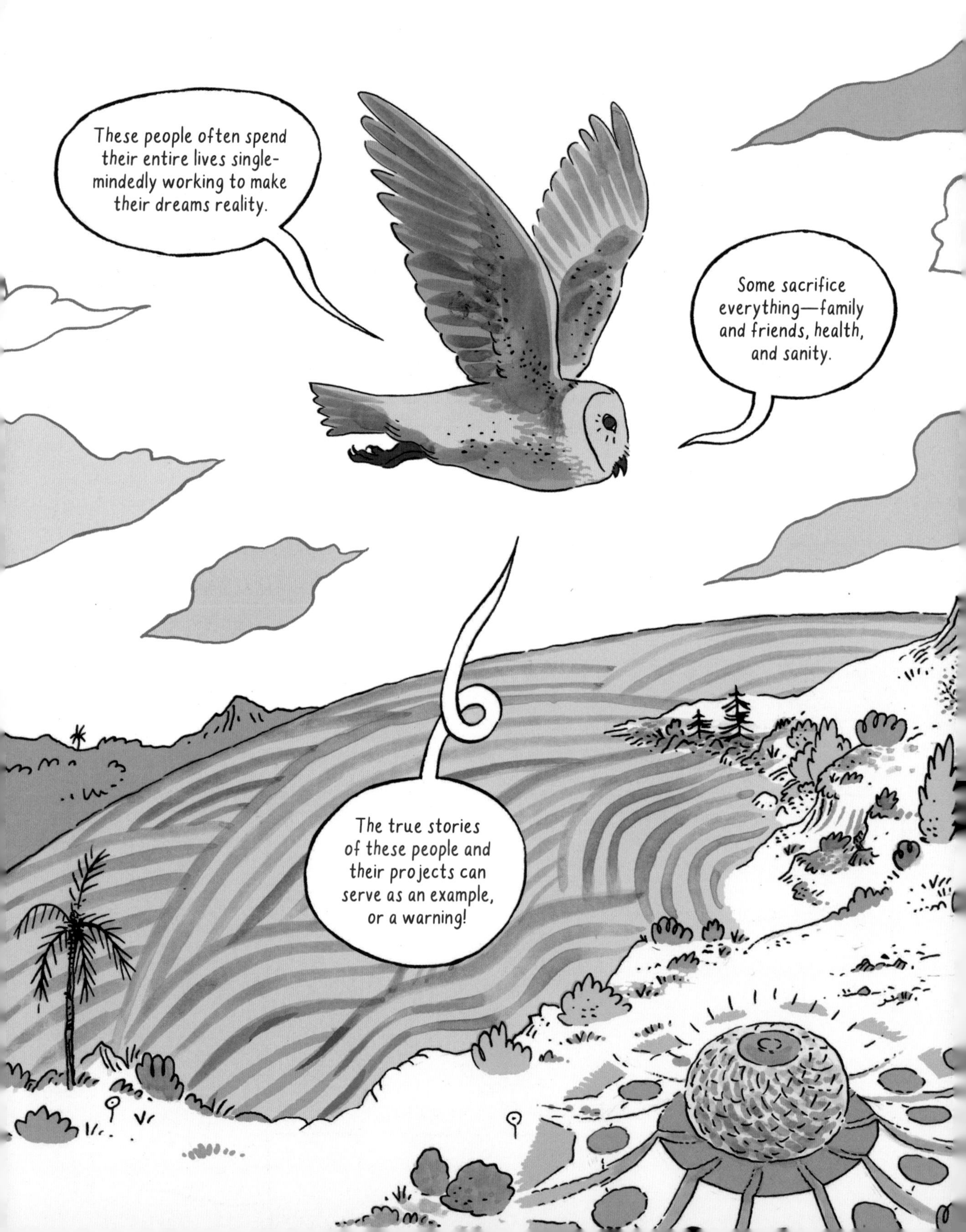
These people often spend their entire lives single-mindedly working to make their dreams reality.
Some sacrifice everything—family and friends, health, and sanity.
The true stories of these people and their projects can serve as an example, or a warning!

This book is divided into five chapters:

I Intentional Communities
Groups of people who choose to radically remake their social structures.

II Micronations
Brief histories of the tiny, unrecognized nations of the world.

III Failed Utopias
The bigger the experiment, the harder it falls.

IV Visionary Environments
Stories of wonderful and bizarre places where individuals make their visions reality.

V Strange Dreams
Proposals, plans, and schemes, never brought to pass.

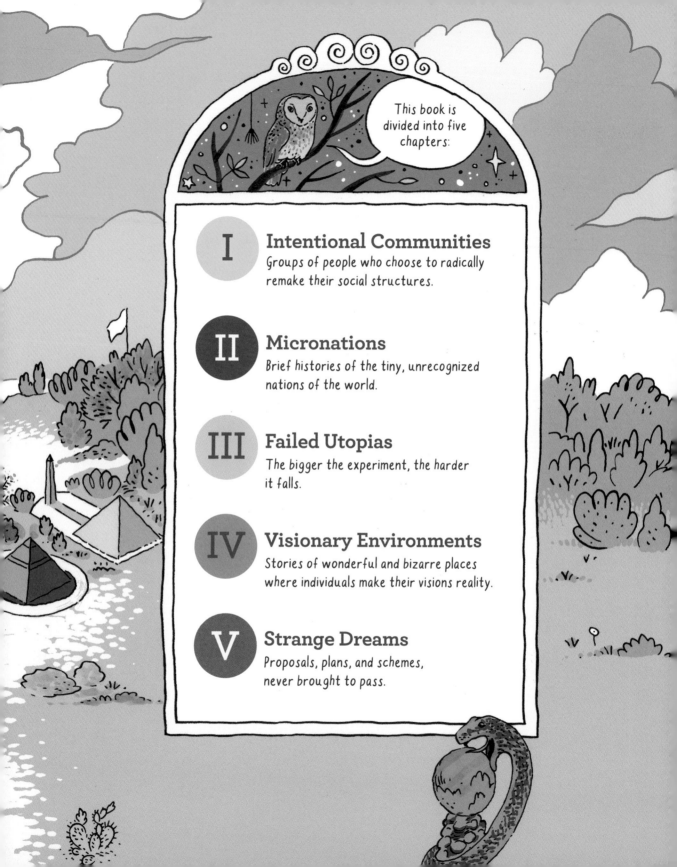

Contents

I

II

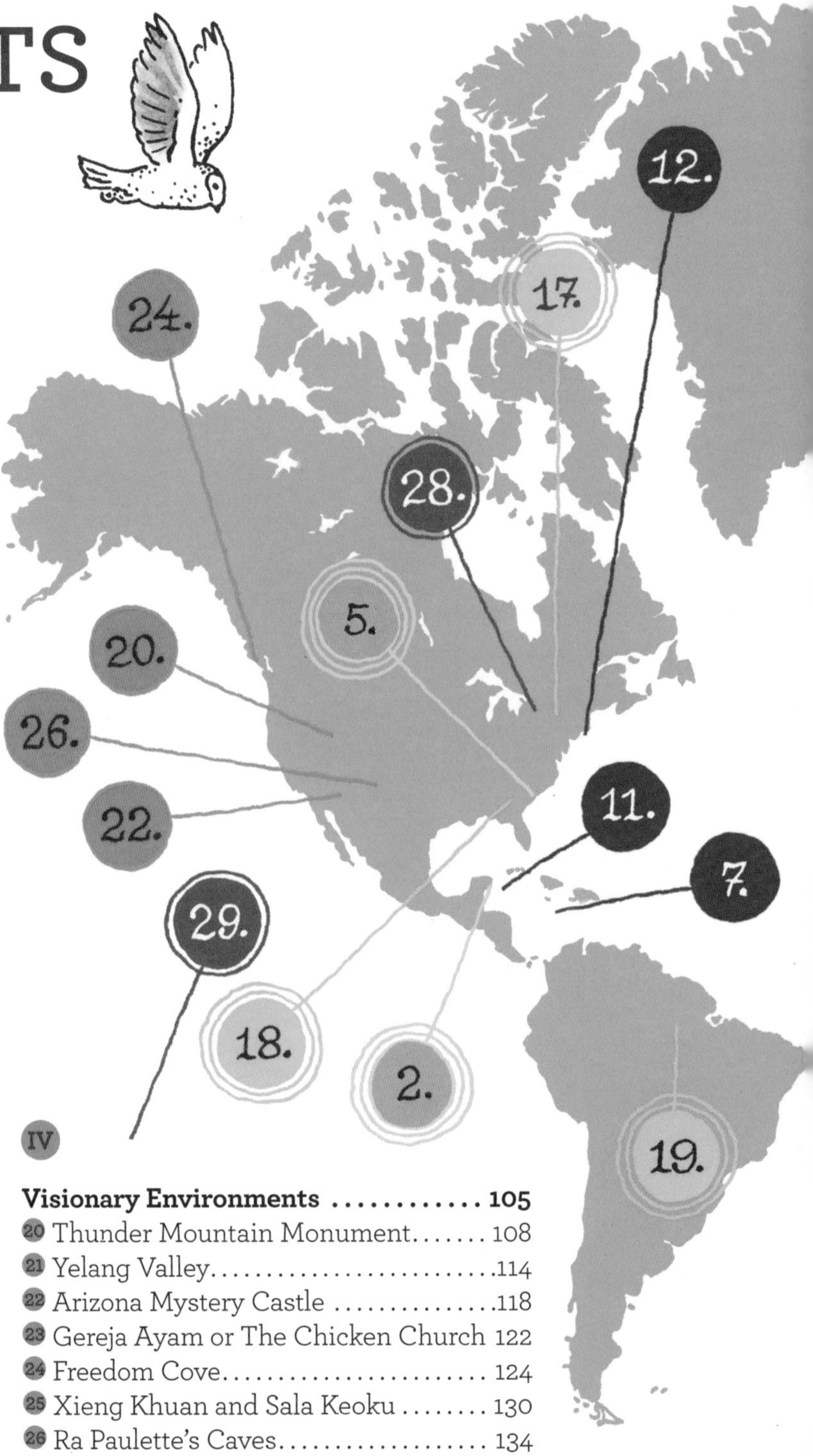
24.
17.
12.
28.
5.
20.
26.
22.
11.
7.
29.
18.
2.
19.

III

IV

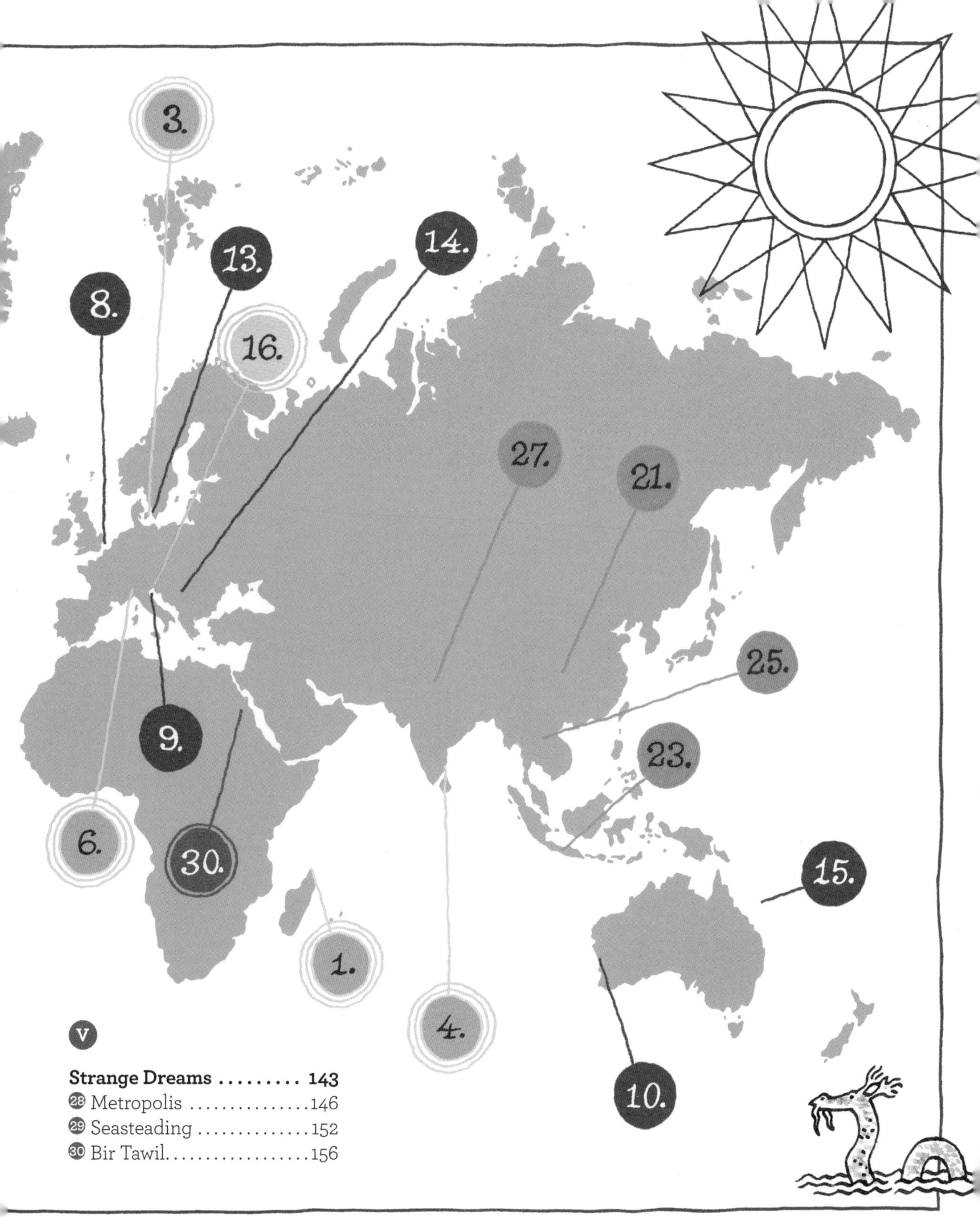
3.
8.
13.
14.
16.
27.
21.
25.
9.
23.
6.
30.
15.
1.
4.
10.

V

Strange Dreams **143**

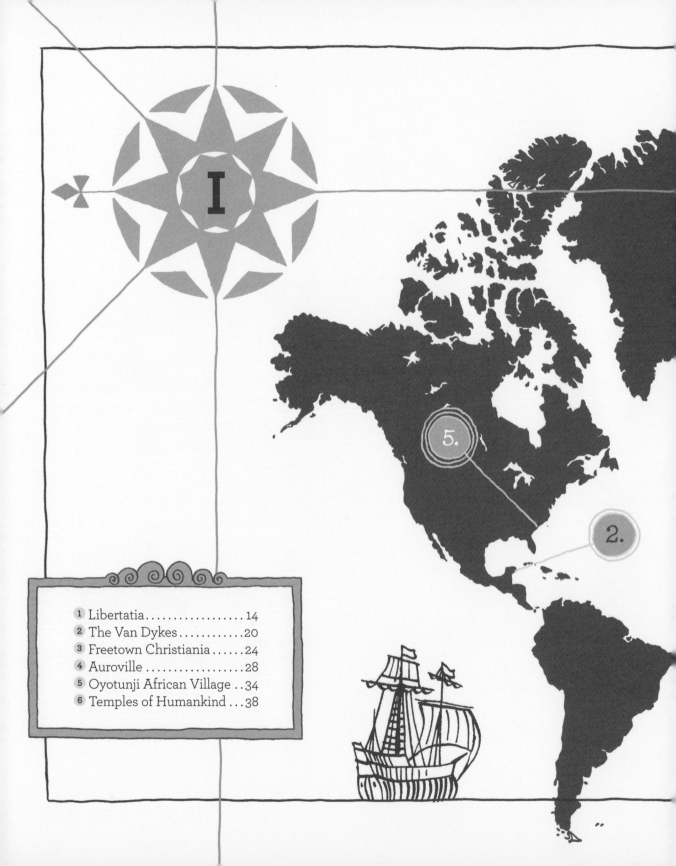

I

INTENTIONAL COMMUNITIES

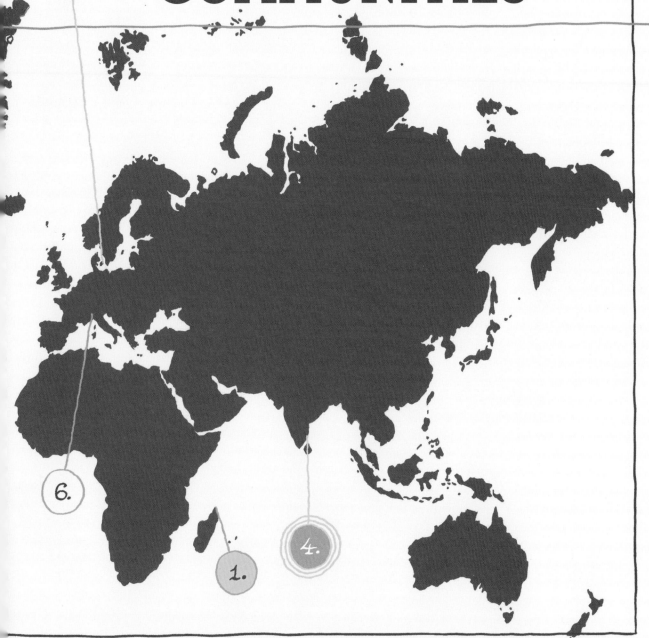

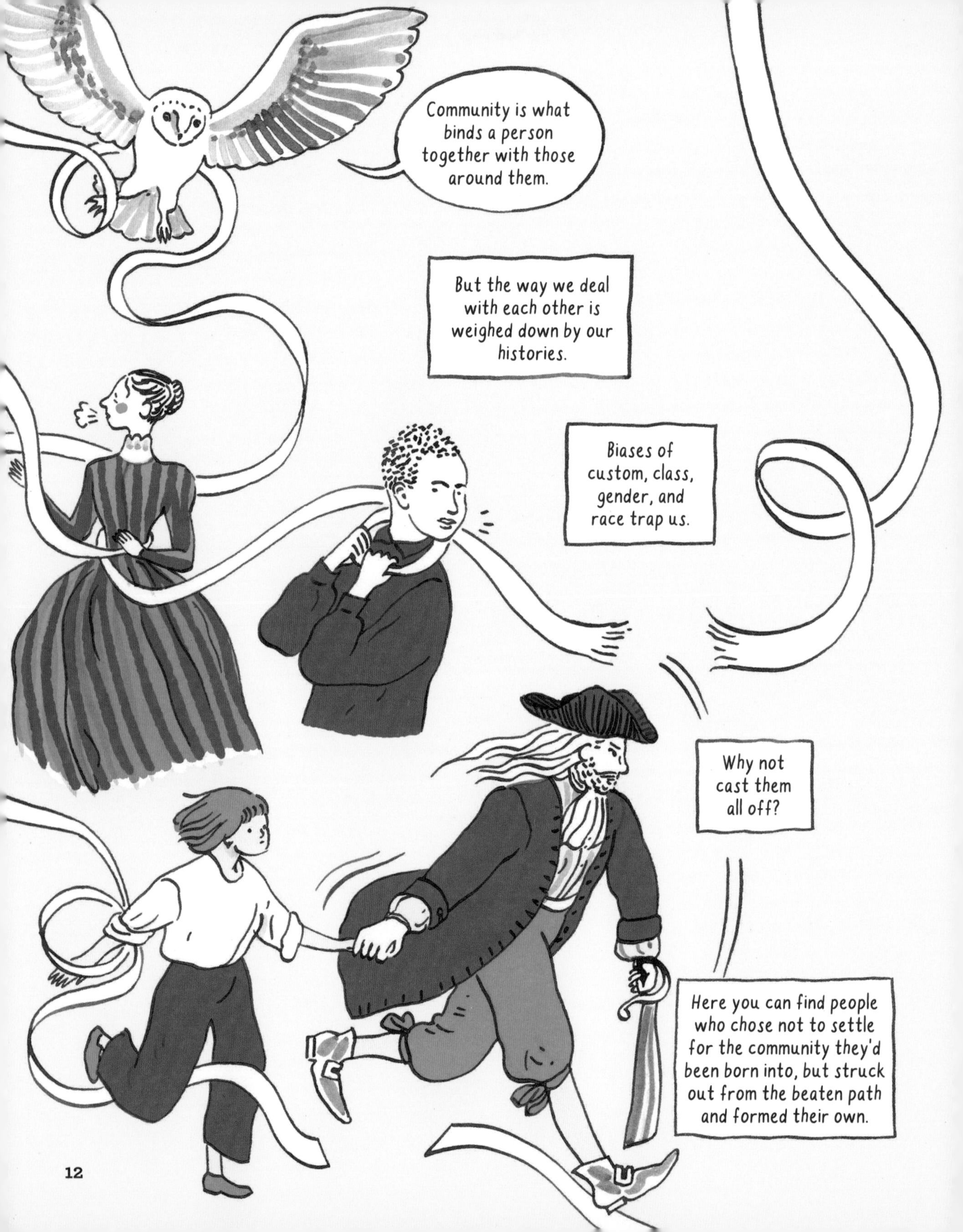
Community is what binds a person together with those around them.
But the way we deal with each other is weighed down by our histories.
Biases of custom, class, gender, and race trap us.
Why not cast them all off?
Here you can find people who chose not to settle for the community they'd been born into, but struck out from the beaten path and formed their own.

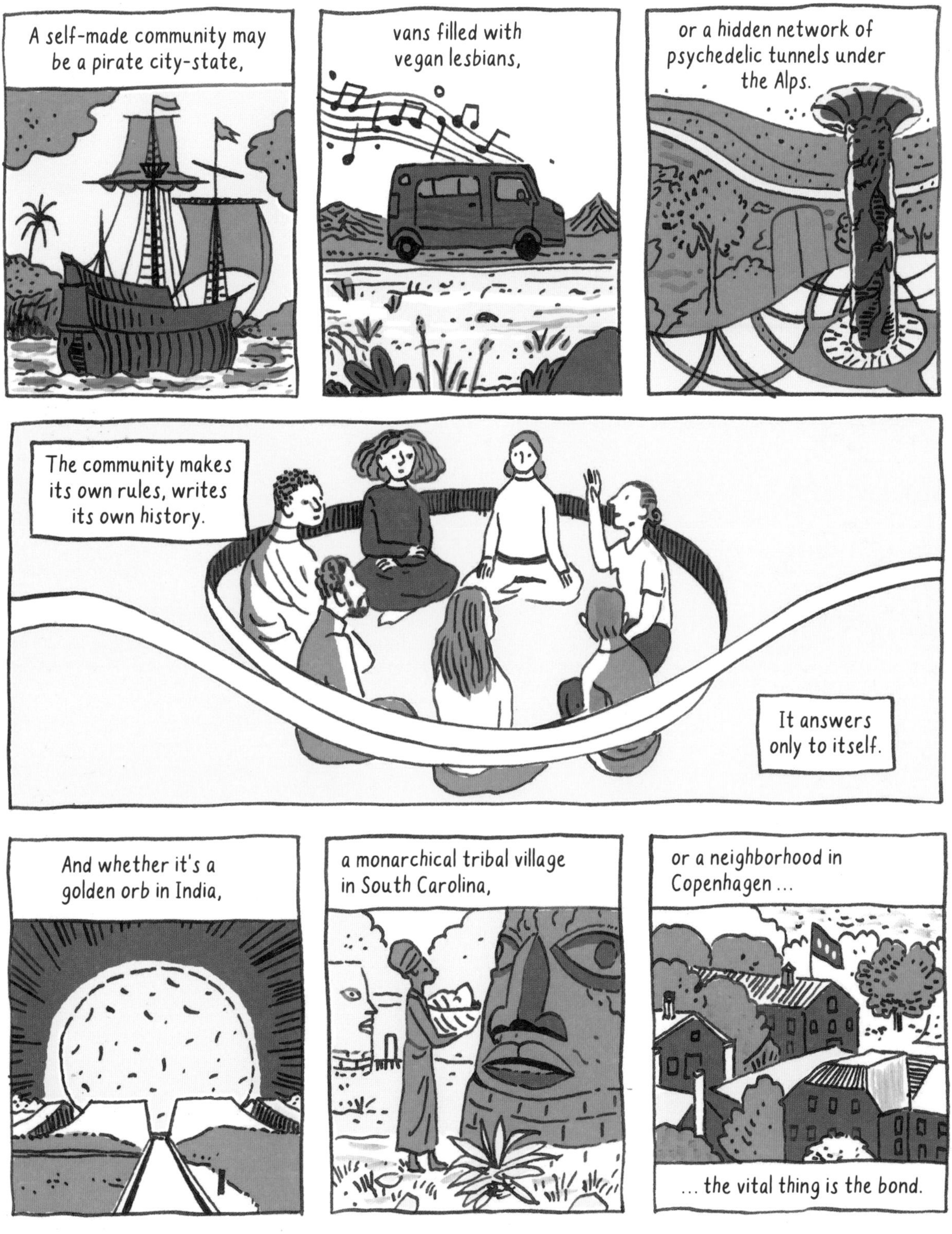
A self-made community may be a pirate city-state,
vans filled with vegan lesbians,
or a hidden network of psychedelic tunnels under the Alps.
The community makes its own rules, writes its own history.
It answers only to itself.
And whether it's a golden orb in India,
a monarchical tribal village in South Carolina,
or a neighborhood in Copenhagen ...
... the vital thing is the bond.

Libertatia

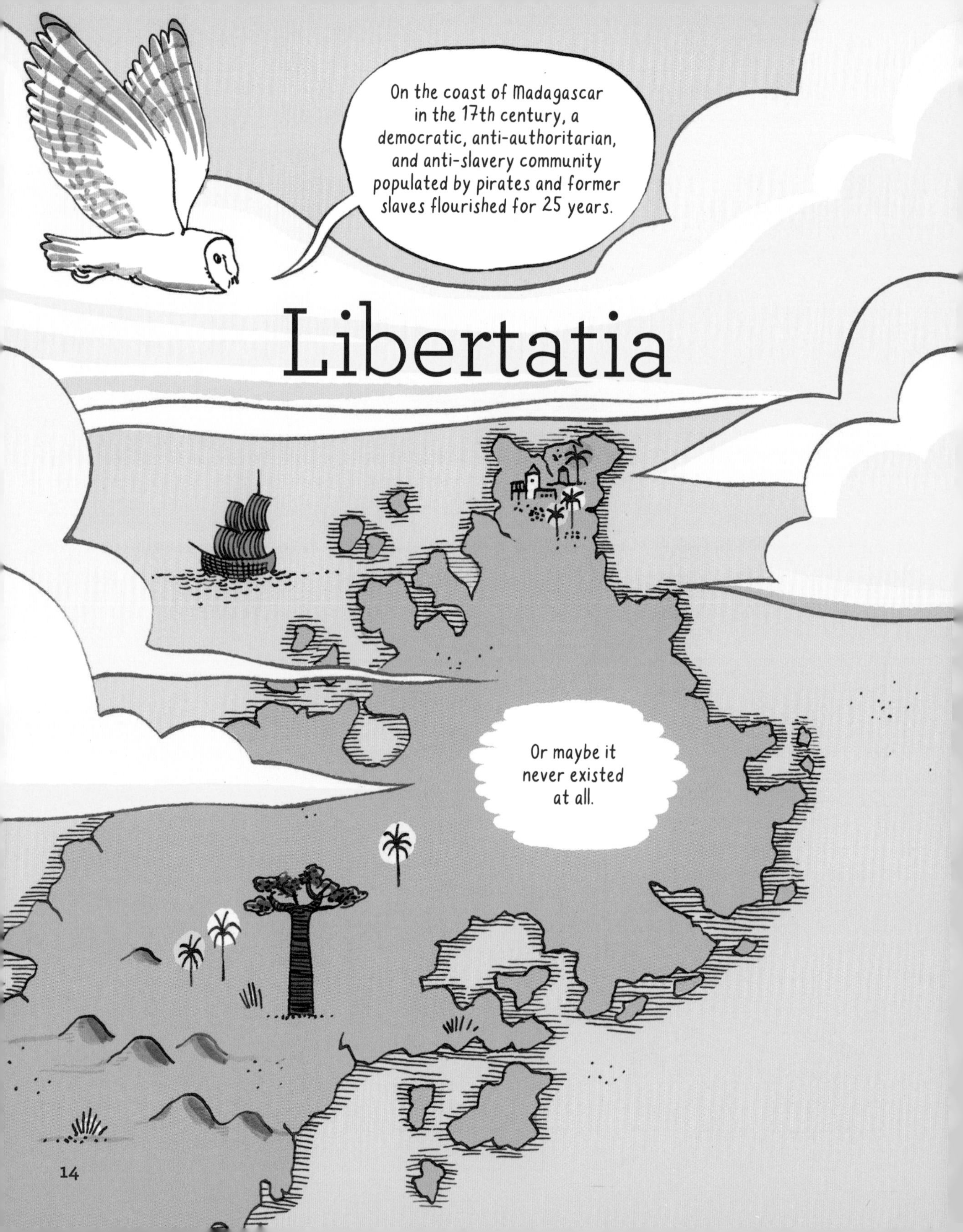

On the coast of Madagascar in the 17th century, a democratic, anti-authoritarian, and anti-slavery community populated by pirates and former slaves flourished for 25 years.
Or maybe it never existed at all.

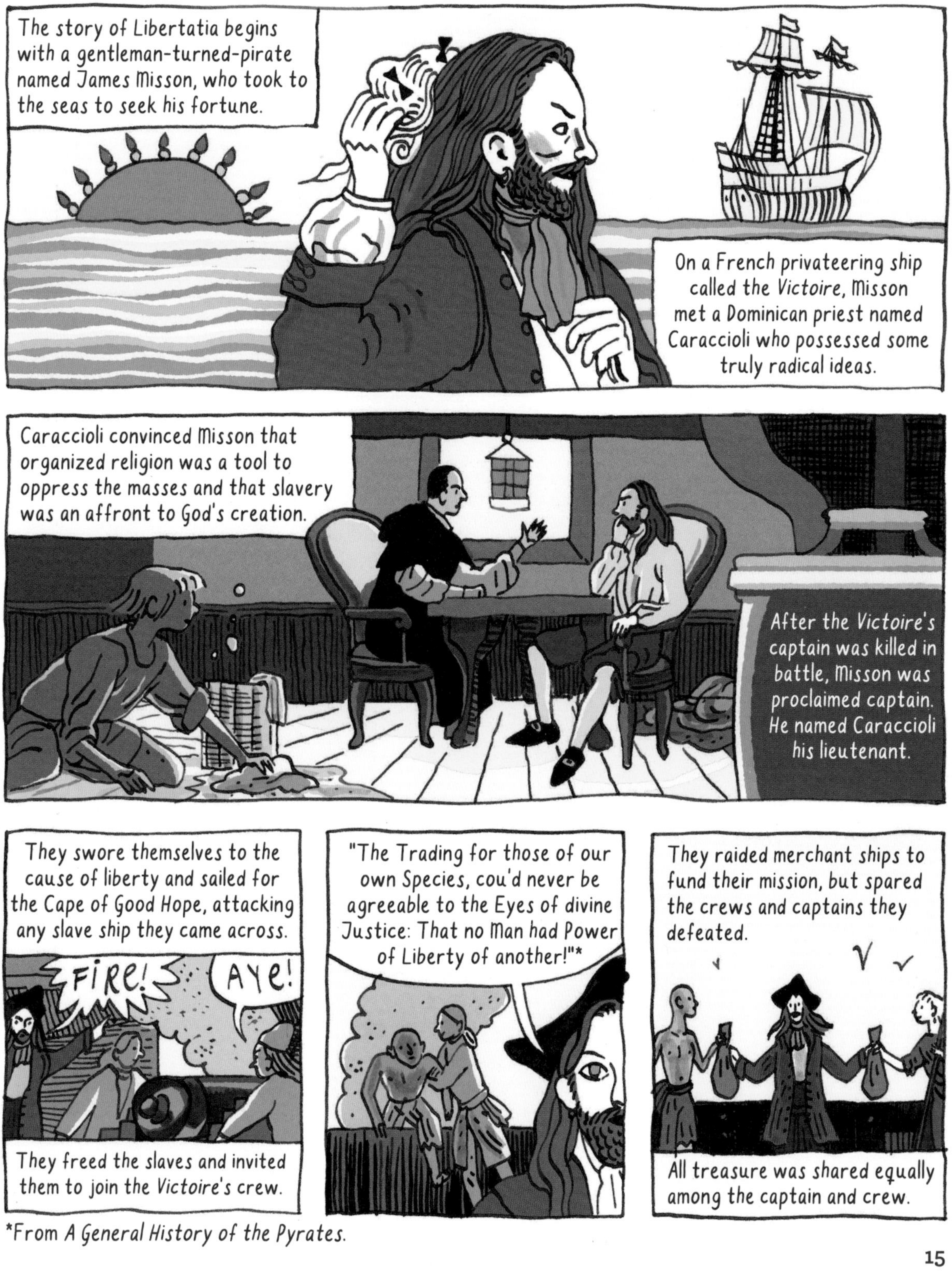
The story of Libertatia begins with a gentleman-turned-pirate named James Misson, who took to the seas to seek his fortune.
On a French privateering ship called the *Victoire*, Misson met a Dominican priest named Caraccioli who possessed some truly radical ideas.
Caraccioli convinced Misson that organized religion was a tool to oppress the masses and that slavery was an affront to God's creation.
After the *Victoire*'s captain was killed in battle, Misson was proclaimed captain. He named Caraccioli his lieutenant.
They swore themselves to the cause of liberty and sailed for the Cape of Good Hope, attacking any slave ship they came across.
FIRE!
AYE!
They freed the slaves and invited them to join the *Victoire*'s crew.
"The Trading for those of our own Species, cou'd never be agreeable to the Eyes of divine Justice: That no Man had Power of Liberty of another!"*
They raided merchant ships to fund their mission, but spared the crews and captains they defeated.
All treasure was shared equally among the captain and crew.

*From *A General History of the Pyrates*.

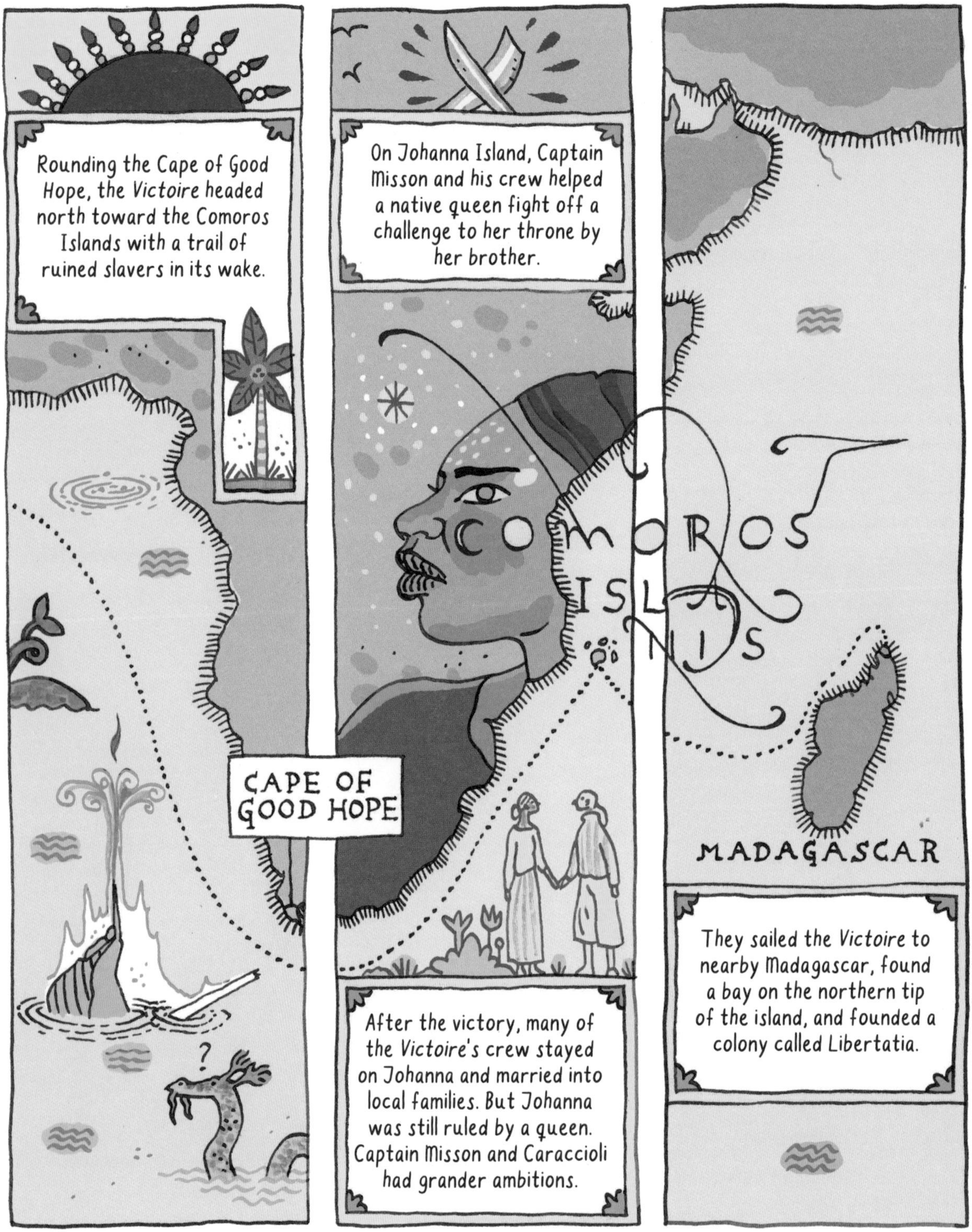
Rounding the Cape of Good Hope, the *Victoire* headed north toward the Comoros Islands with a trail of ruined slavers in its wake.
?
CAPE OF GOOD HOPE
On Johanna Island, Captain Misson and his crew helped a native queen fight off a challenge to her throne by her brother.
COMOROS ISLANDS
After the victory, many of the *Victoire*'s crew stayed on Johanna and married into local families. But Johanna was still ruled by a queen. Captain Misson and Caraccioli had grander ambitions.
MADAGASCAR
They sailed the *Victoire* to nearby Madagascar, found a bay on the northern tip of the island, and founded a colony called Libertatia.

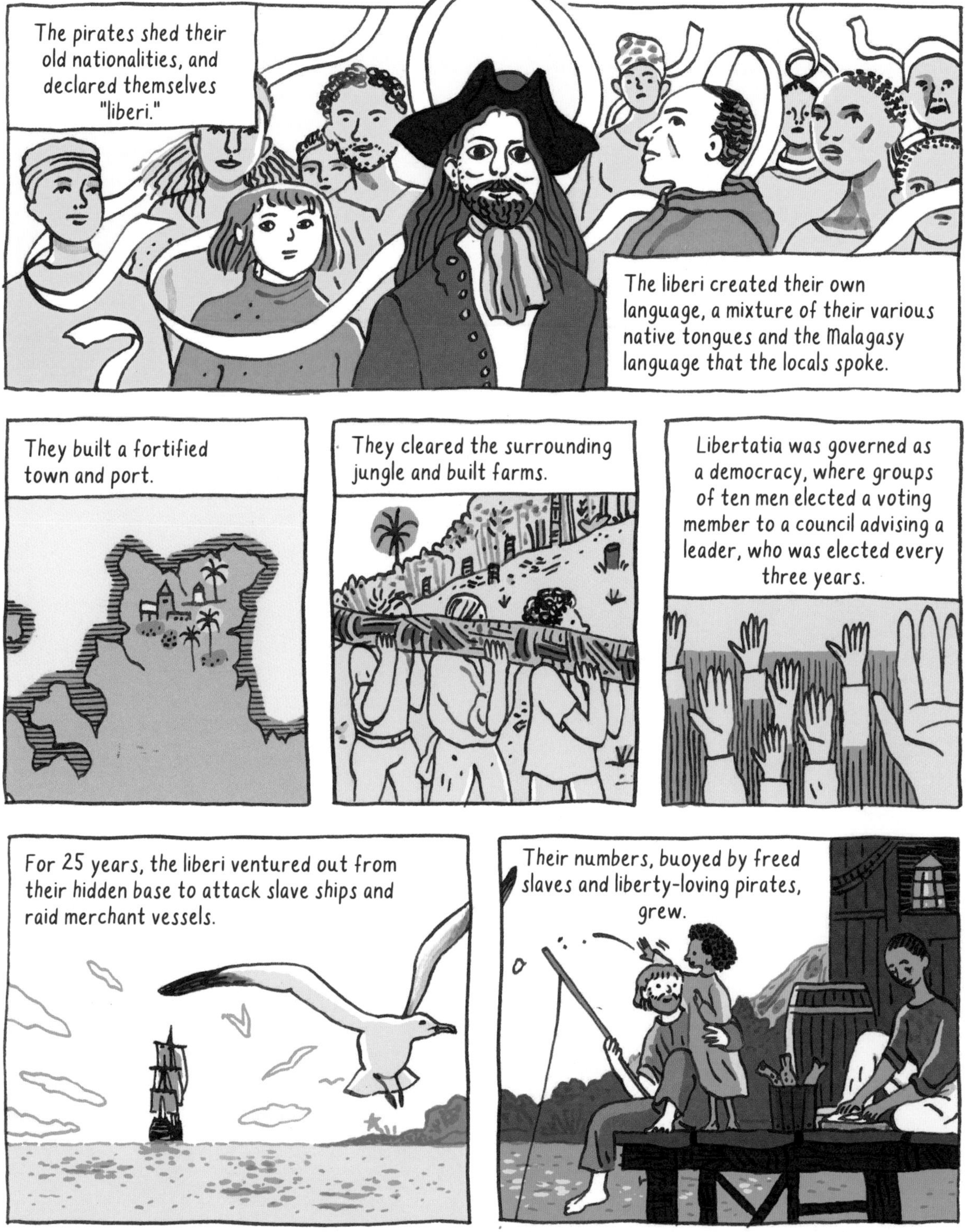
The pirates shed their old nationalities, and declared themselves "liberi."
The liberi created their own language, a mixture of their various native tongues and the Malagasy language that the locals spoke.
They built a fortified town and port.
They cleared the surrounding jungle and built farms.
Libertatia was governed as a democracy, where groups of ten men elected a voting member to a council advising a leader, who was elected every three years.
For 25 years, the liberi ventured out from their hidden base to attack slave ships and raid merchant vessels.
Their numbers, buoyed by freed slaves and liberty-loving pirates, grew.

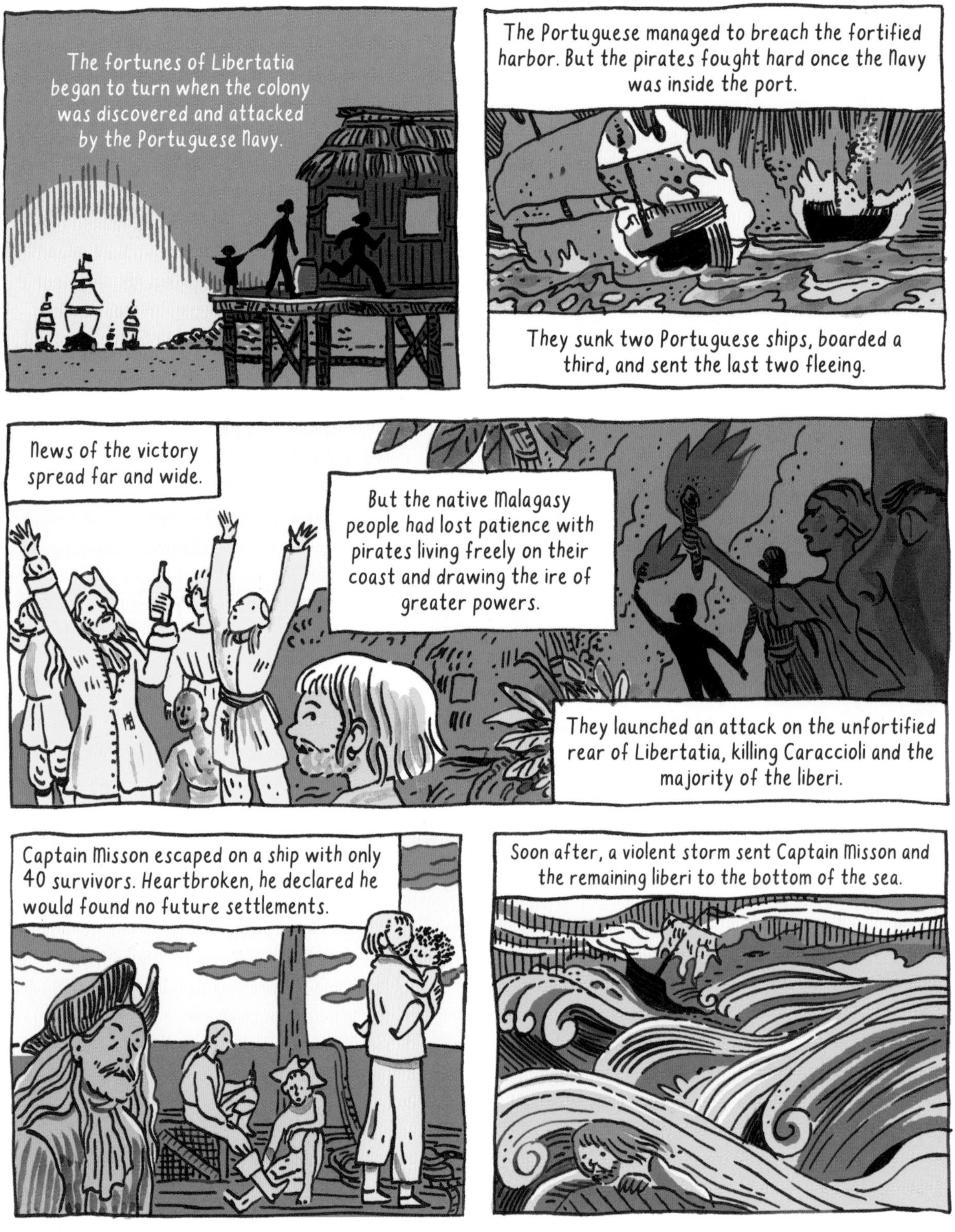
The fortunes of Libertatia began to turn when the colony was discovered and attacked by the Portuguese Navy.
The Portuguese managed to breach the fortified harbor. But the pirates fought hard once the Navy was inside the port.
They sunk two Portuguese ships, boarded a third, and sent the last two fleeing.
News of the victory spread far and wide.
But the native Malagasy people had lost patience with pirates living freely on their coast and drawing the ire of greater powers.
They launched an attack on the unfortified rear of Libertatia, killing Caraccioli and the majority of the liberi.
Captain Misson escaped on a ship with only 40 survivors. Heartbroken, he declared he would found no future settlements.
Soon after, a violent storm sent Captain Misson and the remaining liberi to the bottom of the sea.

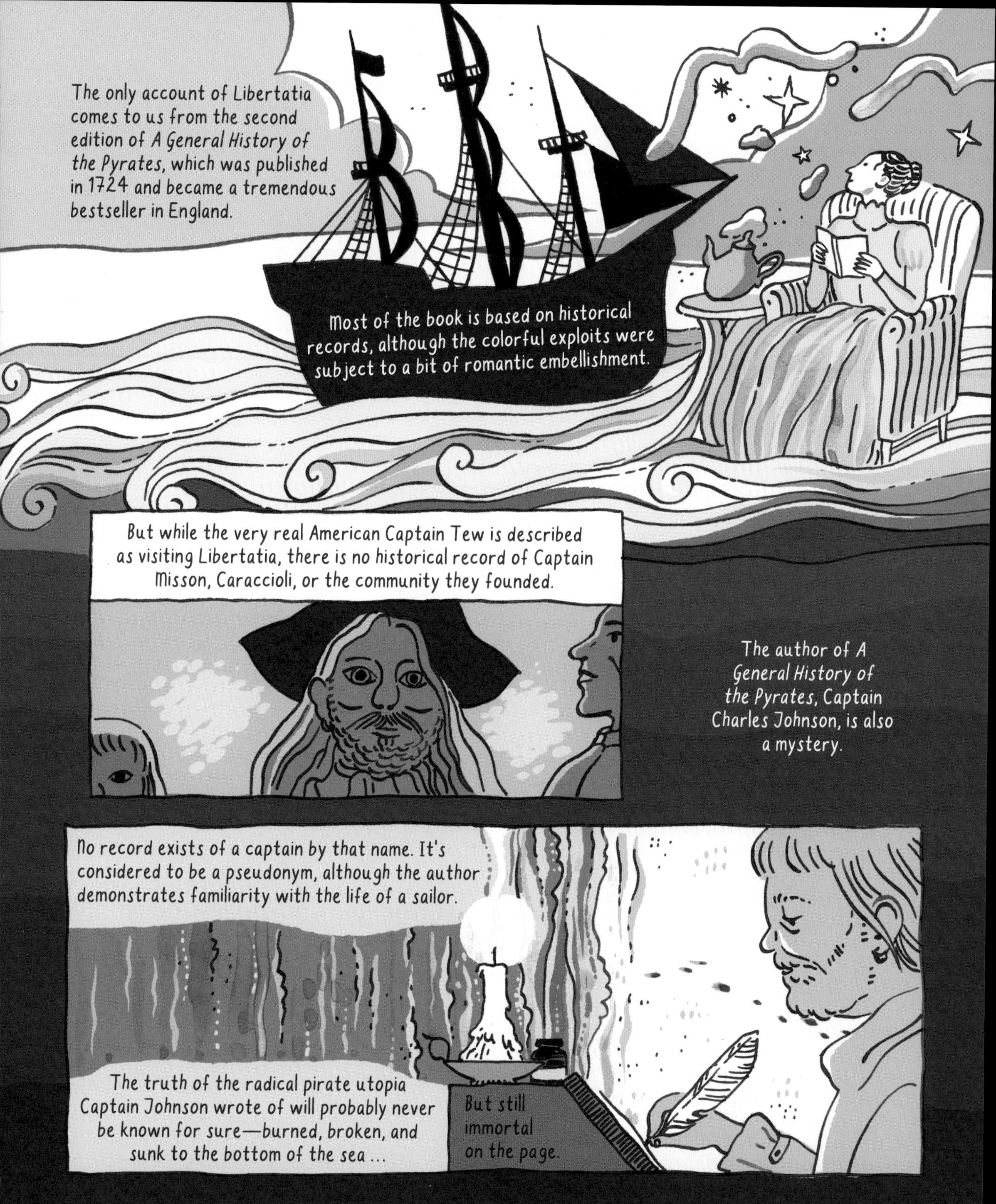
The only account of Libertatia comes to us from the second edition of *A General History of the Pyrates*, which was published in 1724 and became a tremendous bestseller in England.
Most of the book is based on historical records, although the colorful exploits were subject to a bit of romantic embellishment.
But while the very real American Captain Tew is described as visiting Libertatia, there is no historical record of Captain Misson, Caraccioli, or the community they founded.
The author of *A General History of the Pyrates*, Captain Charles Johnson, is also a mystery.
No record exists of a captain by that name. It's considered to be a pseudonym, although the author demonstrates familiarity with the life of a sailor.
The truth of the radical pirate utopia Captain Johnson wrote of will probably never be known for sure—burned, broken, and sunk to the bottom of the sea ...
But still immortal on the page.

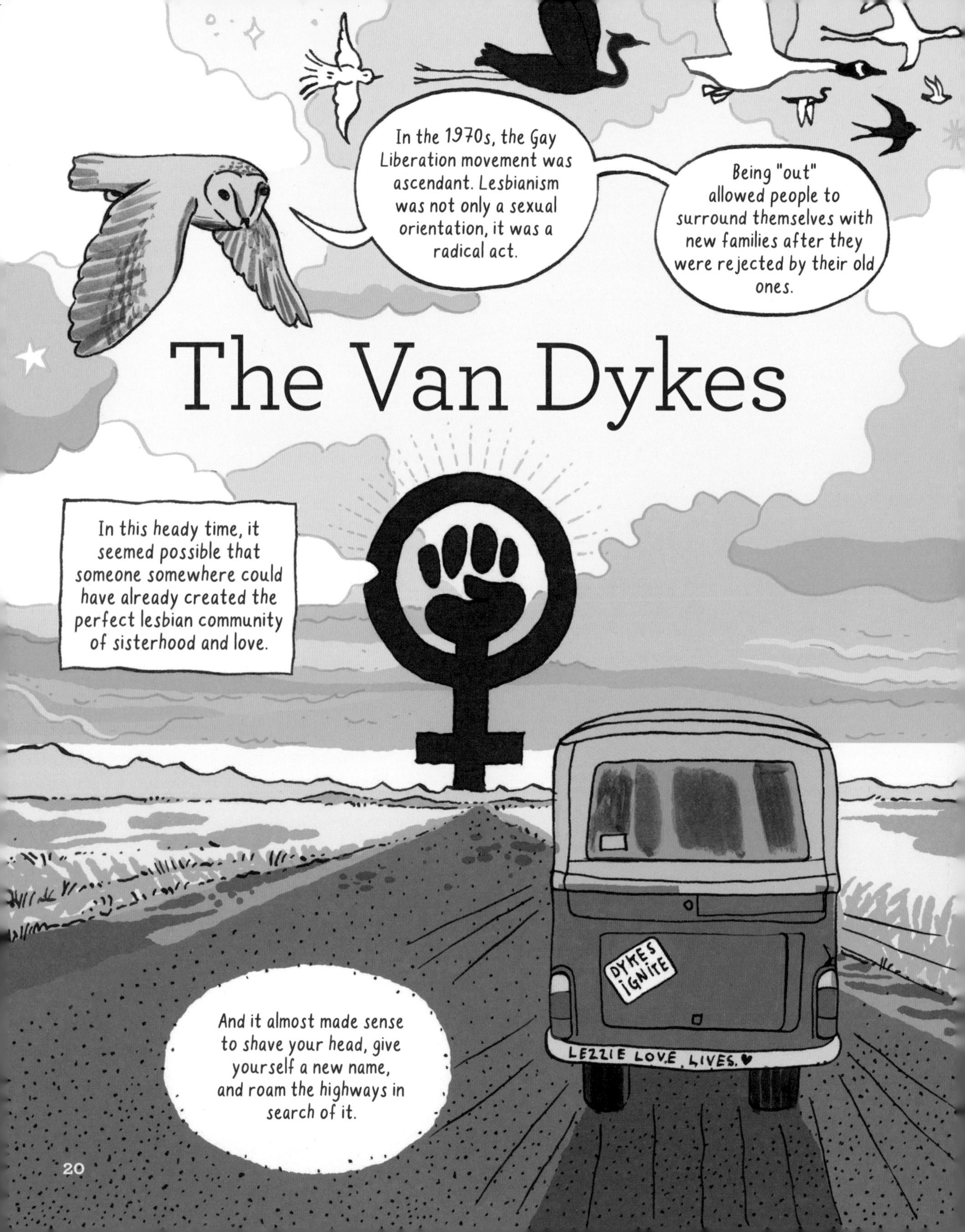
In the 1970s, the Gay Liberation movement was ascendant. Lesbianism was not only a sexual orientation, it was a radical act.
Being "out" allowed people to surround themselves with new families after they were rejected by their old ones.
The Van Dykes
In this heady time, it seemed possible that someone somewhere could have already created the perfect lesbian community of sisterhood and love.
DYKES IGNITE
LEZZIE LOVE LIVES.
And it almost made sense to shave your head, give yourself a new name, and roam the highways in search of it.

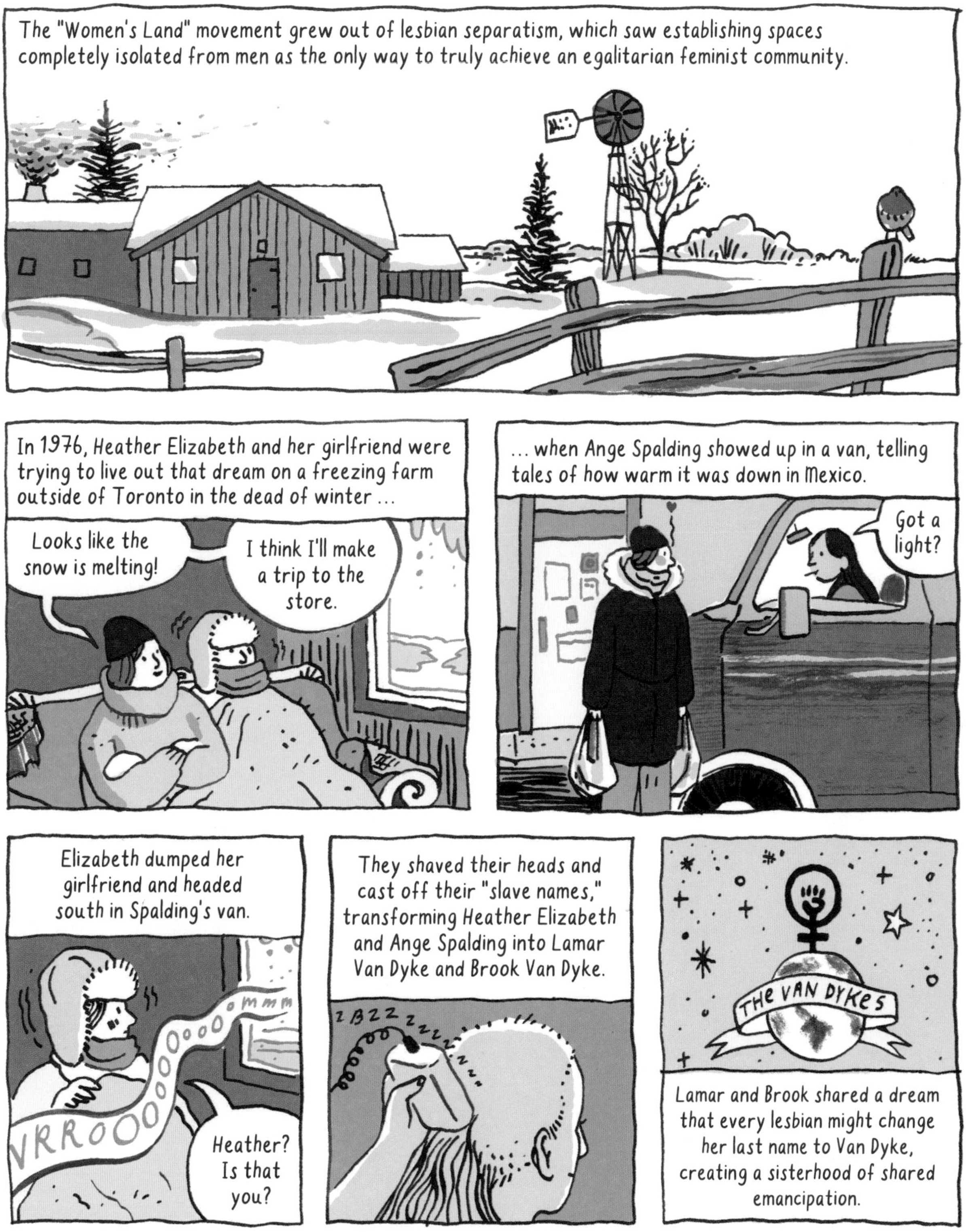
The "Women's Land" movement grew out of lesbian separatism, which saw establishing spaces completely isolated from men as the only way to truly achieve an egalitarian feminist community.
In 1976, Heather Elizabeth and her girlfriend were trying to live out that dream on a freezing farm outside of Toronto in the dead of winter ...
Looks like the snow is melting!
I think I'll make a trip to the store.
... when Ange Spalding showed up in a van, telling tales of how warm it was down in Mexico.
Got a light?
Elizabeth dumped her girlfriend and headed south in Spalding's van.
VRROOOOOOOOooommm
Heather? Is that you?
They shaved their heads and cast off their "slave names," transforming Heather Elizabeth and Ange Spalding into Lamar Van Dyke and Brook Van Dyke.
ZBZZ zzzz
THE VAN DYKES
Lamar and Brook shared a dream that every lesbian might change her last name to Van Dyke, creating a sisterhood of shared emancipation.

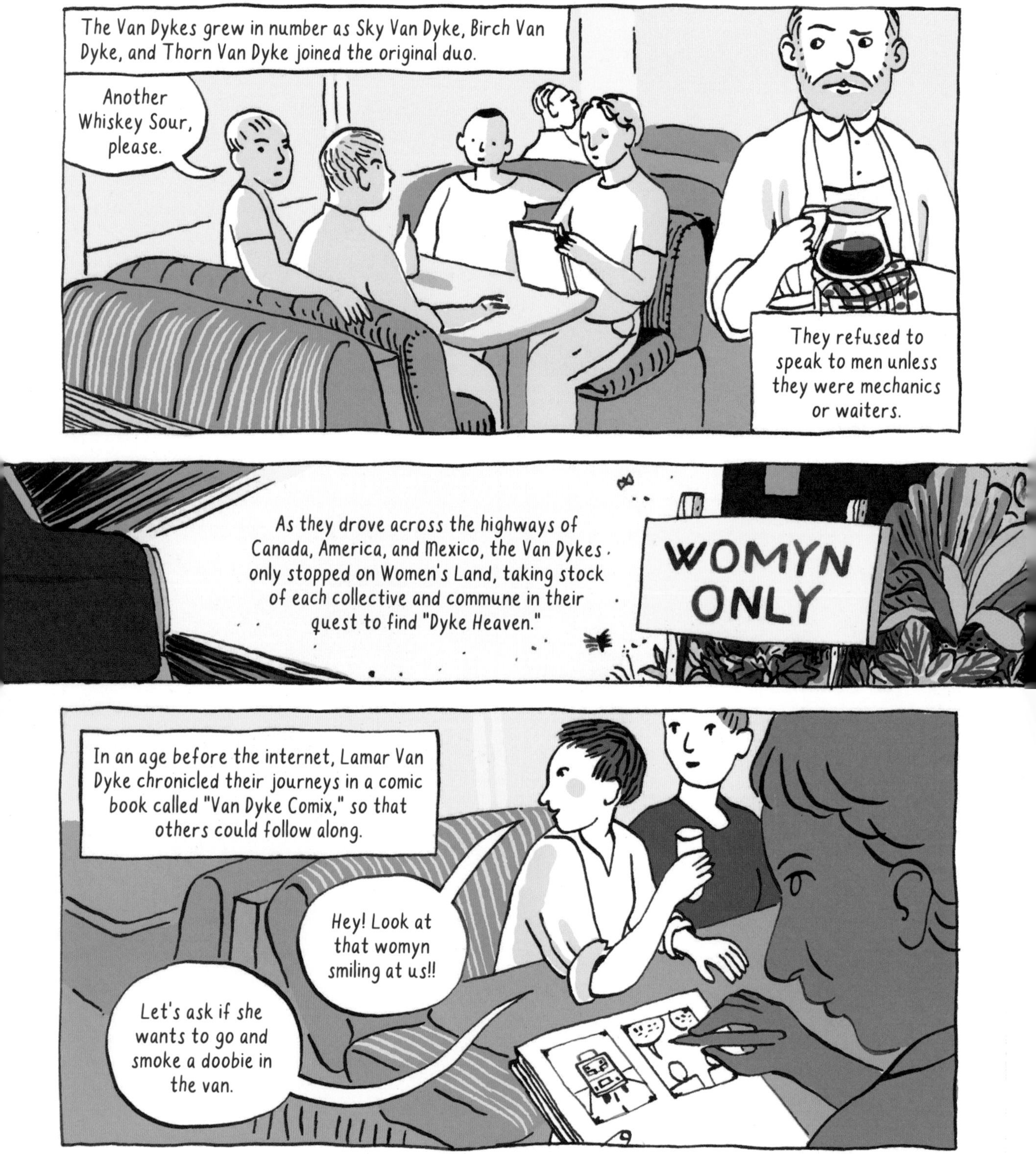
The Van Dykes grew in number as Sky Van Dyke, Birch Van Dyke, and Thorn Van Dyke joined the original duo.
Another Whiskey Sour, please.
They refused to speak to men unless they were mechanics or waiters.
As they drove across the highways of Canada, America, and Mexico, the Van Dykes only stopped on Women's Land, taking stock of each collective and commune in their quest to find "Dyke Heaven."
WOMYN ONLY
In an age before the internet, Lamar Van Dyke chronicled their journeys in a comic book called "Van Dyke Comix," so that others could follow along.
Hey! Look at that womyn smiling at us!!
Let's ask if she wants to go and smoke a doobie in the van.

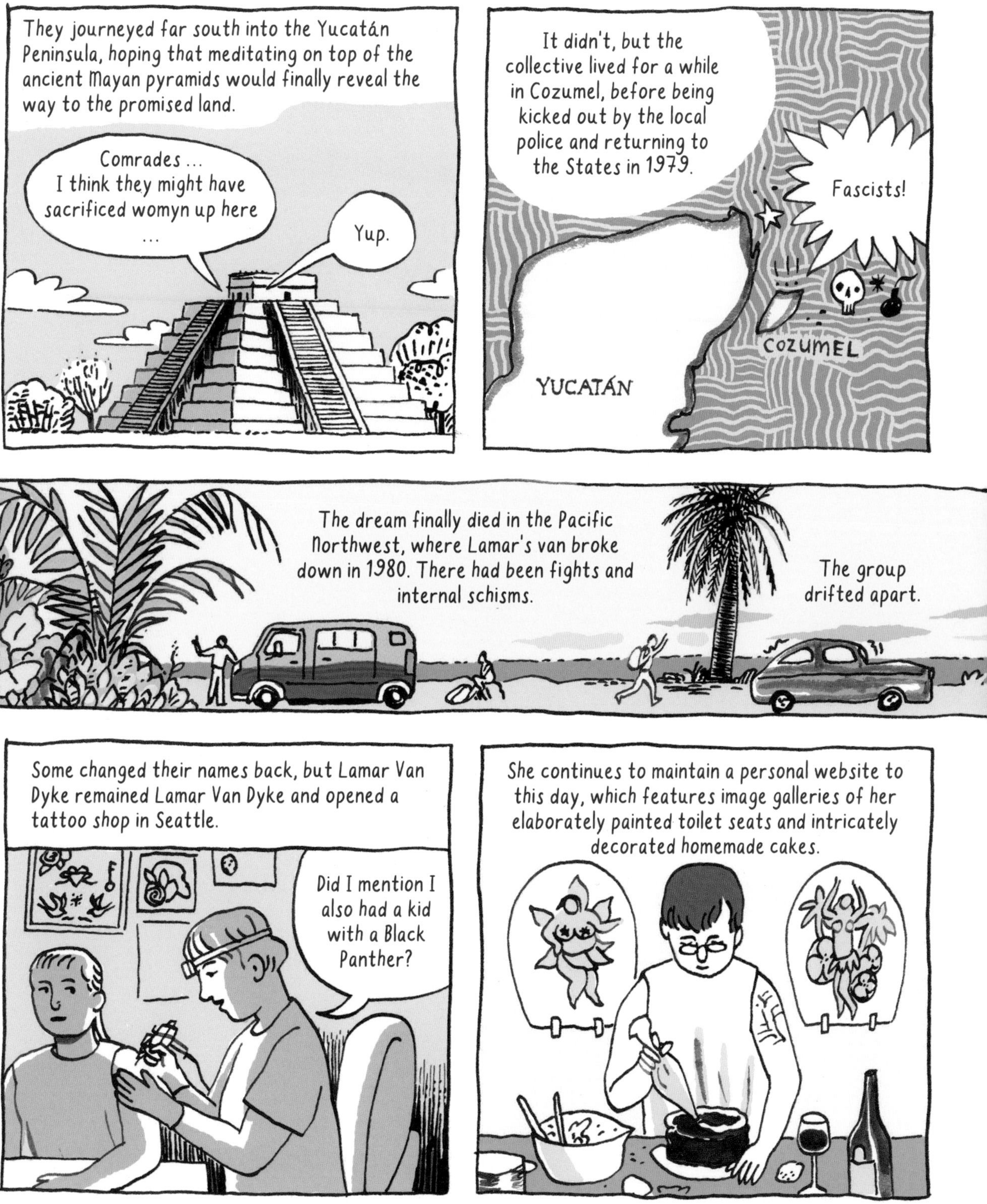
They journeyed far south into the Yucatán Peninsula, hoping that meditating on top of the ancient Mayan pyramids would finally reveal the way to the promised land.
Comrades ... I think they might have sacrificed womyn up here ...
Yup.
It didn't, but the collective lived for a while in Cozumel, before being kicked out by the local police and returning to the States in 1979.
Fascists!
COZUMEL
YUCATÁN
The dream finally died in the Pacific Northwest, where Lamar's van broke down in 1980. There had been fights and internal schisms.
The group drifted apart.
Some changed their names back, but Lamar Van Dyke remained Lamar Van Dyke and opened a tattoo shop in Seattle.
Did I mention I also had a kid with a Black Panther?
She continues to maintain a personal website to this day, which features image galleries of her elaborately painted toilet seats and intricately decorated homemade cakes.

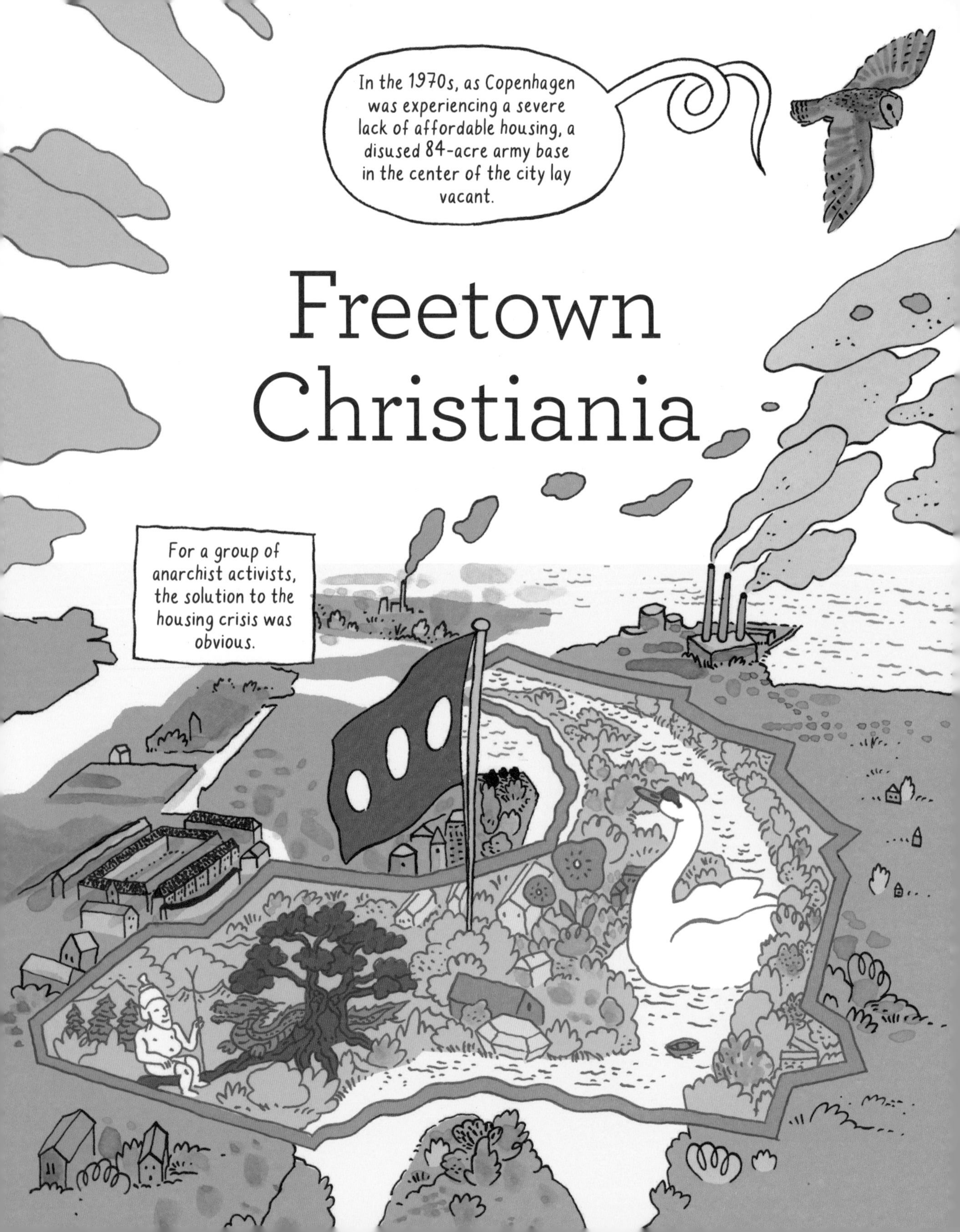
In the 1970s, as Copenhagen was experiencing a severe lack of affordable housing, a disused 84-acre army base in the center of the city lay vacant.
Freetown Christiania
For a group of anarchist activists, the solution to the housing crisis was obvious.

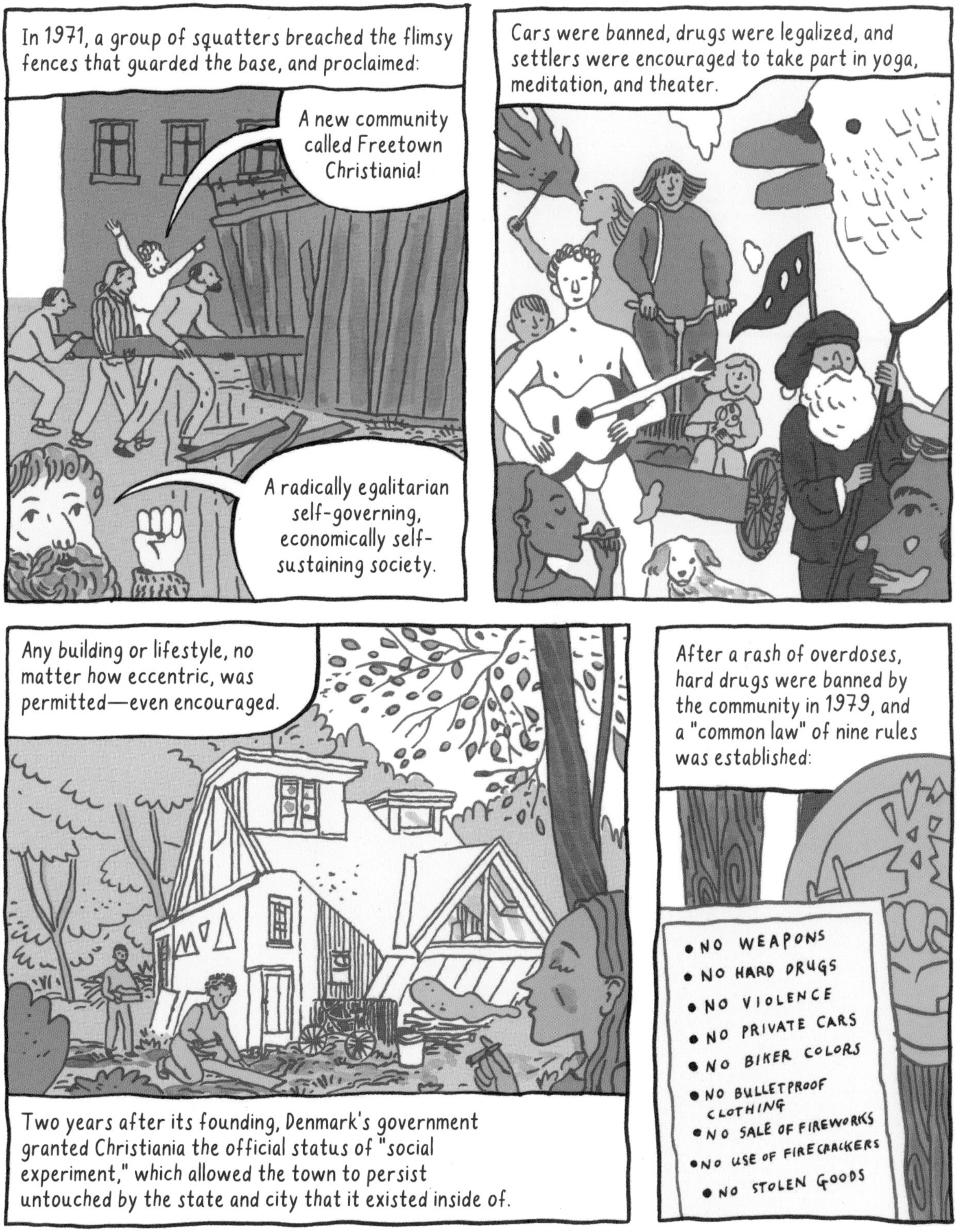
In 1971, a group of squatters breached the flimsy fences that guarded the base, and proclaimed:
A new community called Freetown Christiania!
A radically egalitarian self-governing, economically self-sustaining society.
Cars were banned, drugs were legalized, and settlers were encouraged to take part in yoga, meditation, and theater.
Any building or lifestyle, no matter how eccentric, was permitted—even encouraged.
Two years after its founding, Denmark's government granted Christiania the official status of "social experiment," which allowed the town to persist untouched by the state and city that it existed inside of.
After a rash of overdoses, hard drugs were banned by the community in 1979, and a "common law" of nine rules was established:
• NO WEAPONS
• NO HARD DRUGS
• NO VIOLENCE
• NO PRIVATE CARS
• NO BIKER COLORS
• NO BULLETPROOF CLOTHING
• NO SALE OF FIREWORKS
• NO USE OF FIRECRACKERS
• NO STOLEN GOODS

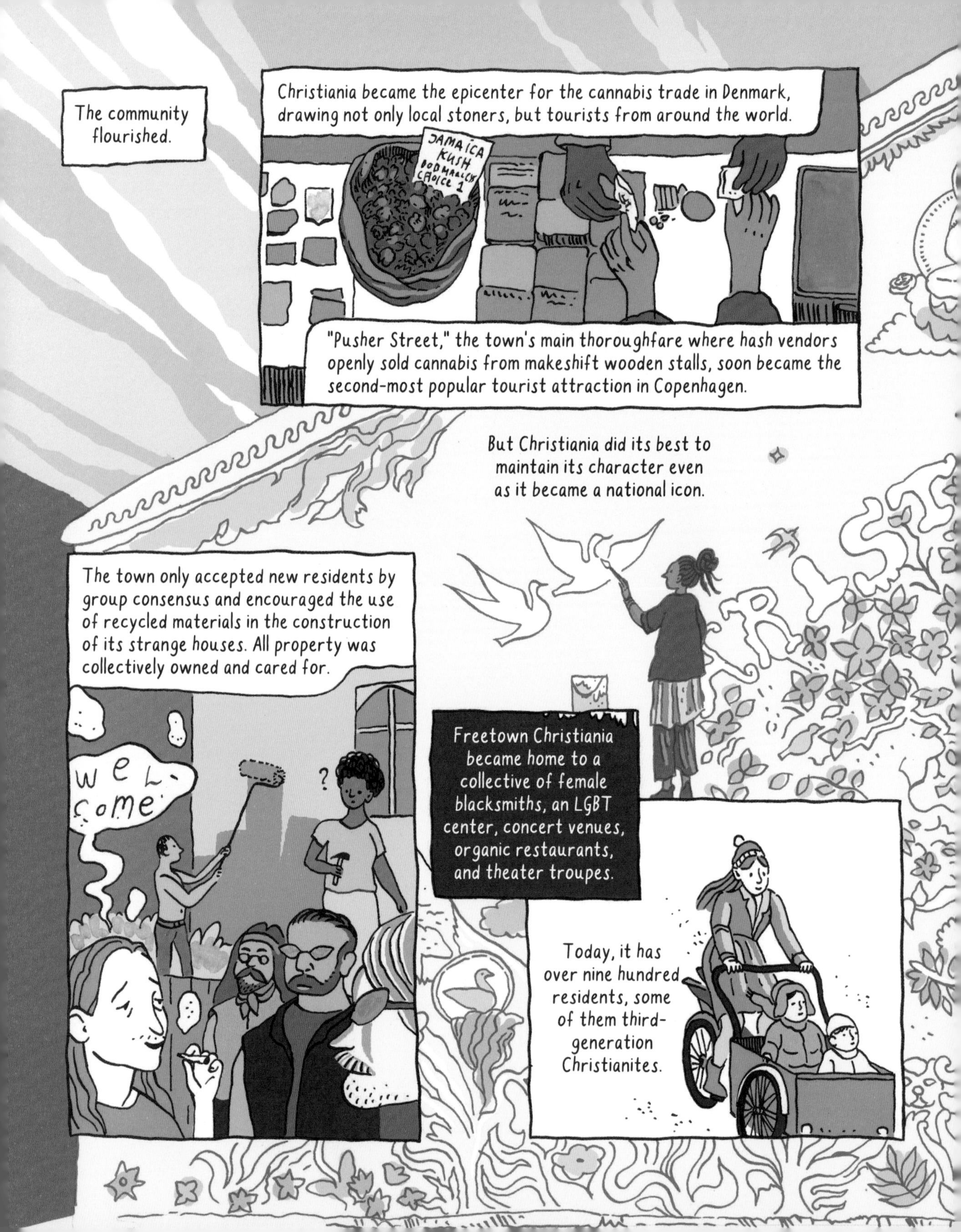
The community flourished.
Christiania became the epicenter for the cannabis trade in Denmark, drawing not only local stoners, but tourists from around the world.
JAMAICA KUSH
"Pusher Street," the town's main thoroughfare where hash vendors openly sold cannabis from makeshift wooden stalls, soon became the second-most popular tourist attraction in Copenhagen.
But Christiania did its best to maintain its character even as it became a national icon.
The town only accepted new residents by group consensus and encouraged the use of recycled materials in the construction of its strange houses. All property was collectively owned and cared for.
WEL-COME
?
Freetown Christiania became home to a collective of female blacksmiths, an LGBT center, concert venues, organic restaurants, and theater troupes.
Today, it has over nine hundred residents, some of them third-generation Christianites.

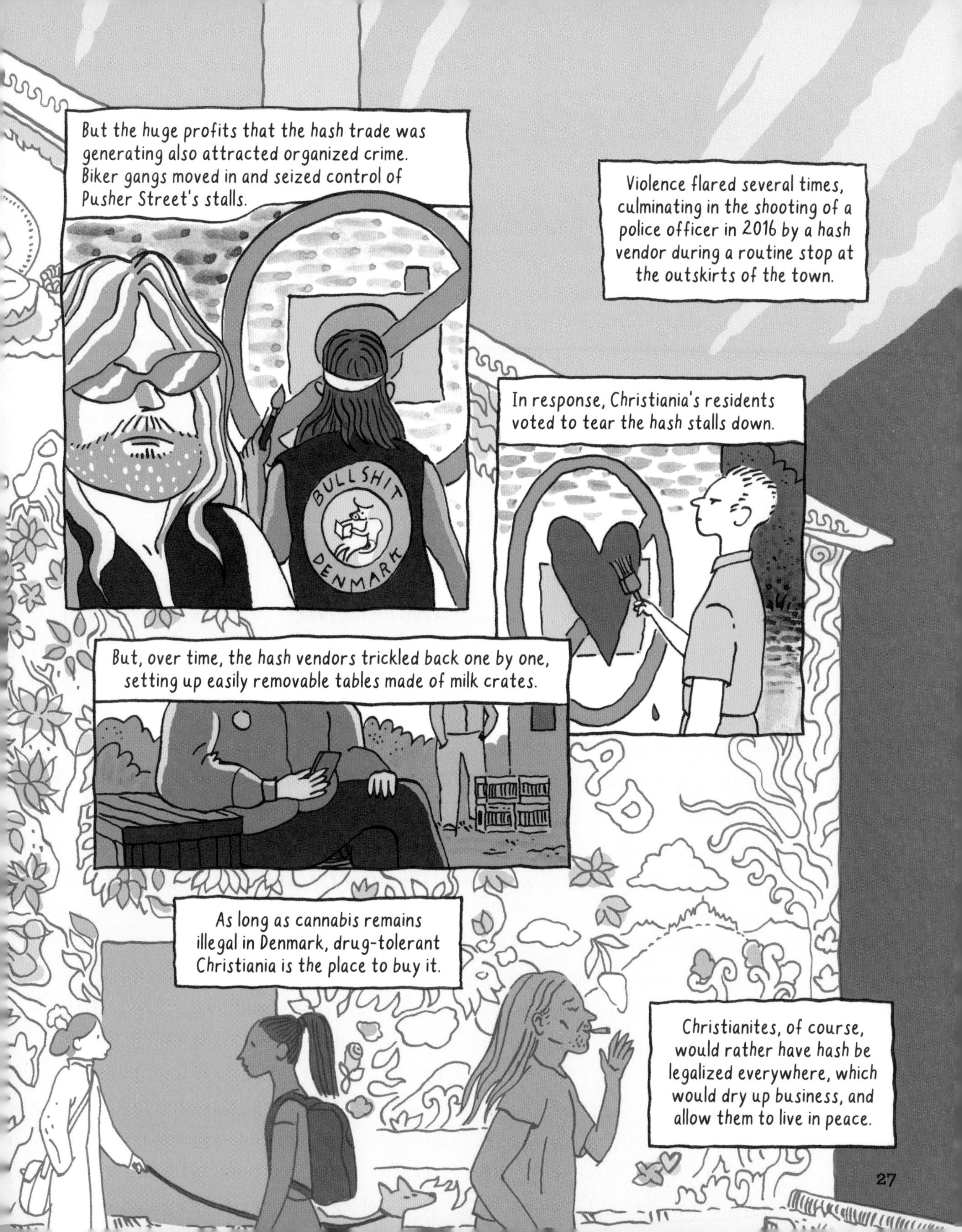
But the huge profits that the hash trade was generating also attracted organized crime. Biker gangs moved in and seized control of Pusher Street's stalls.
BULLSHIT DENMARK
Violence flared several times, culminating in the shooting of a police officer in 2016 by a hash vendor during a routine stop at the outskirts of the town.
In response, Christiania's residents voted to tear the hash stalls down.
But, over time, the hash vendors trickled back one by one, setting up easily removable tables made of milk crates.
As long as cannabis remains illegal in Denmark, drug-tolerant Christiania is the place to buy it.
Christianites, of course, would rather have hash be legalized everywhere, which would dry up business, and allow them to live in peace.

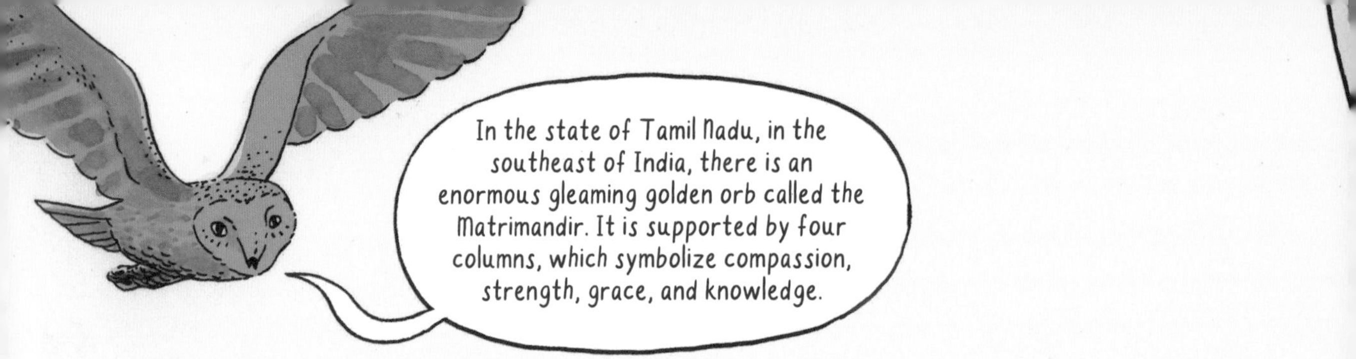
In the state of Tamil Nadu, in the southeast of India, there is an enormous gleaming golden orb called the Matrimandir. It is supported by four columns, which symbolize compassion, strength, grace, and knowledge.

Auroville

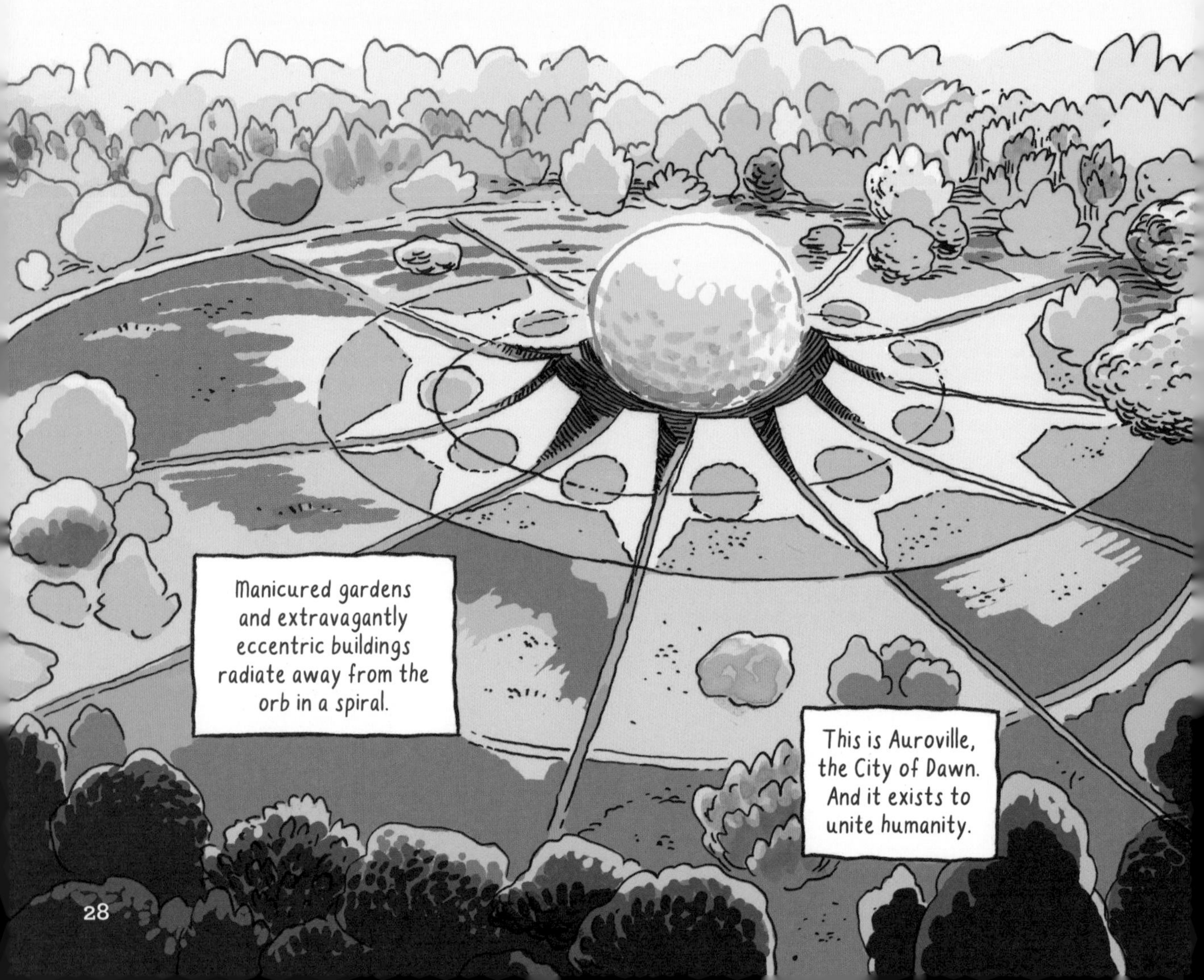
Manicured gardens and extravagantly eccentric buildings radiate away from the orb in a spiral.
This is Auroville, the City of Dawn. And it exists to unite humanity.

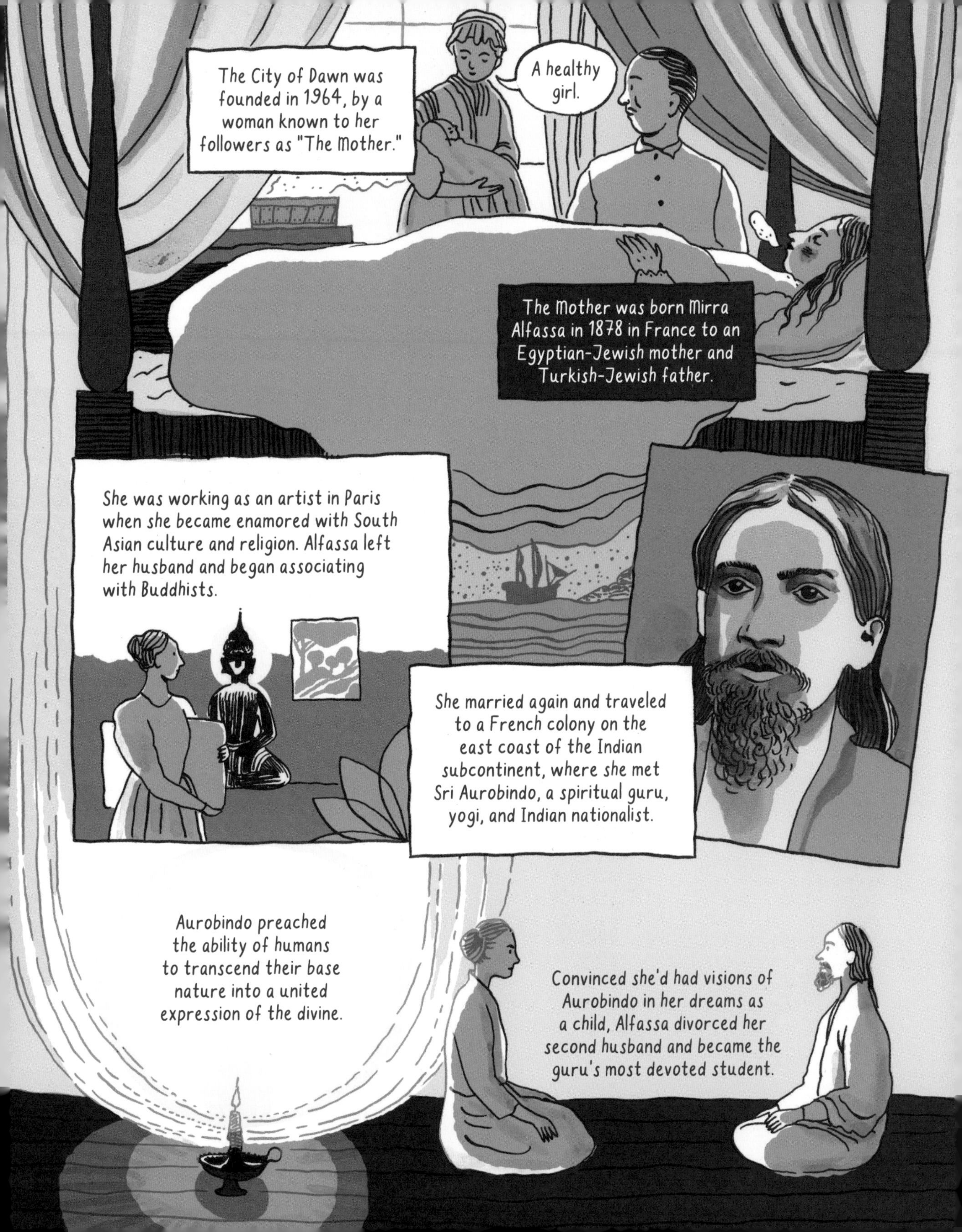
The City of Dawn was founded in 1964, by a woman known to her followers as "The Mother."
A healthy girl.
The Mother was born Mirra Alfassa in 1878 in France to an Egyptian-Jewish mother and Turkish-Jewish father.
She was working as an artist in Paris when she became enamored with South Asian culture and religion. Alfassa left her husband and began associating with Buddhists.
She married again and traveled to a French colony on the east coast of the Indian subcontinent, where she met Sri Aurobindo, a spiritual guru, yogi, and Indian nationalist.
Aurobindo preached the ability of humans to transcend their base nature into a united expression of the divine.
Convinced she'd had visions of Aurobindo in her dreams as a child, Alfassa divorced her second husband and became the guru's most devoted student.

Aurobindo renamed Alfassa "The Mother" and appointed her the second-in-command of his ashram.

Aurobindo's "integral yoga" posited that internal reflection, rather than movement or breathing, was the path to a spiritual transformation of the entire being.

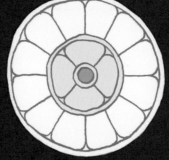

Over the next two and a half decades, his followers grew and grew.

In 1950, Sri Aurobindo died unexpectedly. The Mother assumed responsibility for the ashram and his message of universality.

The ashram flourished under The Mother's watchful eye. She even became a close friend of future Indian Prime Minister Indira Gandhi.

In 1964, at the age of 86, The Mother declared that the rest of her life would be dedicated to building a city called Auroville on seven-and-a-half square miles of empty scrubland north of the ashram as the final expression of her guru's ideals.

"Auroville wants to be a universal town where men and women of all countries are able to live in peace and progressive harmony, above all creeds, all politics and all nationalities. The purpose of Auroville is to realize human unity."

Spiritual seekers flocked to her from the world over.

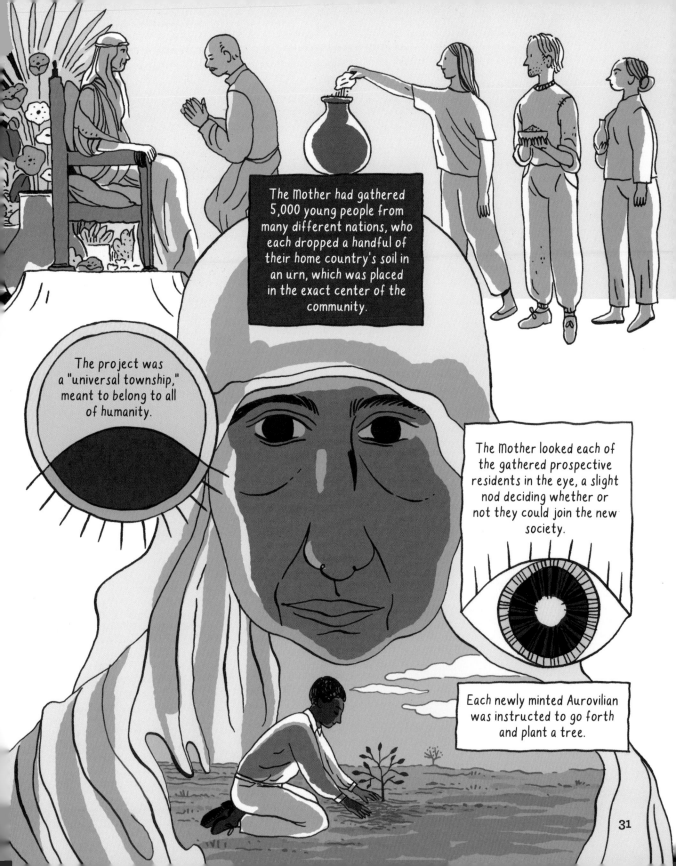

The Mother had gathered 5,000 young people from many different nations, who each dropped a handful of their home country's soil in an urn, which was placed in the exact center of the community.

The project was a "universal township," meant to belong to all of humanity.

The Mother looked each of the gathered prospective residents in the eye, a slight nod deciding whether or not they could join the new society.

Each newly minted Aurovilian was instructed to go forth and plant a tree.

31

At sunrise on February 21, 1971, the Aurovilians began work on the Matrimandir, the gleaming golden dome at the center of their community.

It was The Mother's 92nd birthday.

She died two years later.

It took another 35 years to finish the Matrimandir, which houses a white marble meditation chamber at its core.

In 1980, after complaints from residents of Auroville, the Indian government took over administration of the City of Dawn, which it passed on to a foundation insulated with several layers of confusing bureaucracy.

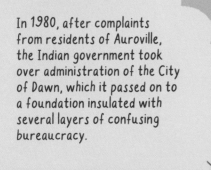

Auroville's permanent status became enshrined in law when the Indian Supreme Court ruled in 1982 that it was in "conformity with India's highest ideals and aspirations." It is also a UNESCO Heritage Site.

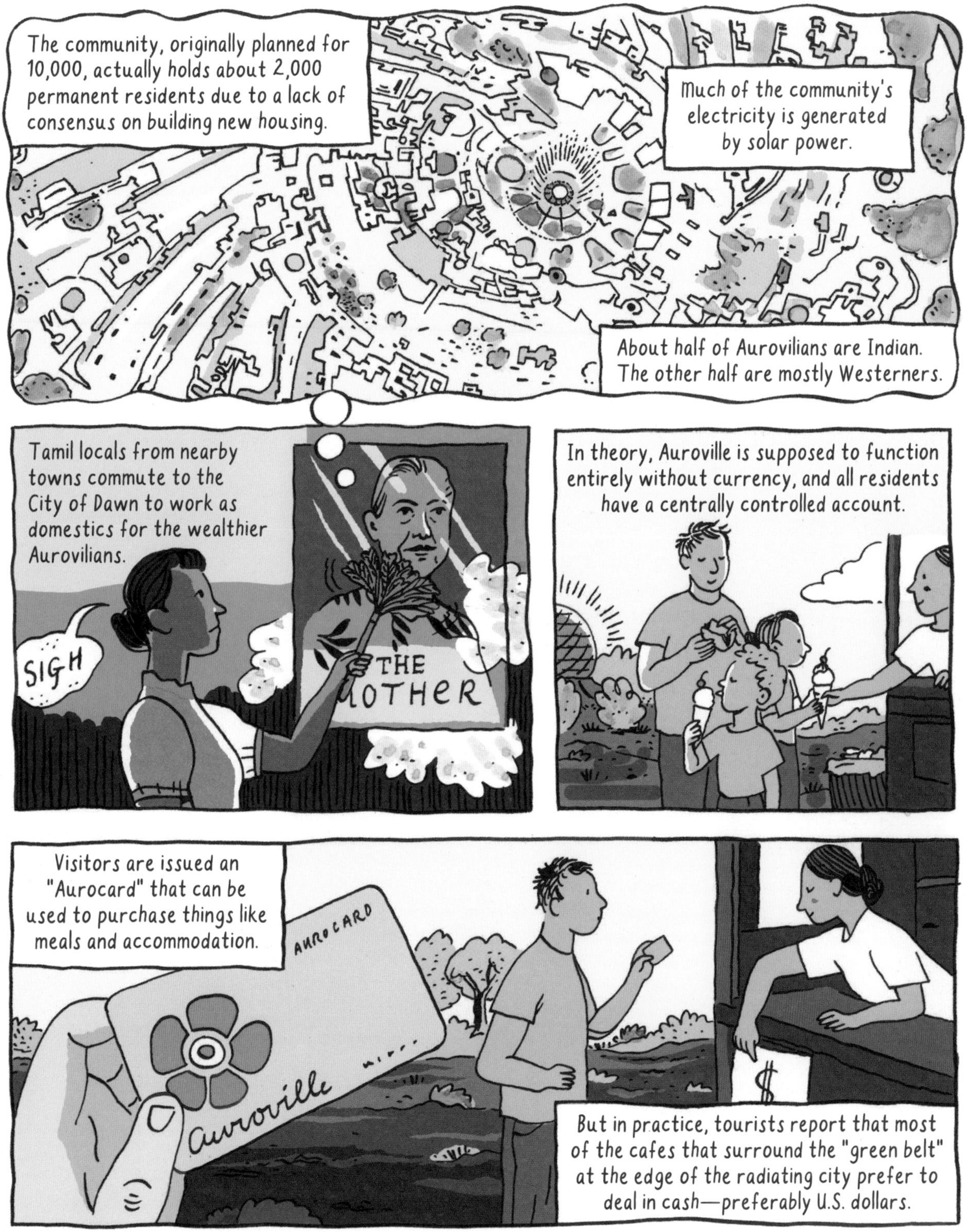

The community, originally planned for 10,000, actually holds about 2,000 permanent residents due to a lack of consensus on building new housing.
Much of the community's electricity is generated by solar power.
About half of Aurovilians are Indian. The other half are mostly Westerners.
Tamil locals from nearby towns commute to the City of Dawn to work as domestics for the wealthier Aurovilians.
SIGH
THE
OTHER
In theory, Auroville is supposed to function entirely without currency, and all residents have a centrally controlled account.
Visitors are issued an "Aurocard" that can be used to purchase things like meals and accommodation.
AUROCARD
auroville
$
But in practice, tourists report that most of the cafes that surround the "green belt" at the edge of the radiating city prefer to deal in cash—preferably U.S. dollars.

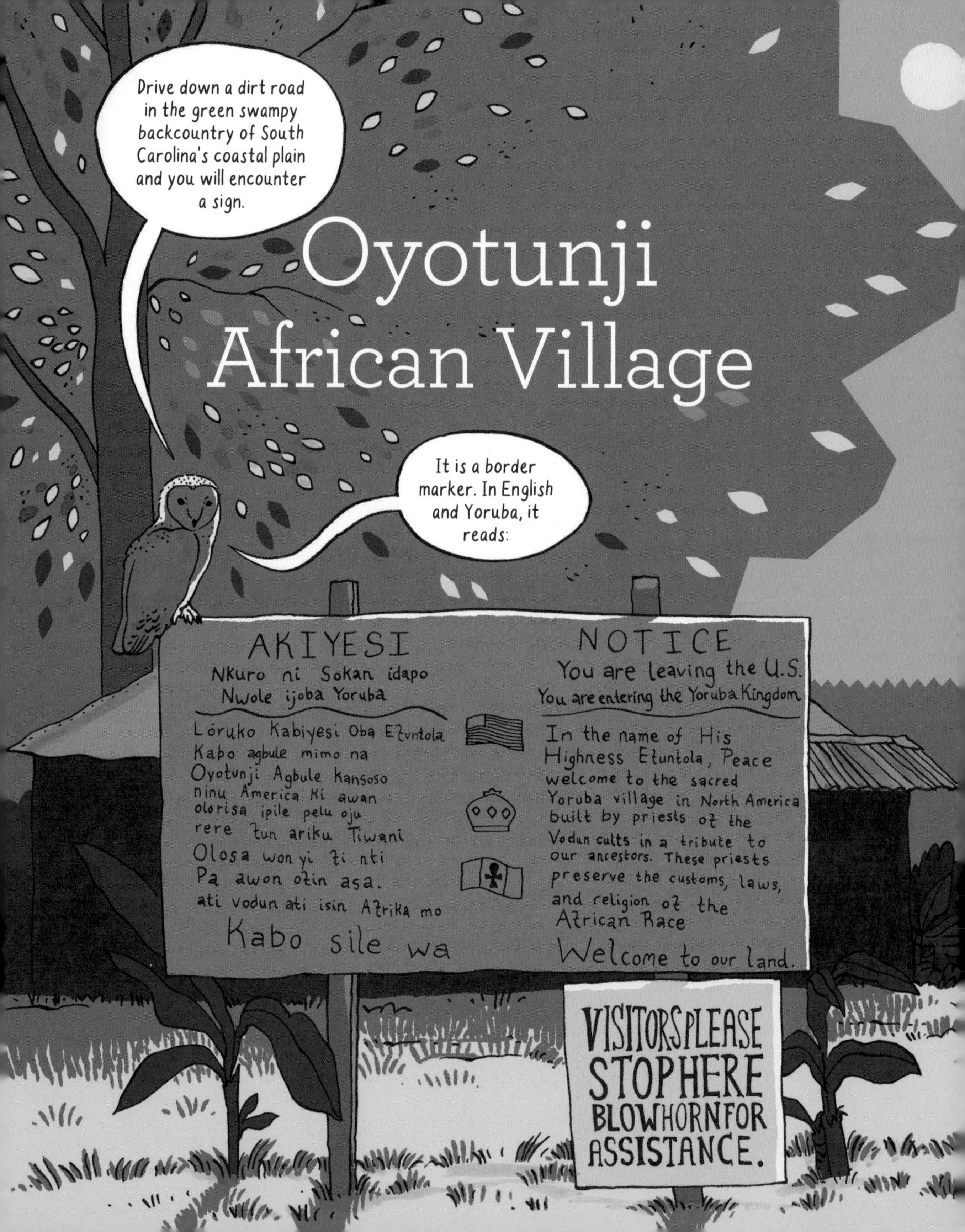
Drive down a dirt road in the green swampy backcountry of South Carolina's coastal plain and you will encounter a sign.
Oyotunji African Village
It is a border marker. In English and Yoruba, it reads:
AKIYESI
Nkuro ni Sokan idapo
Nwole ijoba Yoruba
Lóruko Kabiyesi Oba Efuntola
Kabo agbule mimo na
Oyotunji Agbule kansoso
ninu America ki awan
olorisa ipile pelu oju
rere fun ariku Tiwani
Olosa won yi fi nti
Pa awon ofin asa.
ati vodun ati isin Afrika mo
Kabo sile wa
NOTICE
You are leaving the U.S.
You are entering the Yoruba Kingdom
In the name of His
Highness Efuntola, Peace
welcome to the sacred
Yoruba village in North America
built by priests of the
Vodun cults in a tribute to
our ancestors. These priests
preserve the customs, laws,
and religion of the
African Race
Welcome to our land.
VISITORS PLEASE
STOP HERE
BLOW HORN FOR
ASSISTANCE.

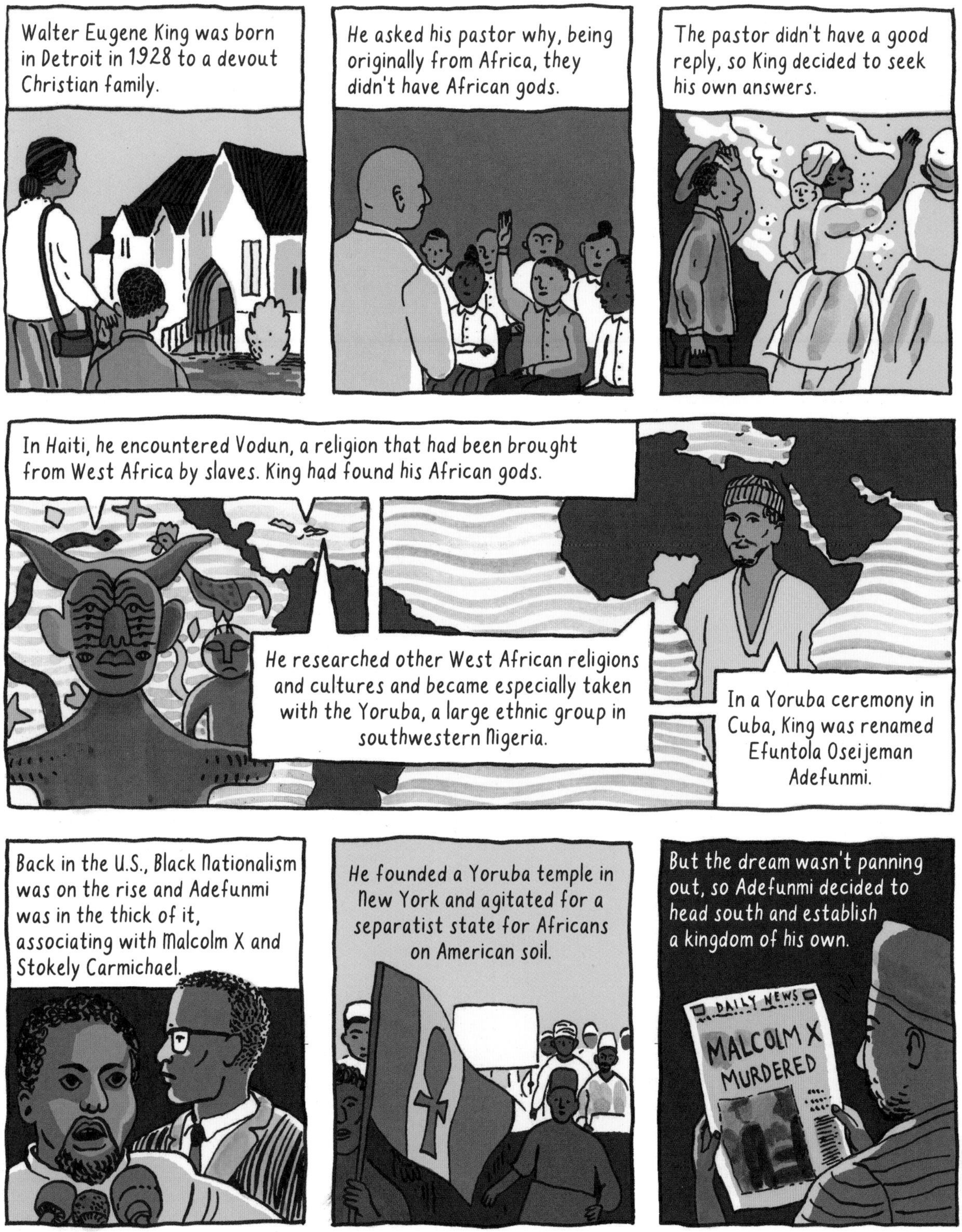
Walter Eugene King was born in Detroit in 1928 to a devout Christian family.
He asked his pastor why, being originally from Africa, they didn't have African gods.
The pastor didn't have a good reply, so King decided to seek his own answers.
In Haiti, he encountered Vodun, a religion that had been brought from West Africa by slaves. King had found his African gods.
He researched other West African religions and cultures and became especially taken with the Yoruba, a large ethnic group in southwestern Nigeria.
In a Yoruba ceremony in Cuba, King was renamed Efuntola Oseijeman Adefunmi.
Back in the U.S., Black Nationalism was on the rise and Adefunmi was in the thick of it, associating with Malcolm X and Stokely Carmichael.
He founded a Yoruba temple in New York and agitated for a separatist state for Africans on American soil.
But the dream wasn't panning out, so Adefunmi decided to head south and establish a kingdom of his own.
DAILY NEWS
MALCOLM X MURDERED

In 1970, Oyotunji was founded on land that had once been a plantation in the South Carolina Low Country.

It was named for the Oyo Empire, a kingdom in modern-day Nigeria founded in the 15th century that had persisted for almost 600 years and was famous for its cavalry and wealth.

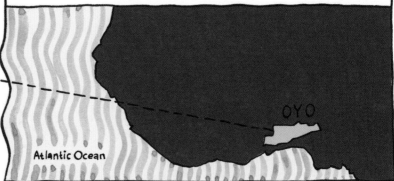

OYOTUNJI African Village

Atlantic Ocean

OYO

Oyotunji's residents taught themselves the Yoruba language,

E kaasan, Iye Agba!*

*Good afternoon, Grandma!

donned Yoruba clothes, worshipped Yoruba gods,

and arranged their society in a hierarchy, ruled by a king or Oba.

That Oba, of course, was Adefunmi.

The population of Oyotunji fluctuated from highs of 150 to lows of 25.

Despite occasional sensational news coverage driven by its adherence to traditional West African polygamy, the community has persisted for 47 years.

Oyotunji's recreation of a traditional Yoruba lifestyle was so immersive that its residents have been hired to play West Africans in television shows and movies.

AFRICAN VILLAGE OYOTUNJI
AS SEEN ON TV

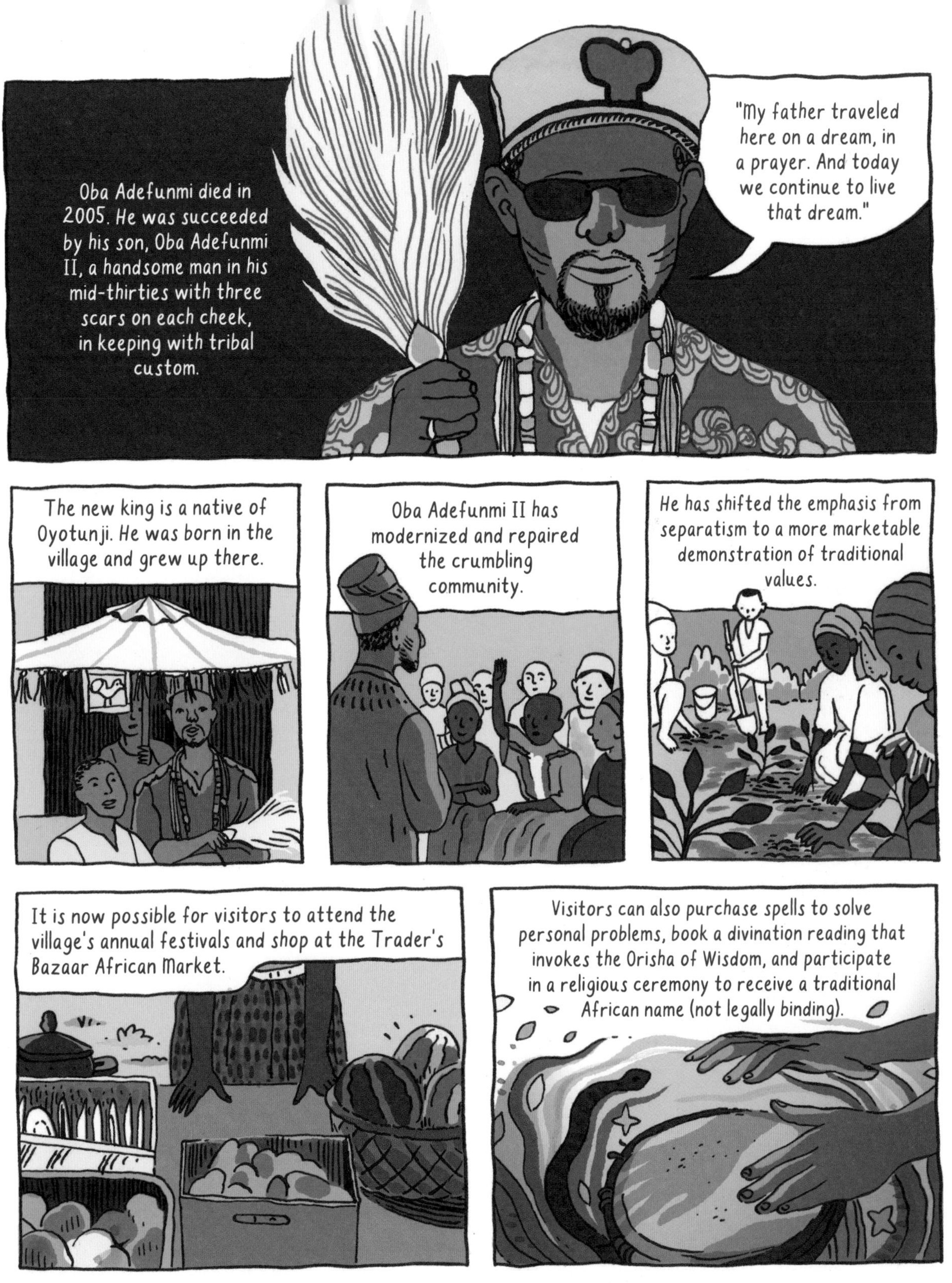
Oba Adefunmi died in 2005. He was succeeded by his son, Oba Adefunmi II, a handsome man in his mid-thirties with three scars on each cheek, in keeping with tribal custom.
"My father traveled here on a dream, in a prayer. And today we continue to live that dream."
The new king is a native of Oyotunji. He was born in the village and grew up there.
Oba Adefunmi II has modernized and repaired the crumbling community.
He has shifted the emphasis from separatism to a more marketable demonstration of traditional values.
It is now possible for visitors to attend the village's annual festivals and shop at the Trader's Bazaar African Market.
Visitors can also purchase spells to solve personal problems, book a divination reading that invokes the Orisha of Wisdom, and participate in a religious ceremony to receive a traditional African name (not legally binding).

Temples of Humankind

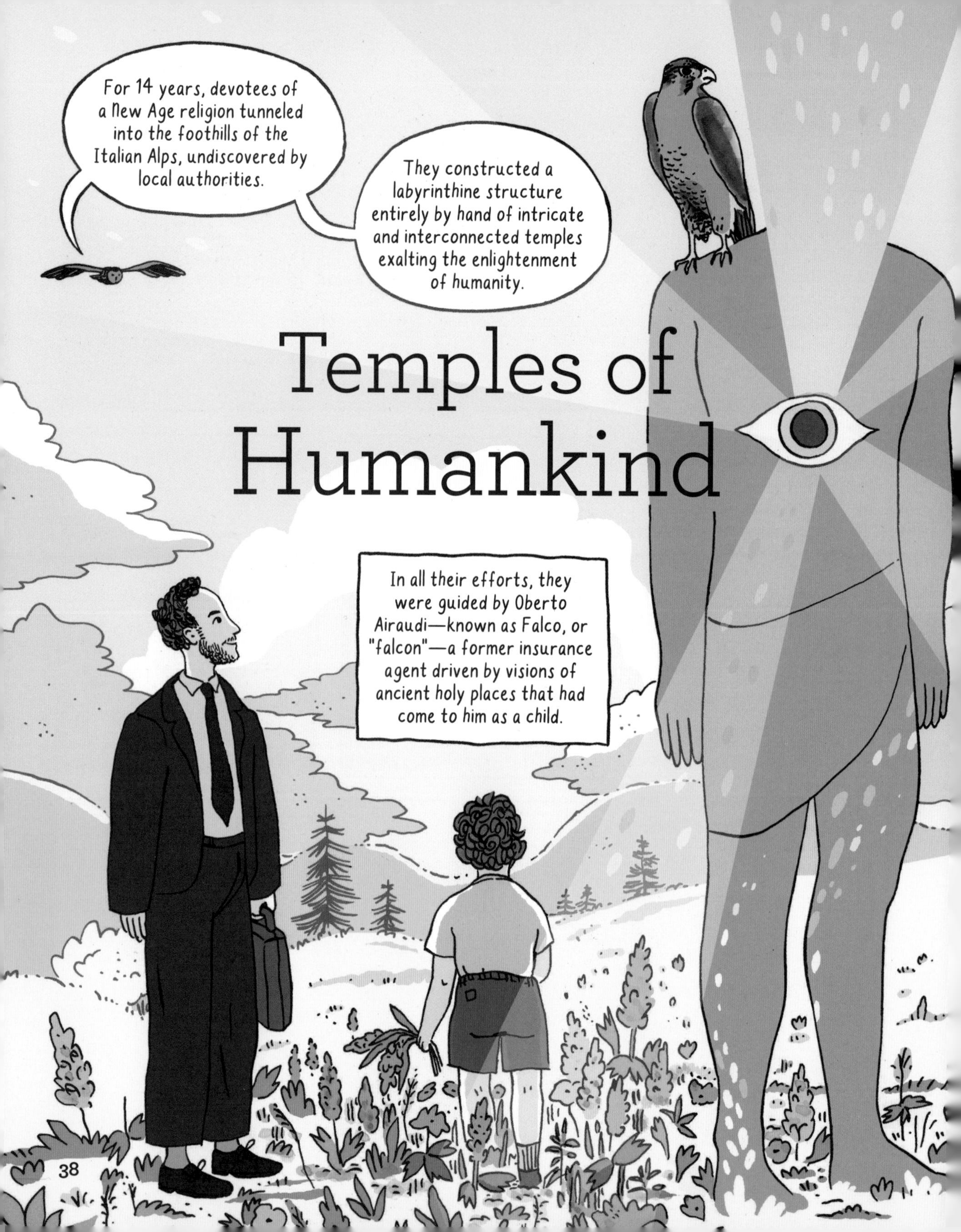
For 14 years, devotees of a New Age religion tunneled into the foothills of the Italian Alps, undiscovered by local authorities.
They constructed a labyrinthine structure entirely by hand of intricate and interconnected temples exalting the enlightenment of humanity.
In all their efforts, they were guided by Oberto Airaudi—known as Falco, or "falcon"—a former insurance agent driven by visions of ancient holy places that had come to him as a child.

Temple construction began in 1978, when Falco bought a house in the mountains and began to dig at a spot he claimed was the intersection of three of the earth's energy lines.

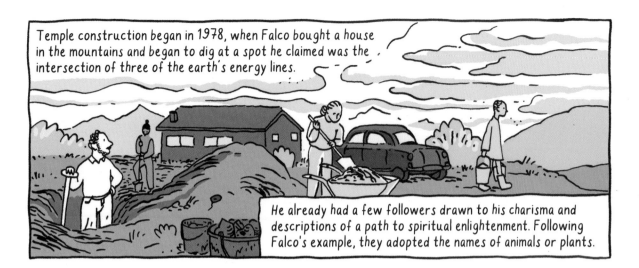

He already had a few followers drawn to his charisma and descriptions of a path to spiritual enlightenment. Following Falco's example, they adopted the names of animals or plants.

Falco called his community "Damanhur" after an Egyptian city with a temple dedicated to Horus.

The Italian authorities finally caught wind of Damanhur's project in 1992.

As unpermitted digging, it was illegal and would have to be shut down.

But no amount of searching revealed the entrance to the tunnels.

HEY!

Frustrated, the police told Falco that they'd dynamite the entire hillside if he didn't reveal where his tunnels were.

So he led them to a shaft hidden behind a door, and showed them.

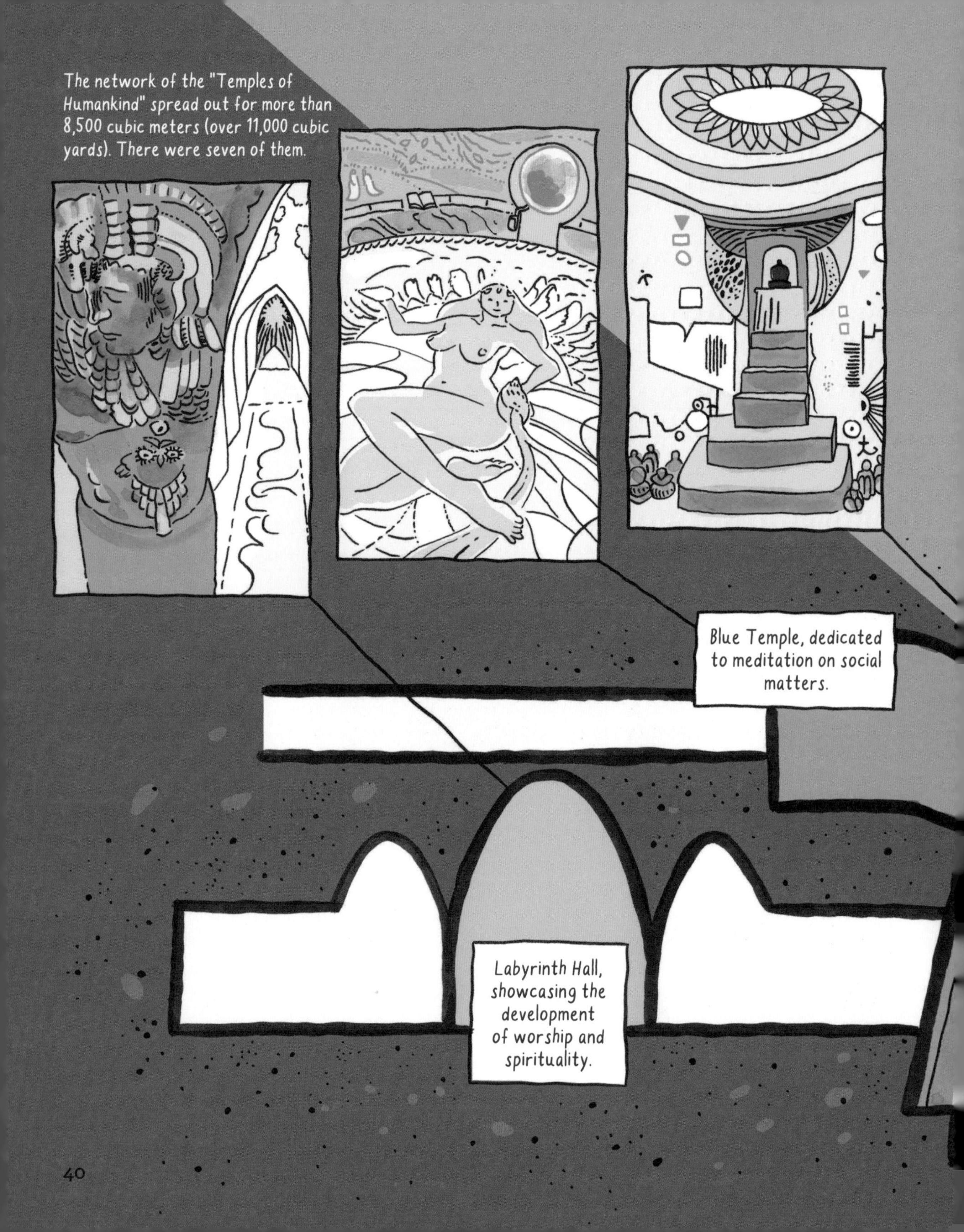
The network of the "Temples of Humankind" spread out for more than 8,500 cubic meters (over 11,000 cubic yards). There were seven of them.
Blue Temple, dedicated to meditation on social matters.
Labyrinth Hall, showcasing the development of worship and spirituality.

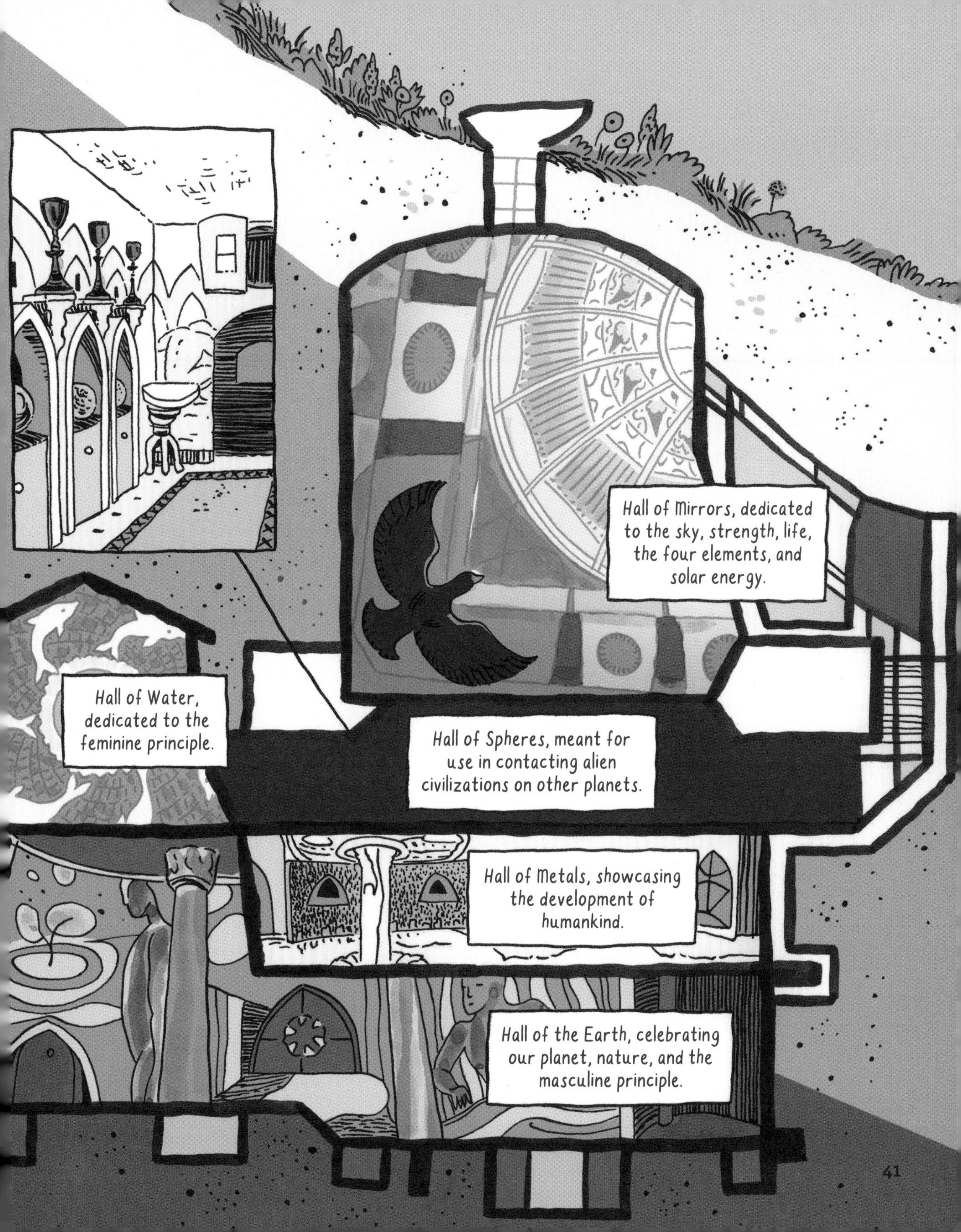
Hall of Mirrors, dedicated to the sky, strength, life, the four elements, and solar energy.
Hall of Water, dedicated to the feminine principle.
Hall of Spheres, meant for use in contacting alien civilizations on other planets.
Hall of Metals, showcasing the development of humankind.
Hall of the Earth, celebrating our planet, nature, and the masculine principle.

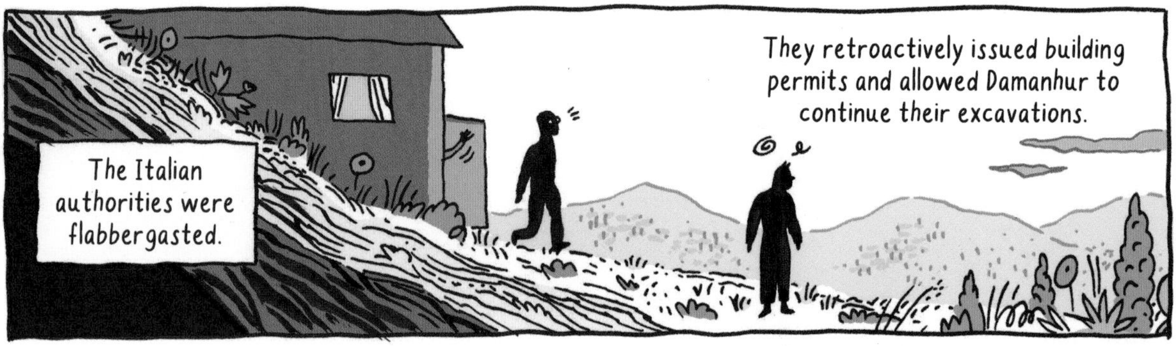
The Italian authorities were flabbergasted.
They retroactively issued building permits and allowed Damanhur to continue their excavations.

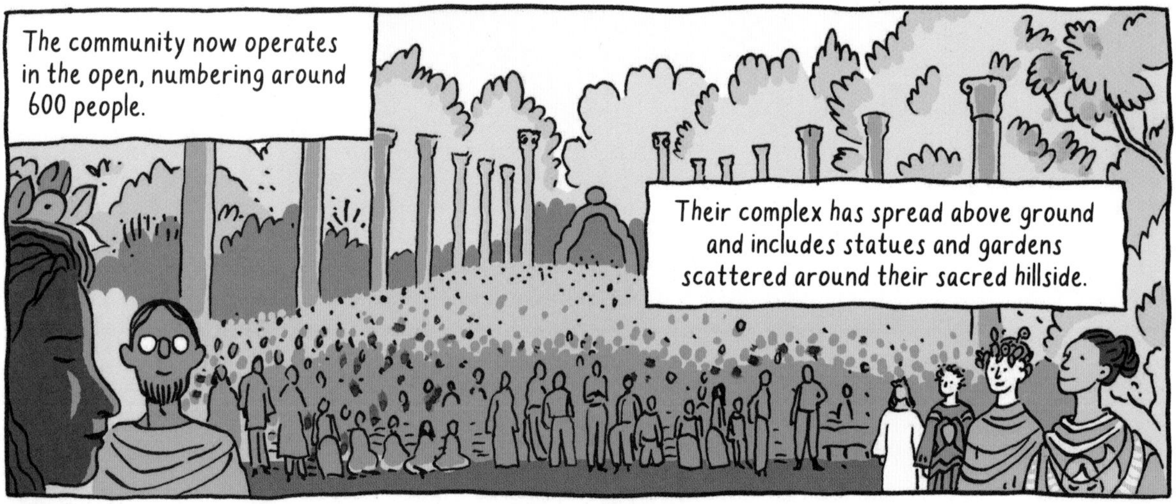
The community now operates in the open, numbering around 600 people.
Their complex has spread above ground and includes statues and gardens scattered around their sacred hillside.

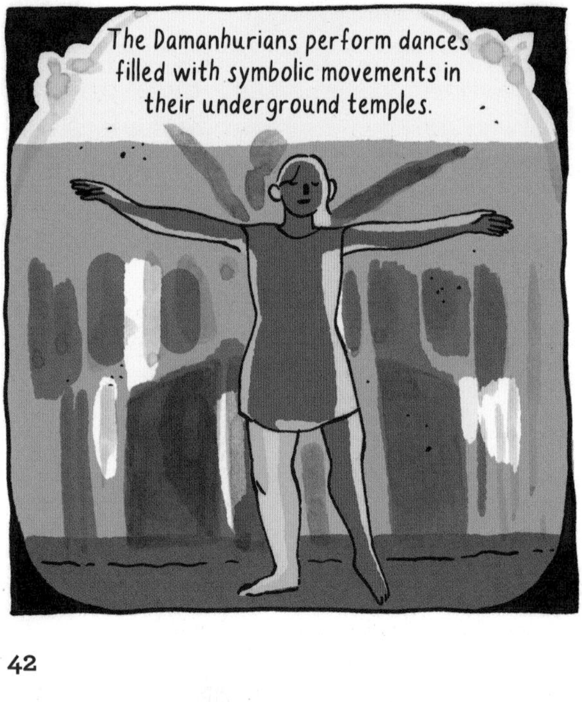
The Damanhurians perform dances filled with symbolic movements in their underground temples.

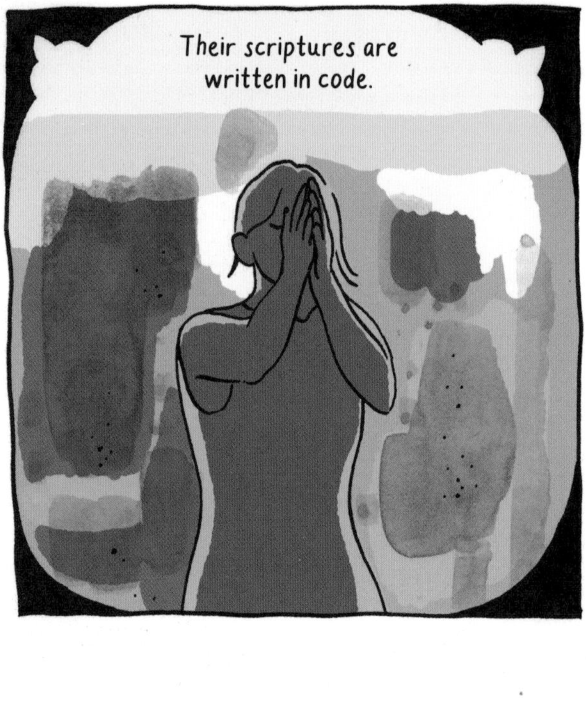
Their scriptures are written in code.

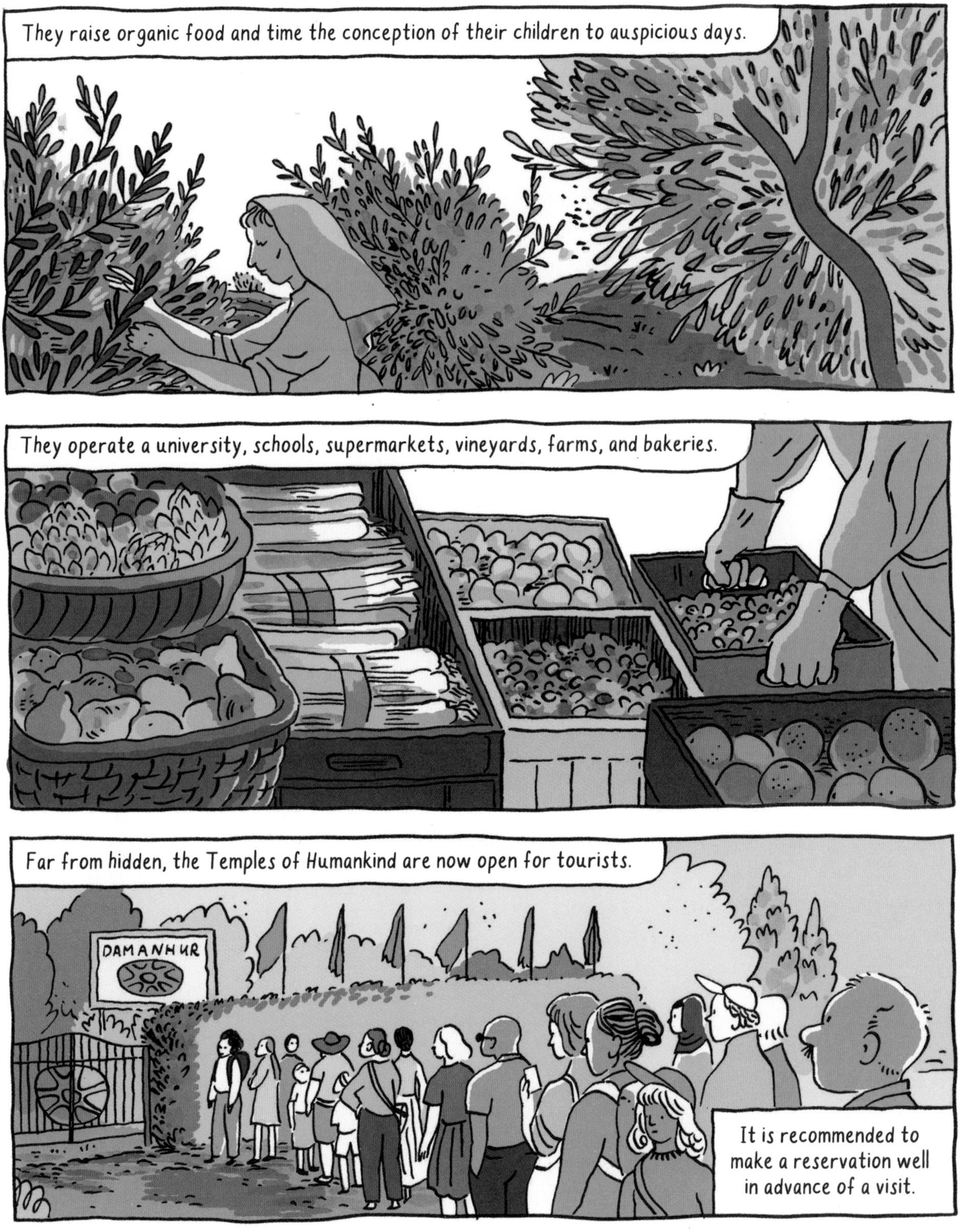
They raise organic food and time the conception of their children to auspicious days.
They operate a university, schools, supermarkets, vineyards, farms, and bakeries.
Far from hidden, the Temples of Humankind are now open for tourists.
DAMANHUR
It is recommended to make a reservation well in advance of a visit.

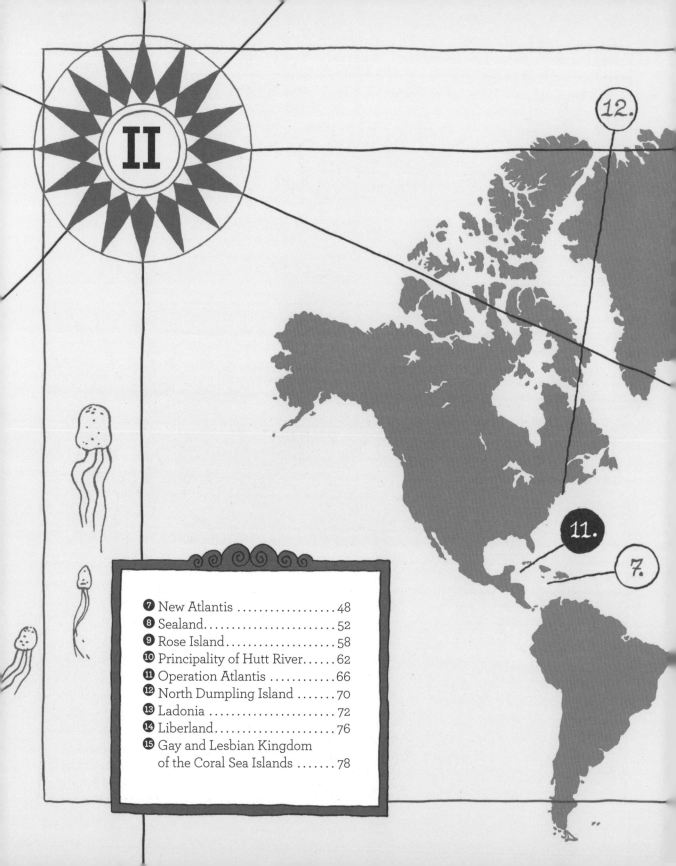

II

12.

11.

7.

MICRONATIONS

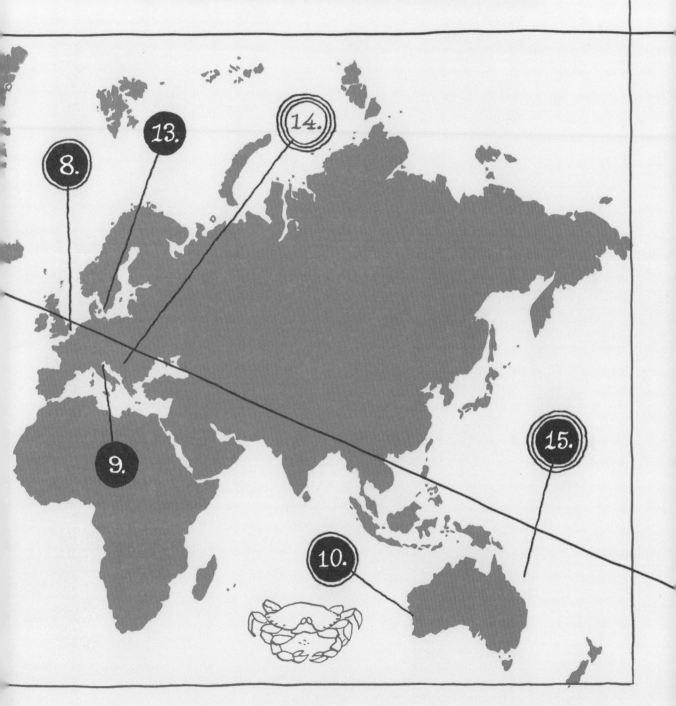

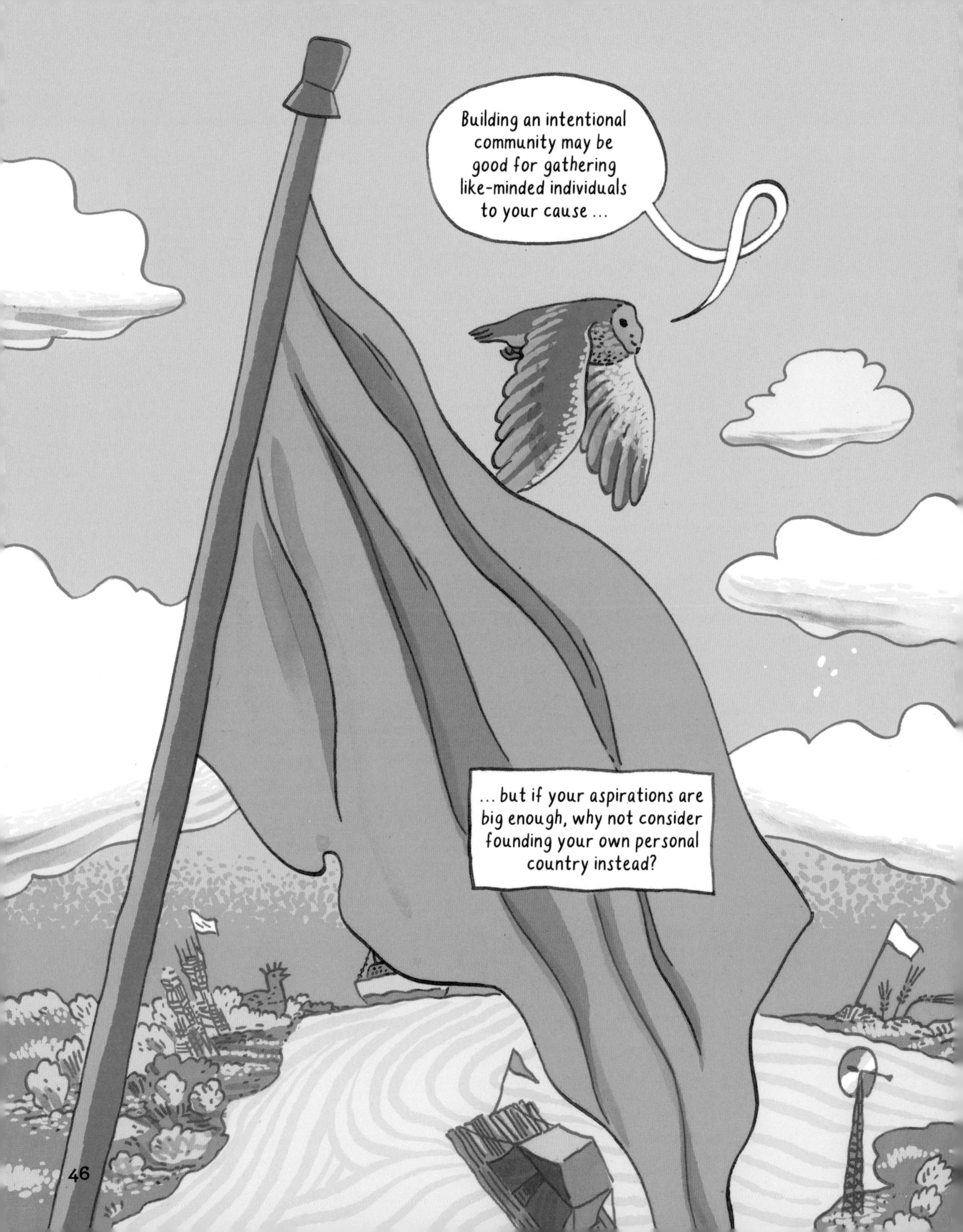
Building an intentional community may be good for gathering like-minded individuals to your cause ...
... but if your aspirations are big enough, why not consider founding your own personal country instead?

Pursuing the dream of sovereignty can be costly, however.

You might have to defend your new nation from armed Dutch mercenaries ...

WAT.

... or go to war with Australia ...

... but if you succeed, you may get to issue your own postage stamps and bestow royal titles!

BECOME A LADY, LORD, BARON, OR BARONESS!

SHOP NOW

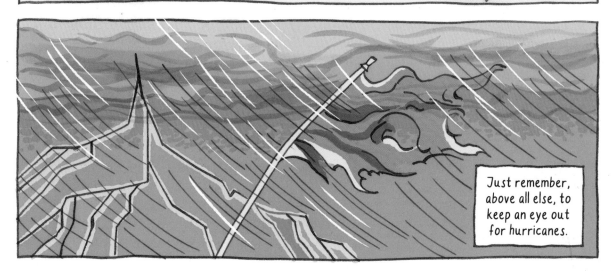

Just remember, above all else, to keep an eye out for hurricanes.

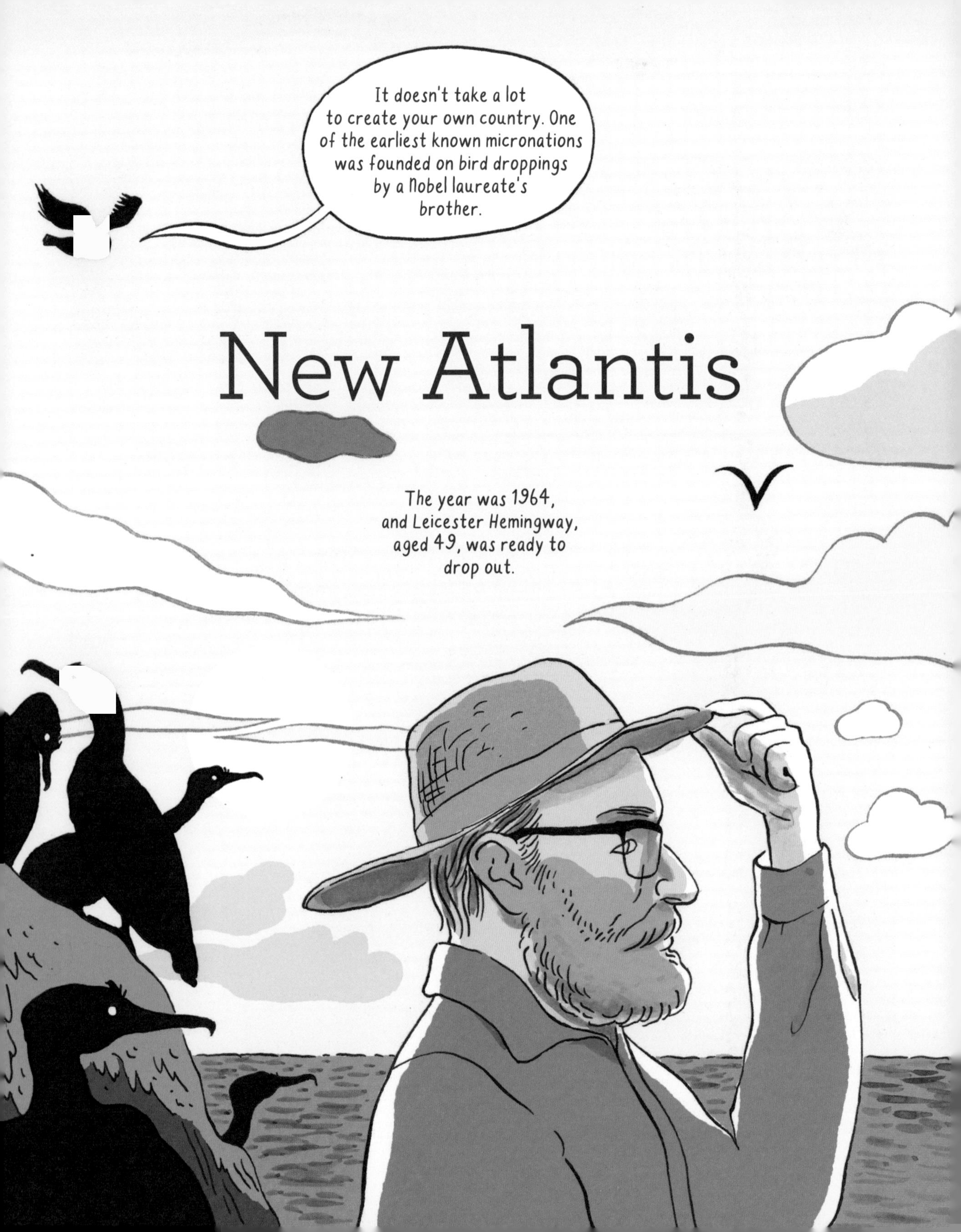
It doesn't take a lot to create your own country. One of the earliest known micronations was founded on bird droppings by a Nobel laureate's brother.
New Atlantis
The year was 1964, and Leicester Hemingway, aged 49, was ready to drop out.

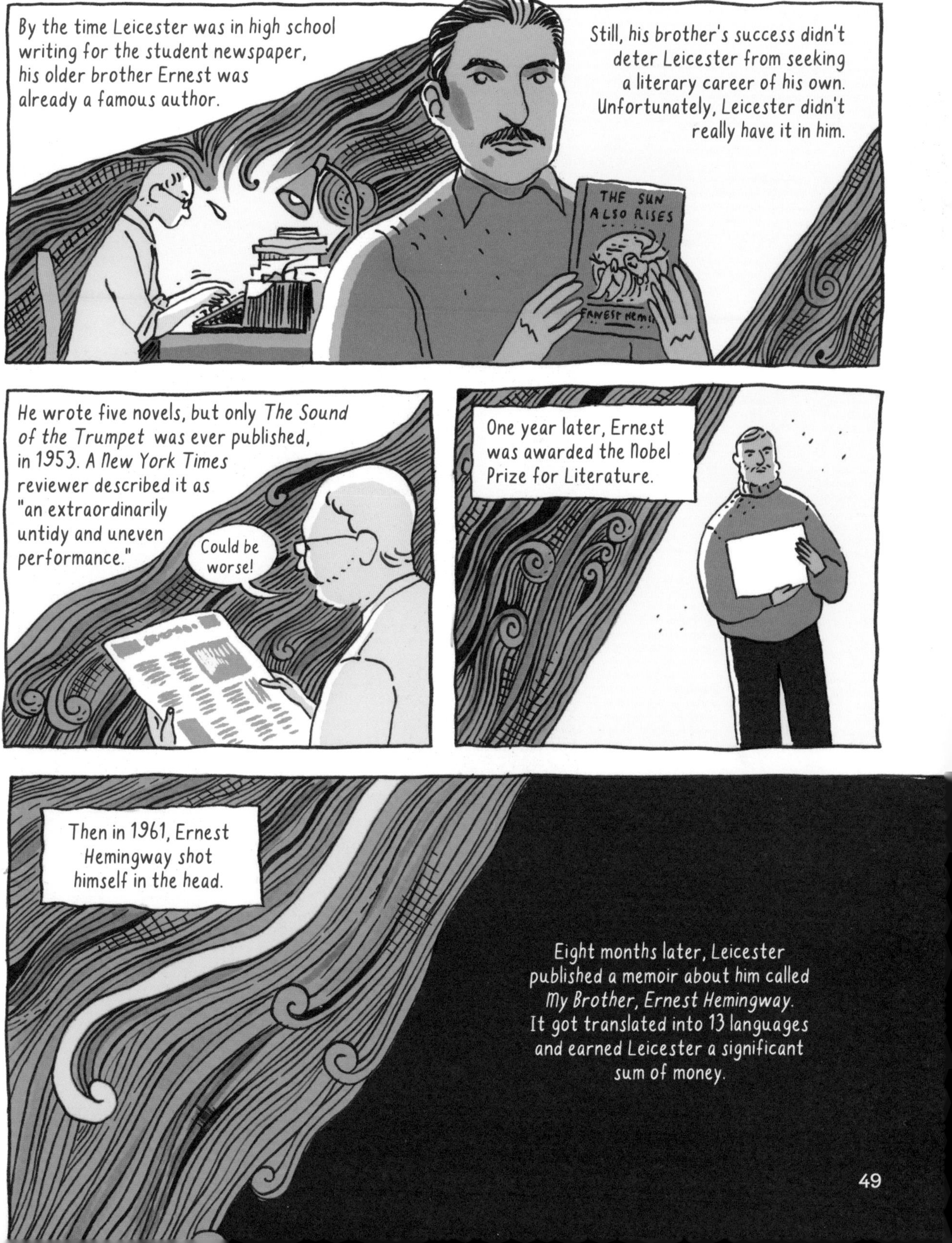
By the time Leicester was in high school writing for the student newspaper, his older brother Ernest was already a famous author.
Still, his brother's success didn't deter Leicester from seeking a literary career of his own. Unfortunately, Leicester didn't really have it in him.
THE SUN ALSO RISES
He wrote five novels, but only *The Sound of the Trumpet* was ever published, in 1953. A *New York Times* reviewer described it as "an extraordinarily untidy and uneven performance."
Could be worse!
One year later, Ernest was awarded the Nobel Prize for Literature.
Then in 1961, Ernest Hemingway shot himself in the head.
Eight months later, Leicester published a memoir about him called *My Brother, Ernest Hemingway*. It got translated into 13 languages and earned Leicester a significant sum of money.

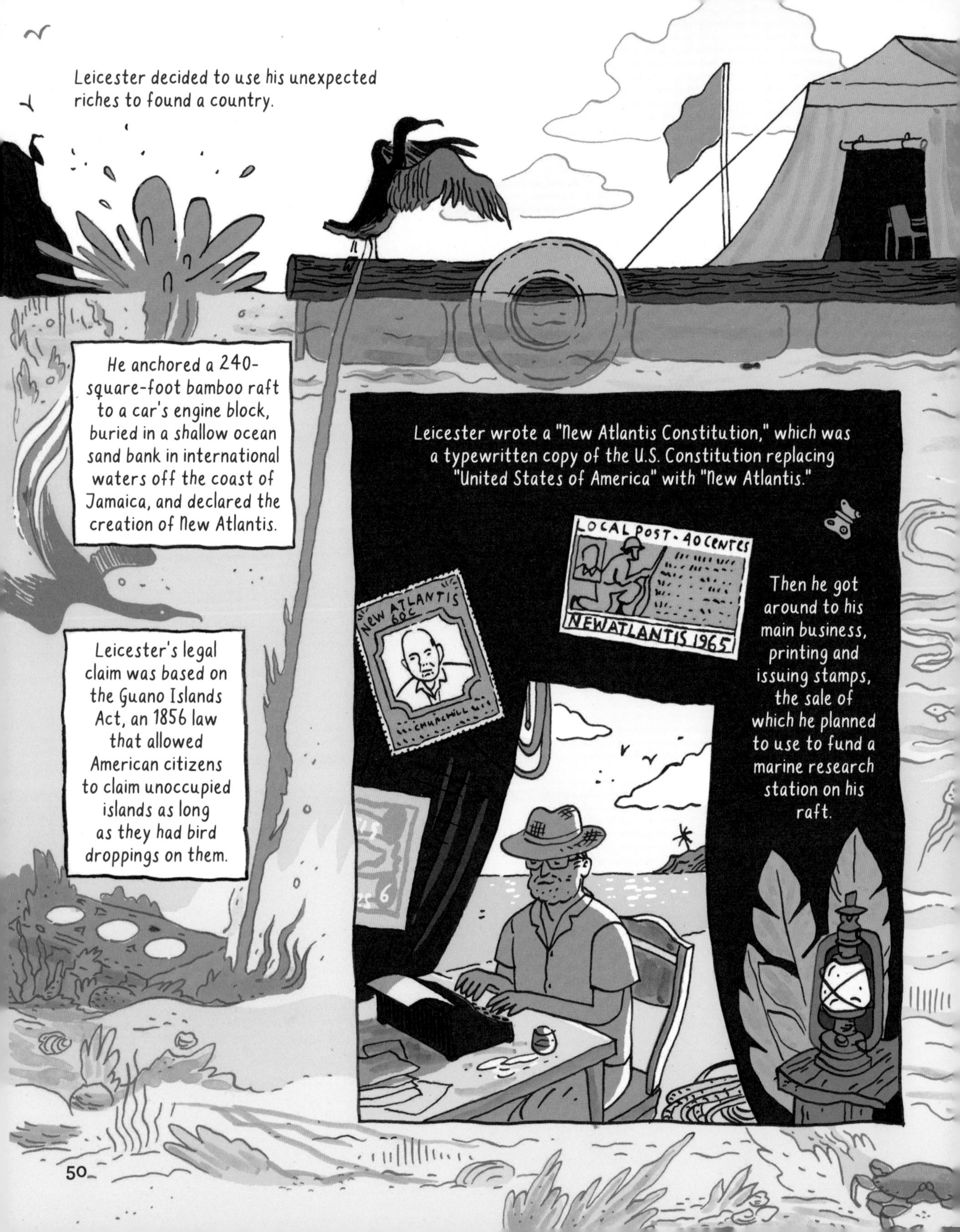
Leicester decided to use his unexpected riches to found a country.
He anchored a 240-square-foot bamboo raft to a car's engine block, buried in a shallow ocean sand bank in international waters off the coast of Jamaica, and declared the creation of New Atlantis.
Leicester's legal claim was based on the Guano Islands Act, an 1856 law that allowed American citizens to claim unoccupied islands as long as they had bird droppings on them.
Leicester wrote a "New Atlantis Constitution," which was a typewritten copy of the U.S. Constitution replacing "United States of America" with "New Atlantis."
LOCAL POST · 40 CENTES
NEWATLANTIS 1965
NEW ATLANTIS 60C
CHURCHILL
Then he got around to his main business, printing and issuing stamps, the sale of which he planned to use to fund a marine research station on his raft.

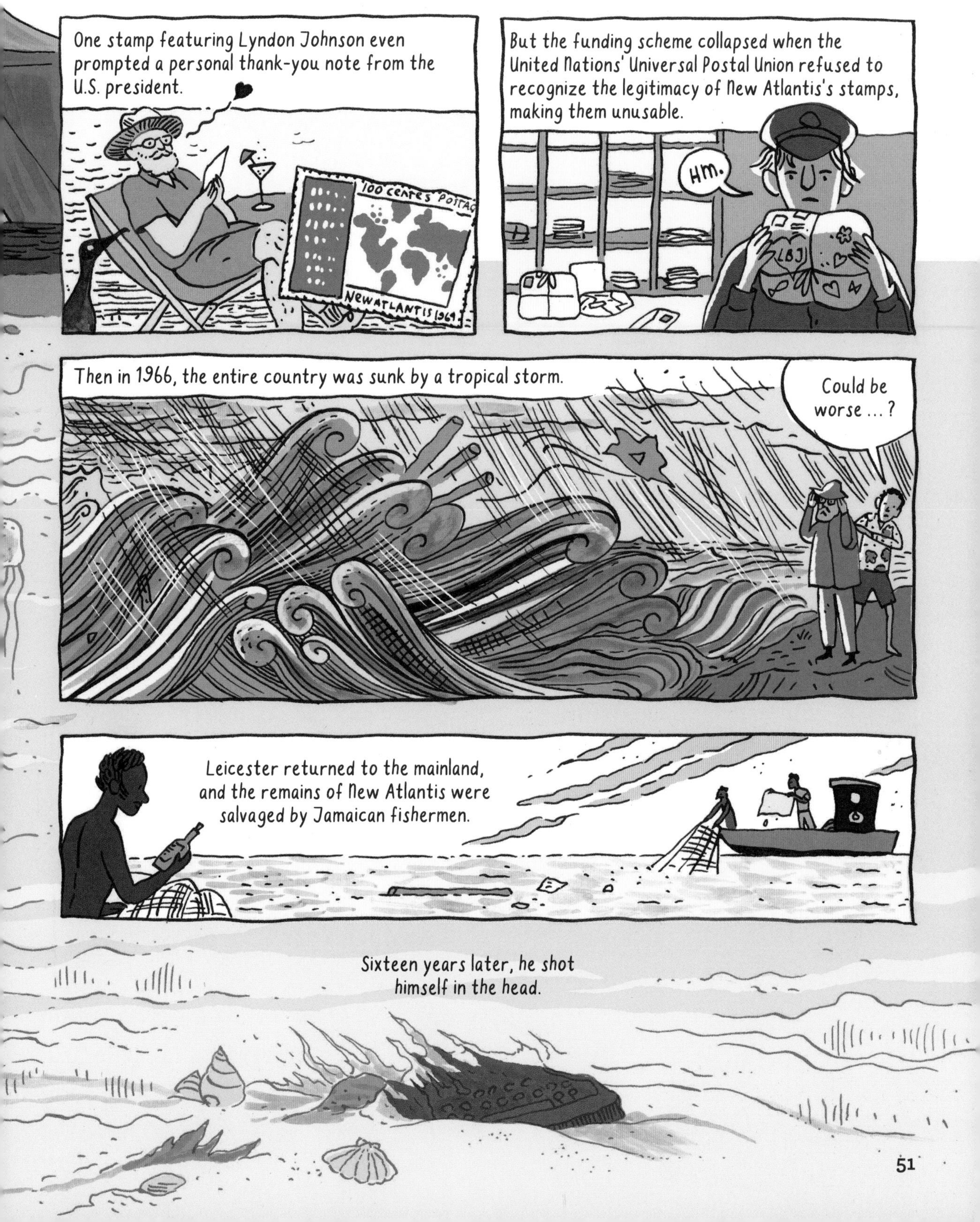
One stamp featuring Lyndon Johnson even prompted a personal thank-you note from the U.S. president.
100 CENTS POSTAG
NEW ATLANTIS 1964
But the funding scheme collapsed when the United Nations' Universal Postal Union refused to recognize the legitimacy of New Atlantis's stamps, making them unusable.
HM.
LBJ
Then in 1966, the entire country was sunk by a tropical storm.
Could be worse ...?
Leicester returned to the mainland, and the remains of New Atlantis were salvaged by Jamaican fishermen.
Sixteen years later, he shot himself in the head.

Sealand

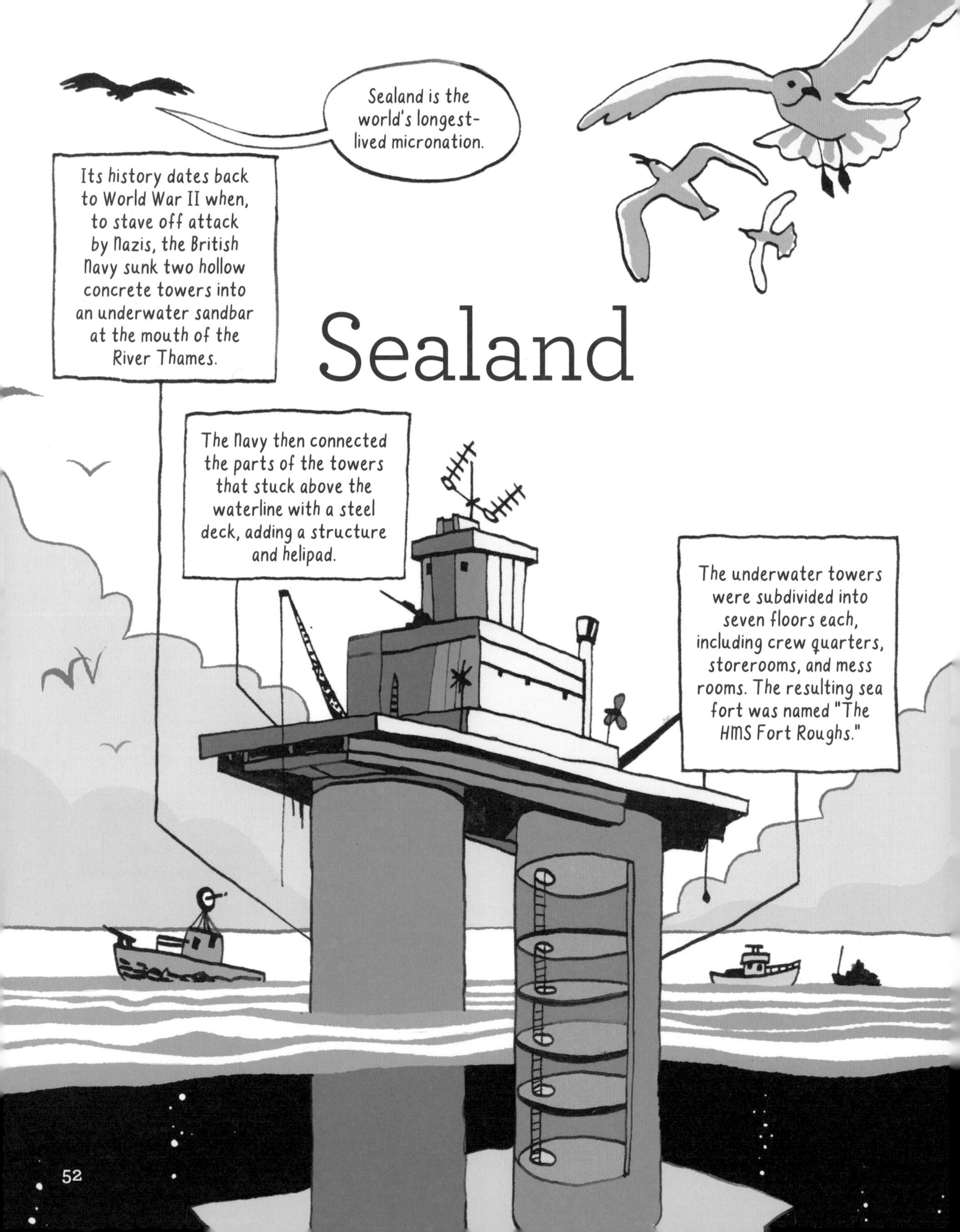
Sealand is the world's longest-lived micronation.
Its history dates back to World War II when, to stave off attack by Nazis, the British Navy sunk two hollow concrete towers into an underwater sandbar at the mouth of the River Thames.
The Navy then connected the parts of the towers that stuck above the waterline with a steel deck, adding a structure and helipad.
The underwater towers were subdivided into seven floors each, including crew quarters, storerooms, and mess rooms. The resulting sea fort was named "The HMS Fort Roughs."

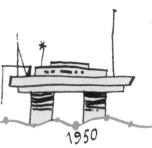

1945

The Nazis never came, and the fort was abandoned in 1956.

1956

1950

1960

In 1966, the pirate radio stations arrived.

1966

Pirate radio existed because the BBC, which had a monopoly over British airwaves, refused to play pop or rock and roll.

And now, the soothing tune "Why" from Anthony Newley.

Renegade DJs established their own stations in international waters, broadcasting music that teenagers could tune into back on the mainland.

Most pirate radio stations were set up on ships, but an empty naval fort promised a more permanent installation.

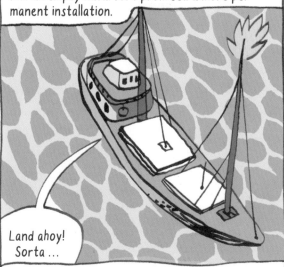

Land ahoy! Sorta ...

Paddy Roy Bates, who operated Radio Essex, and Ronan O'Rahilly, who operated Radio Caroline, sailed to the vacant HMS Fort Roughs and occupied it.

Unsurprisingly, things did not go smoothly.

Let me check if the coast is clear ...

So, is it clear?

Sure!

They were pirates, after all.

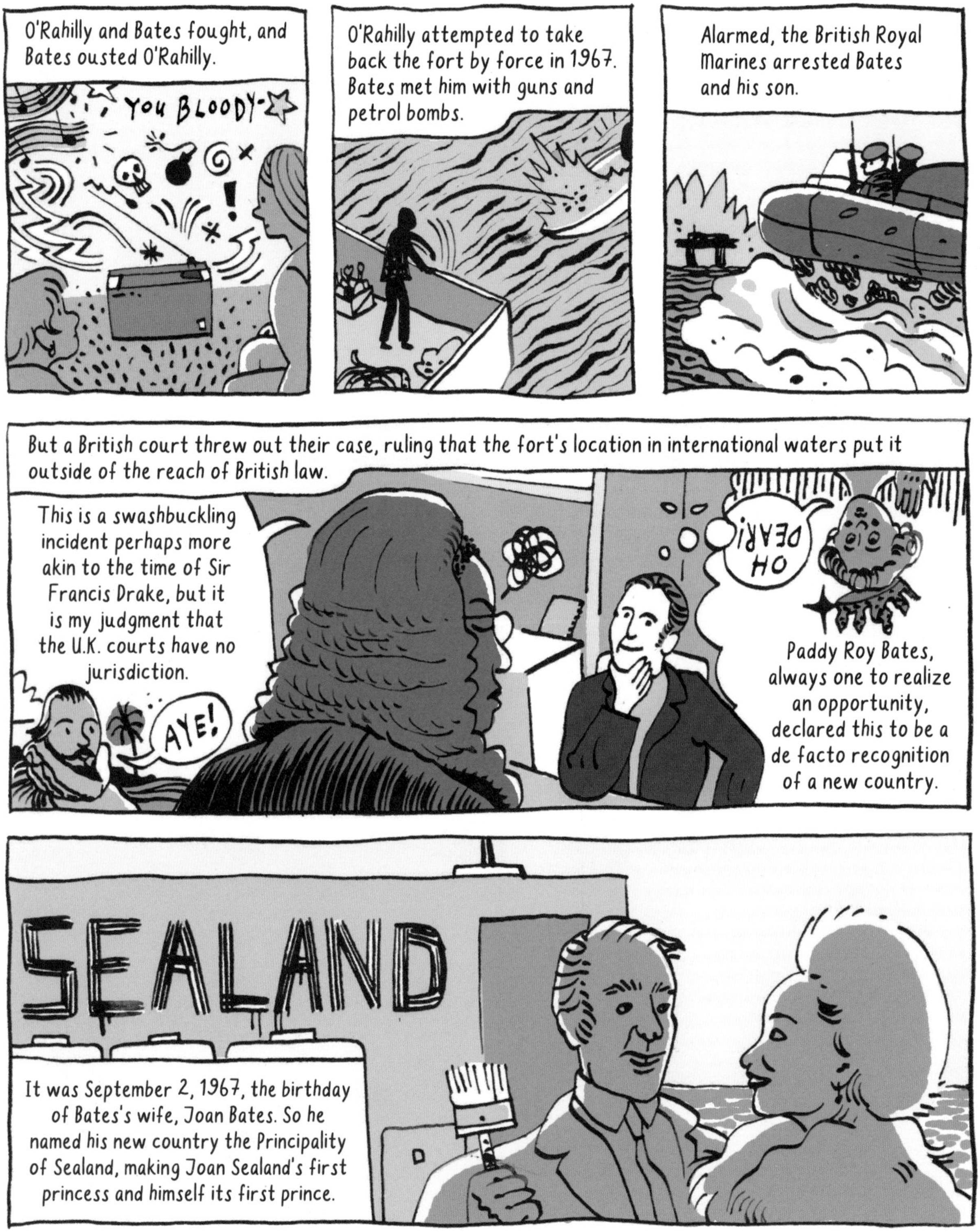
O'Rahilly and Bates fought, and Bates ousted O'Rahilly.
YOU BLOODY-
O'Rahilly attempted to take back the fort by force in 1967. Bates met him with guns and petrol bombs.
Alarmed, the British Royal Marines arrested Bates and his son.
But a British court threw out their case, ruling that the fort's location in international waters put it outside of the reach of British law.
This is a swashbuckling incident perhaps more akin to the time of Sir Francis Drake, but it is my judgment that the U.K. courts have no jurisdiction.
AYE!
OH DEAR!
Paddy Roy Bates, always one to realize an opportunity, declared this to be a de facto recognition of a new country.
SEALAND
It was September 2, 1967, the birthday of Bates's wife, Joan Bates. So he named his new country the Principality of Sealand, making Joan Sealand's first princess and himself its first prince.

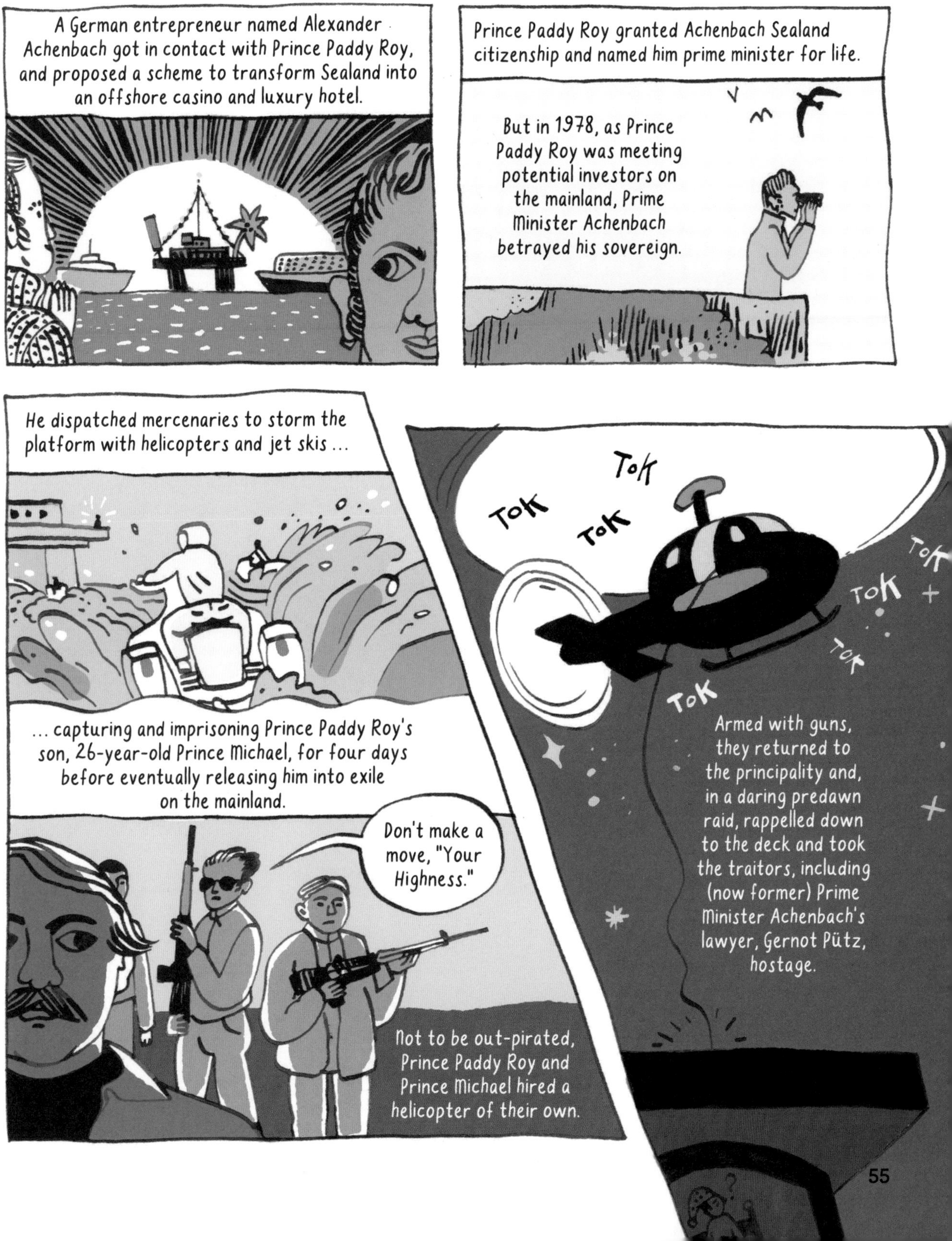
A German entrepreneur named Alexander Achenbach got in contact with Prince Paddy Roy, and proposed a scheme to transform Sealand into an offshore casino and luxury hotel.
Prince Paddy Roy granted Achenbach Sealand citizenship and named him prime minister for life.
But in 1978, as Prince Paddy Roy was meeting potential investors on the mainland, Prime Minister Achenbach betrayed his sovereign.
He dispatched mercenaries to storm the platform with helicopters and jet skis ...
... capturing and imprisoning Prince Paddy Roy's son, 26-year-old Prince Michael, for four days before eventually releasing him into exile on the mainland.
Don't make a move, "Your Highness."
Not to be out-pirated, Prince Paddy Roy and Prince Michael hired a helicopter of their own.
TOK
TOK
TOK
TOK
TOK
TOK
TOK
Armed with guns, they returned to the principality and, in a daring predawn raid, rappelled down to the deck and took the traitors, including (now former) Prime Minister Achenbach's lawyer, Gernot Pütz, hostage.

Since Pütz was a German national, this briefly resulted in an international incident between Britain and Germany.

To Germany's consternation, Britain refused to intercede to free Pütz, citing the 1967 court decision that placed Sealand out of its jurisdiction.

The crisis ended when Germany sent a diplomat from its London embassy to Sealand to negotiate for Pütz's release.

There, there. Now, who would fancy some tea?

Prince Paddy Roy took this as de facto recognition of Sealand by Germany and released Pütz as a gesture of goodwill.

Pütz and Achenbach established a rebel Sealand government-in-exile in Germany, but never troubled Prince Paddy Roy again.

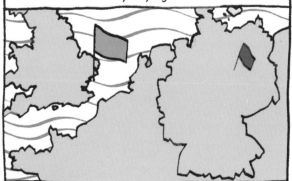

Left undisturbed, the Principality of Sealand did a brisk trade in selling commemorative stamps ...

... and granting noble titles for a fee.

For a brief period in 2000, Sealand acted as an offshore data haven, until the dot-com crash dried up business.

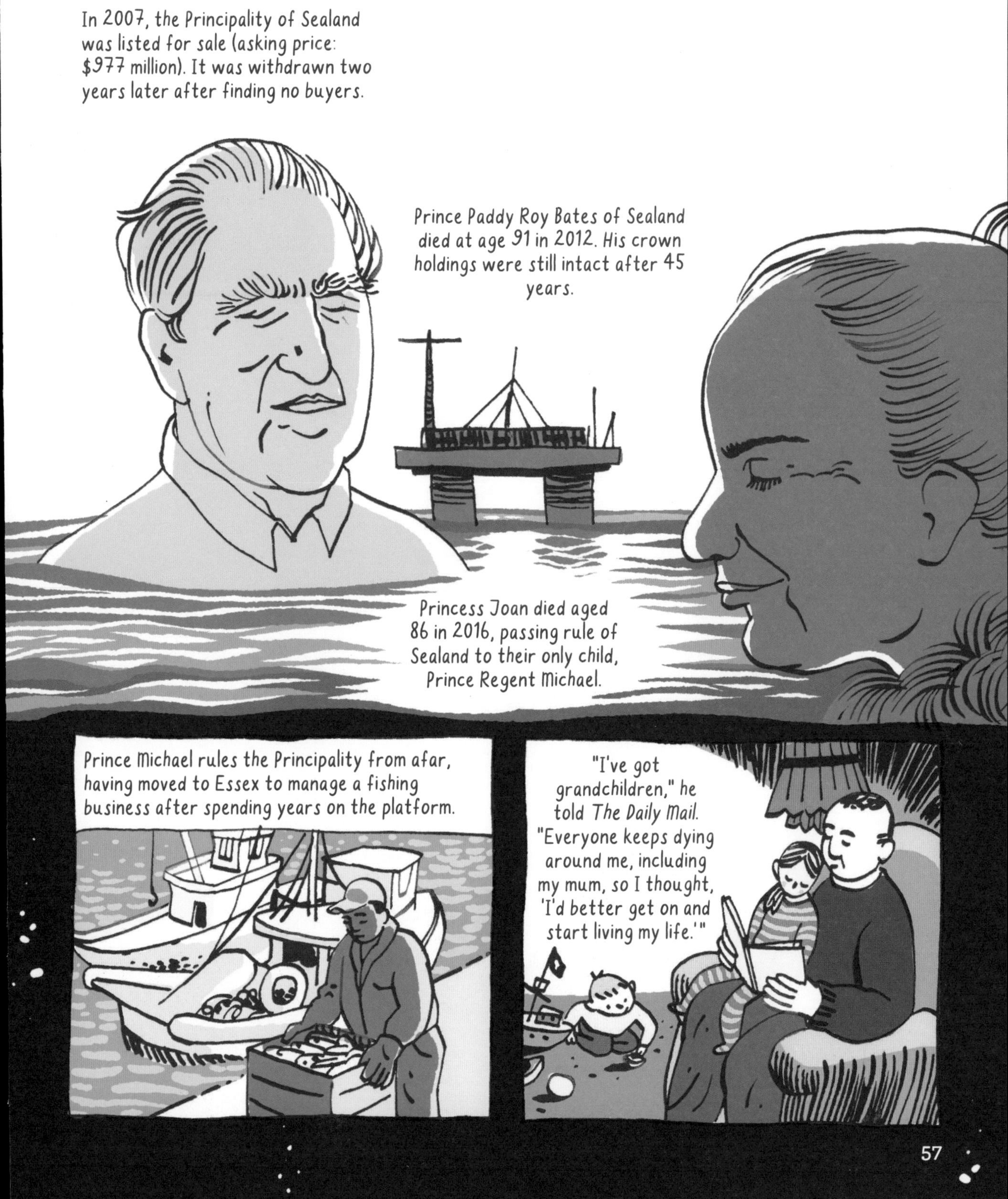
In 2007, the Principality of Sealand was listed for sale (asking price: $977 million). It was withdrawn two years later after finding no buyers.
Prince Paddy Roy Bates of Sealand died at age 91 in 2012. His crown holdings were still intact after 45 years.
Princess Joan died aged 86 in 2016, passing rule of Sealand to their only child, Prince Regent Michael.
Prince Michael rules the Principality from afar, having moved to Essex to manage a fishing business after spending years on the platform.
"I've got grandchildren," he told *The Daily Mail*. "Everyone keeps dying around me, including my mum, so I thought, 'I'd better get on and start living my life.'"

Rose Island

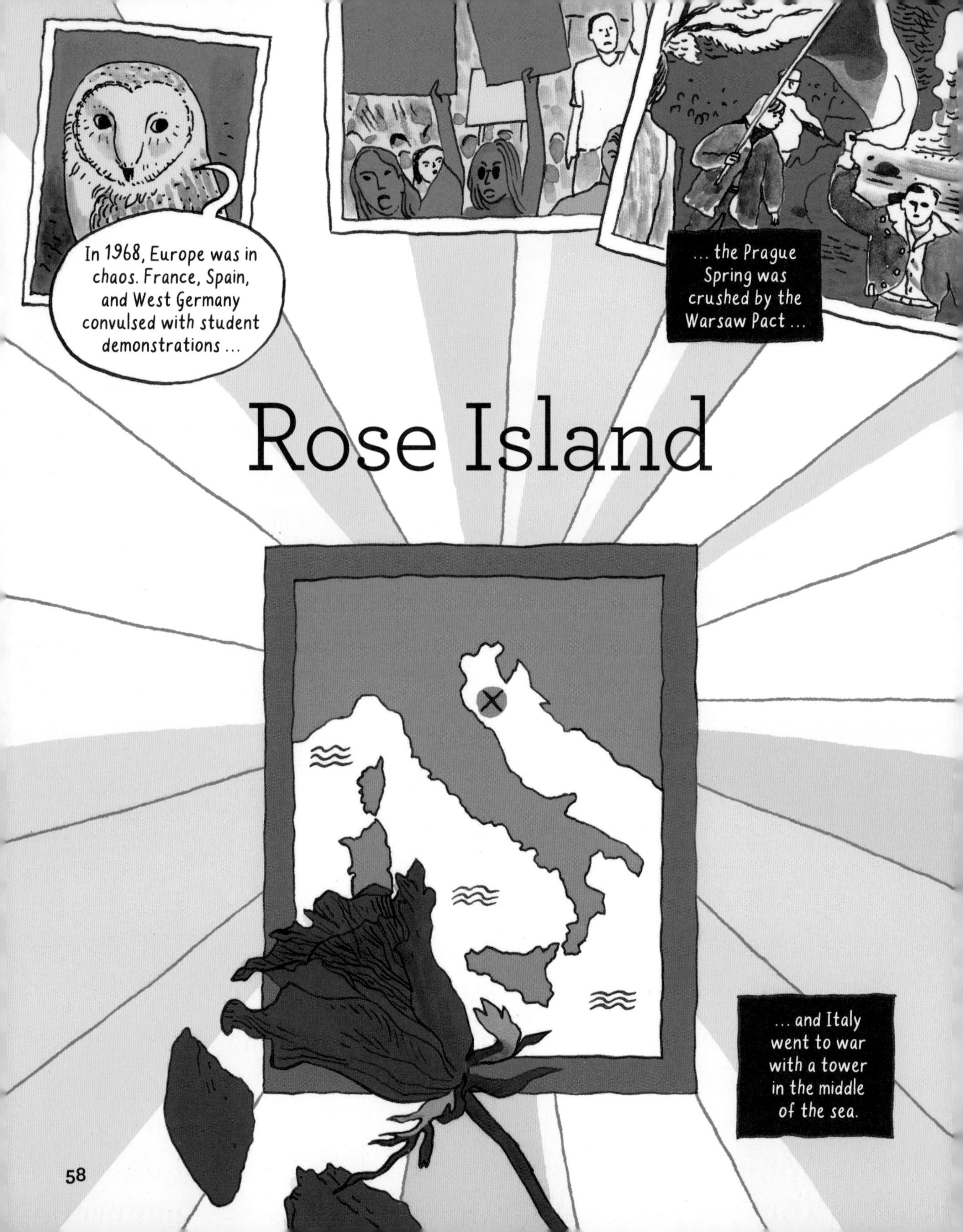
In 1968, Europe was in chaos. France, Spain, and West Germany convulsed with student demonstrations ...
... the Prague Spring was crushed by the Warsaw Pact ...
... and Italy went to war with a tower in the middle of the sea.

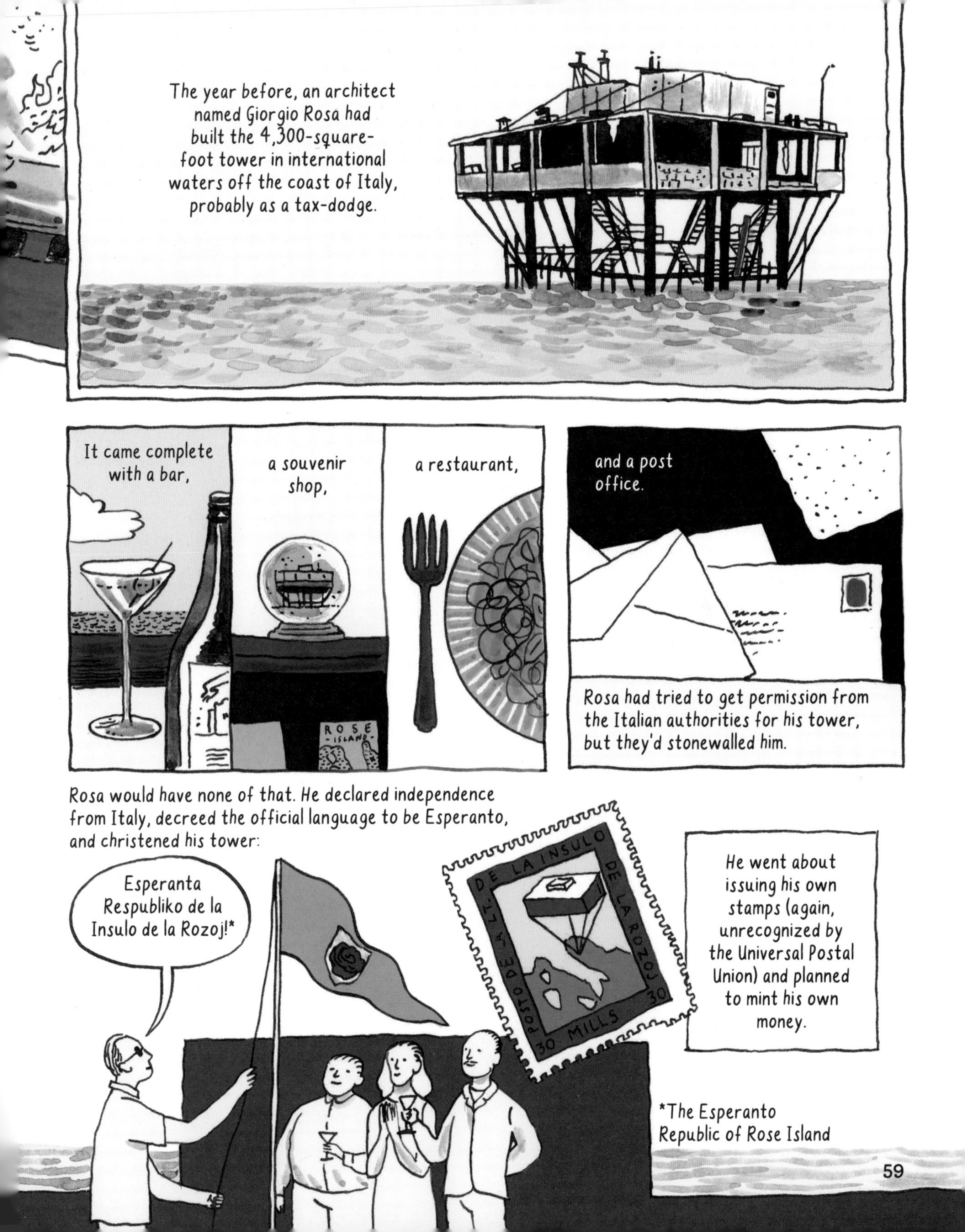
The year before, an architect named Giorgio Rosa had built the 4,300-square-foot tower in international waters off the coast of Italy, probably as a tax-dodge.
It came complete with a bar,
a souvenir shop,
a restaurant,
and a post office.
Rosa had tried to get permission from the Italian authorities for his tower, but they'd stonewalled him.
Rosa would have none of that. He declared independence from Italy, decreed the official language to be Esperanto, and christened his tower:
Esperanta Respubliko de la Insulo de la Rozoj!*
POSTO DE LA I.T. DE LA INSULO DE LA ROZOJ
30 MILLS 30
He went about issuing his own stamps (again, unrecognized by the Universal Postal Union) and planned to mint his own money.
*The Esperanto Republic of Rose Island

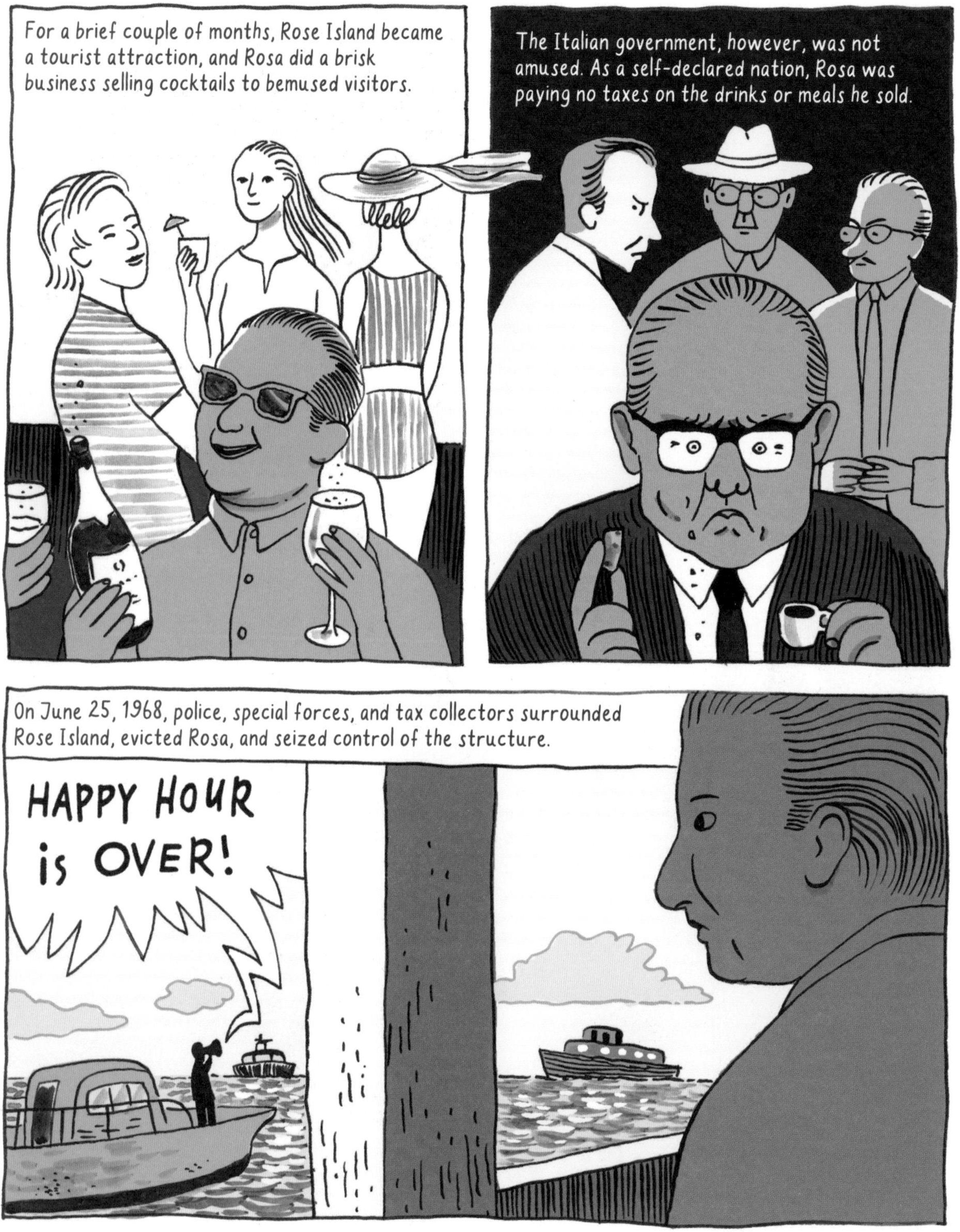
For a brief couple of months, Rose Island became a tourist attraction, and Rosa did a brisk business selling cocktails to bemused visitors.
The Italian government, however, was not amused. As a self-declared nation, Rosa was paying no taxes on the drinks or meals he sold.
On June 25, 1968, police, special forces, and tax collectors surrounded Rose Island, evicted Rosa, and seized control of the structure.
HAPPY HOUR is OVER!

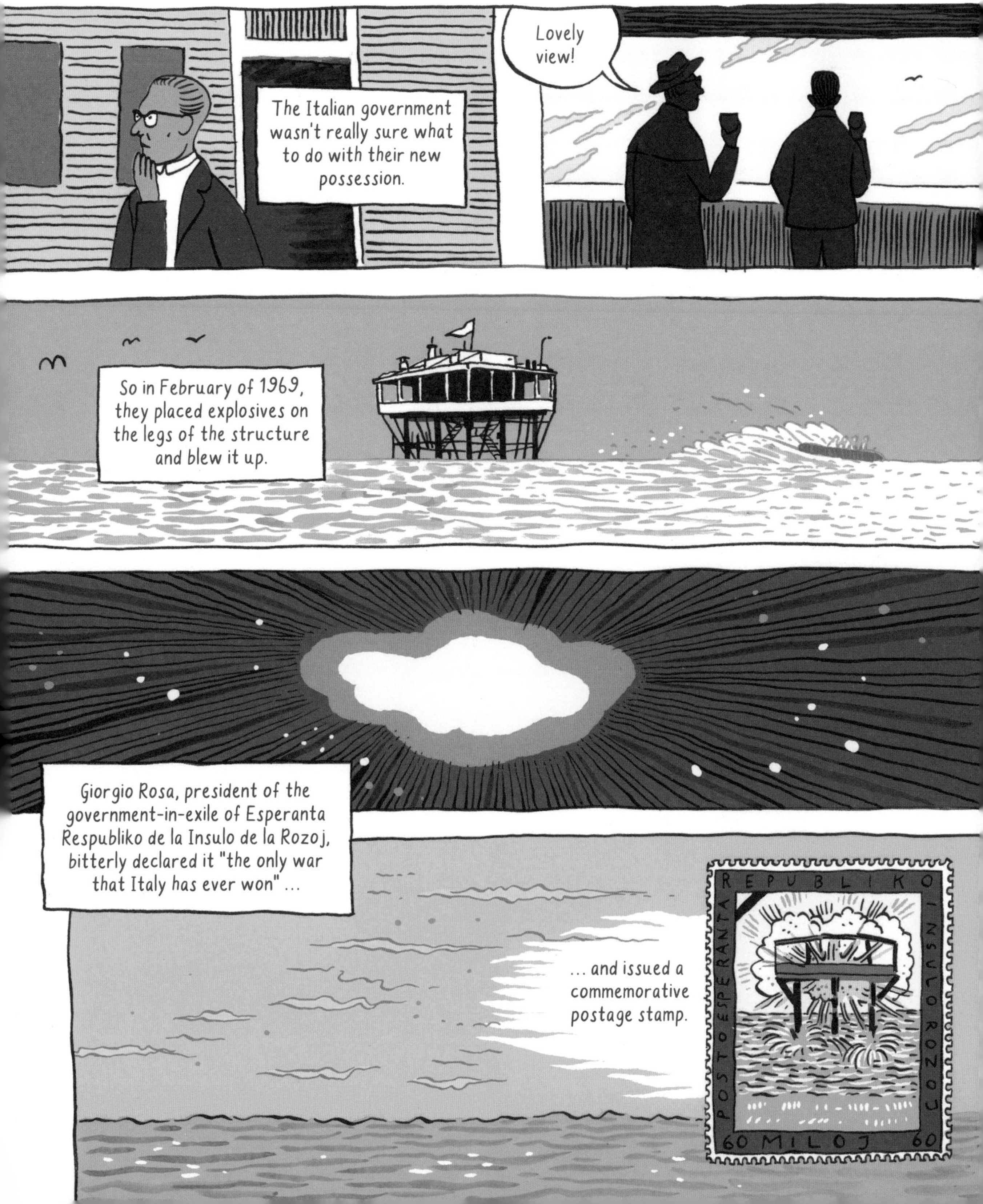
The Italian government wasn't really sure what to do with their new possession.
Lovely view!
So in February of 1969, they placed explosives on the legs of the structure and blew it up.
Giorgio Rosa, president of the government-in-exile of Esperanta Respubliko de la Insulo de la Rozoj, bitterly declared it "the only war that Italy has ever won" ...
... and issued a commemorative postage stamp.
REPUBLIKO
INSULO ROZOJ
POSTO ESPERANTA
60 MILOJ 60

Principality of Hutt River

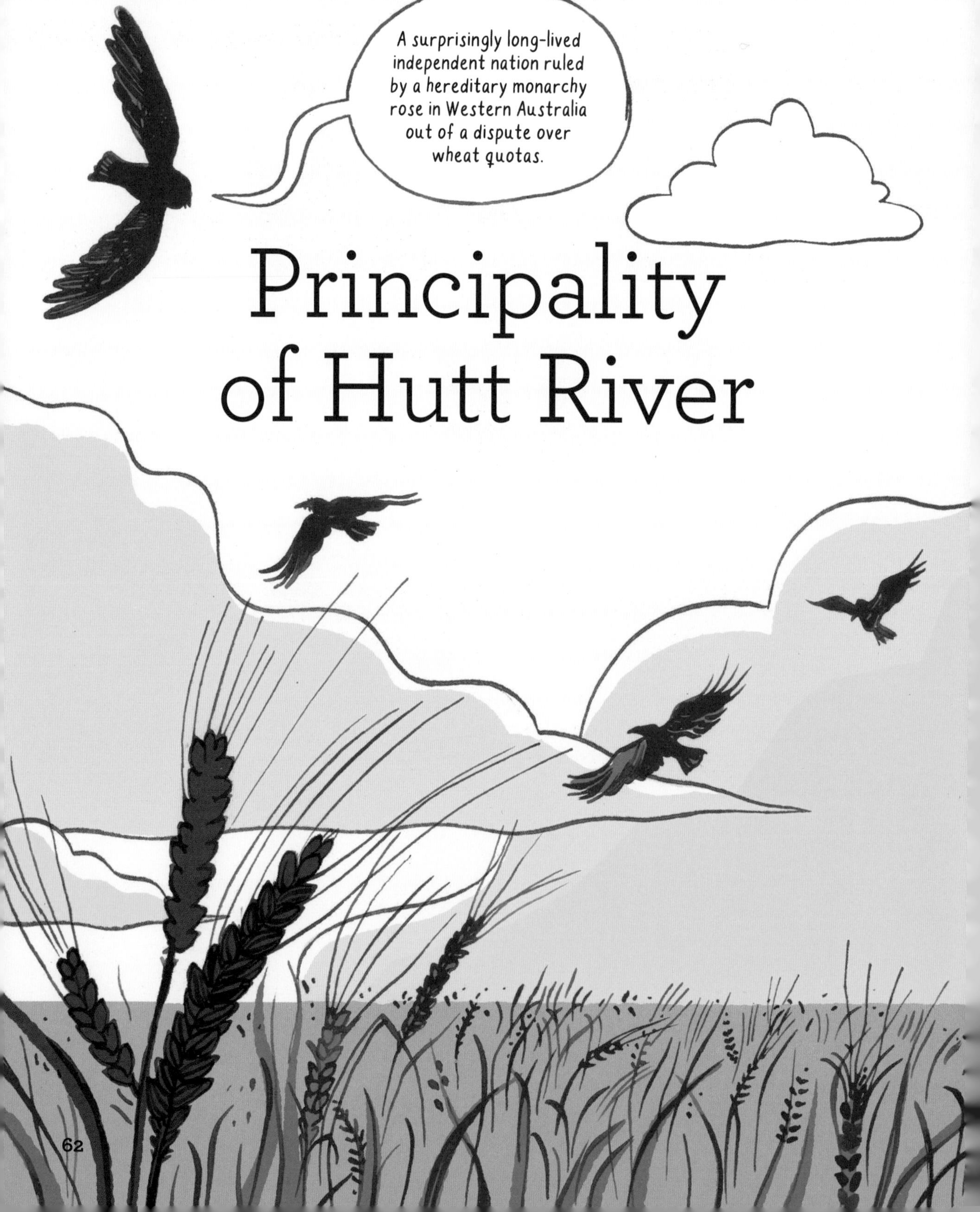
A surprisingly long-lived independent nation ruled by a hereditary monarchy rose in Western Australia out of a dispute over wheat quotas.

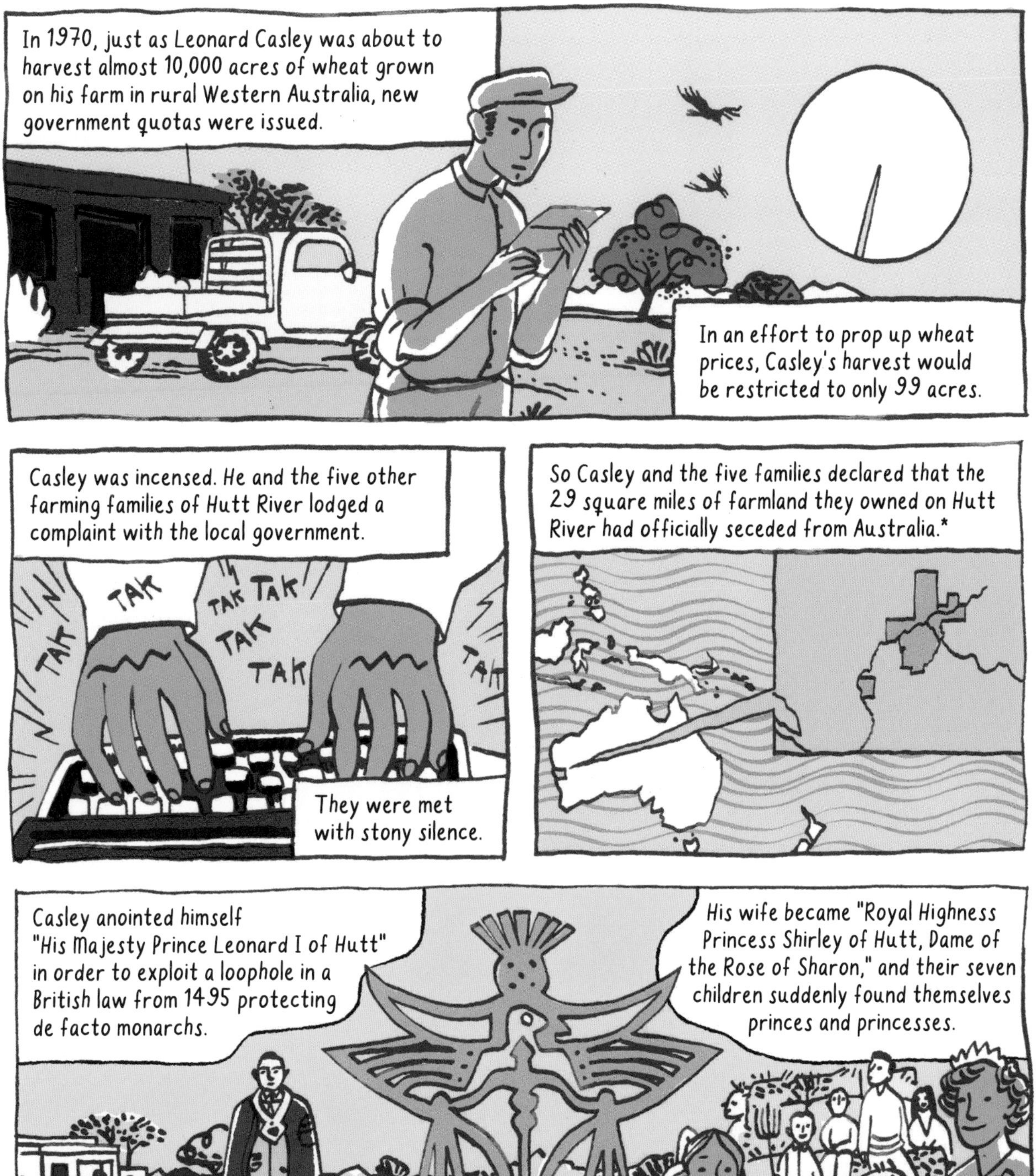
In 1970, just as Leonard Casley was about to harvest almost 10,000 acres of wheat grown on his farm in rural Western Australia, new government quotas were issued.
In an effort to prop up wheat prices, Casley's harvest would be restricted to only 99 acres.
Casley was incensed. He and the five other farming families of Hutt River lodged a complaint with the local government.
TAK
TAK TAK
TAK
TAK
TAK
TAK
They were met with stony silence.
So Casley and the five families declared that the 29 square miles of farmland they owned on Hutt River had officially seceded from Australia.*
Casley anointed himself "His Majesty Prince Leonard I of Hutt" in order to exploit a loophole in a British law from 1495 protecting de facto monarchs.
His wife became "Royal Highness Princess Shirley of Hutt, Dame of the Rose of Sharon," and their seven children suddenly found themselves princes and princesses.

*Although Casley made sure to declare that he remained loyal to Queen Elizabeth II, establishing the Principality of Hutt River as an unrecognized commonwealth of the English Crown.

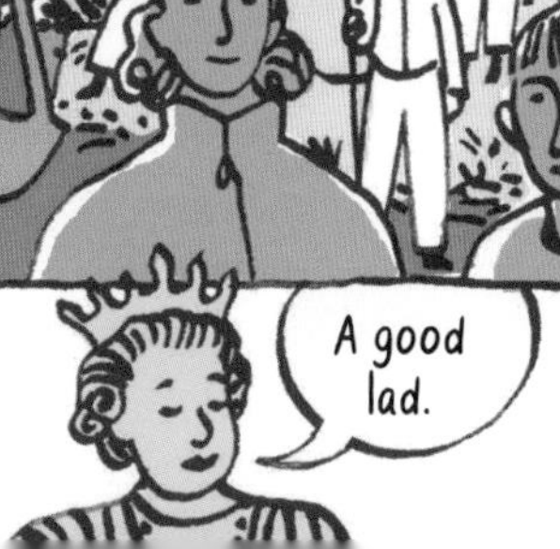
A good lad.

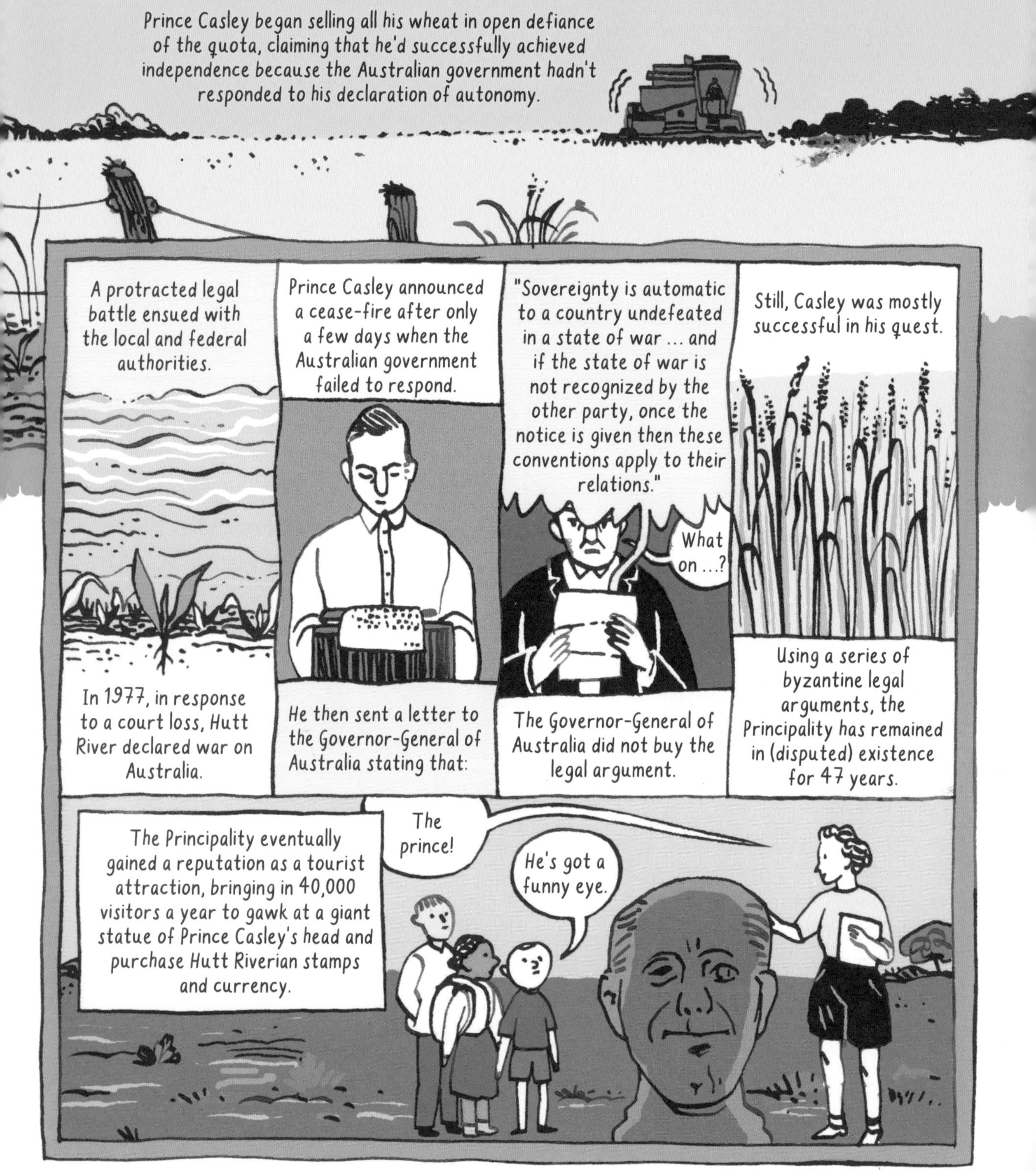
Prince Casley began selling all his wheat in open defiance of the quota, claiming that he'd successfully achieved independence because the Australian government hadn't responded to his declaration of autonomy.
A protracted legal battle ensued with the local and federal authorities.
In 1977, in response to a court loss, Hutt River declared war on Australia.
Prince Casley announced a cease-fire after only a few days when the Australian government failed to respond.
He then sent a letter to the Governor-General of Australia stating that:
"Sovereignty is automatic to a country undefeated in a state of war ... and if the state of war is not recognized by the other party, once the notice is given then these conventions apply to their relations."
What on ...?
The Governor-General of Australia did not buy the legal argument.
Still, Casley was mostly successful in his quest.
Using a series of byzantine legal arguments, the Principality has remained in (disputed) existence for 47 years.
The Principality eventually gained a reputation as a tourist attraction, bringing in 40,000 visitors a year to gawk at a giant statue of Prince Casley's head and purchase Hutt Riverian stamps and currency.
The prince!
He's got a funny eye.

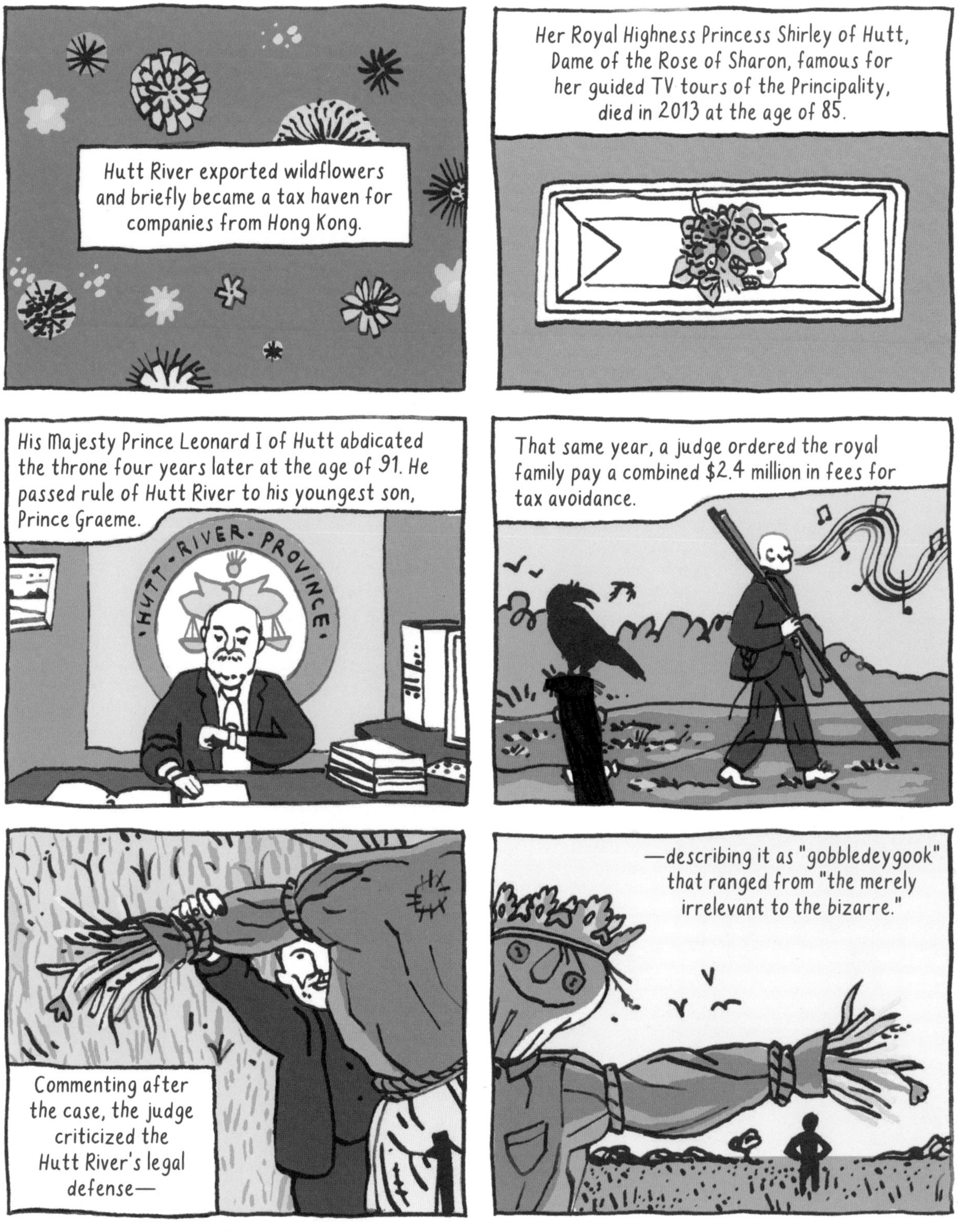
Hutt River exported wildflowers and briefly became a tax haven for companies from Hong Kong.
Her Royal Highness Princess Shirley of Hutt, Dame of the Rose of Sharon, famous for her guided TV tours of the Principality, died in 2013 at the age of 85.
His Majesty Prince Leonard I of Hutt abdicated the throne four years later at the age of 91. He passed rule of Hutt River to his youngest son, Prince Graeme.
HUTT - RIVER - PROVINCE
That same year, a judge ordered the royal family pay a combined $2.4 million in fees for tax avoidance.
Commenting after the case, the judge criticized the Hutt River's legal defense—
—describing it as "gobbledeygook" that ranged from "the merely irrelevant to the bizarre."

Operation Atlantis

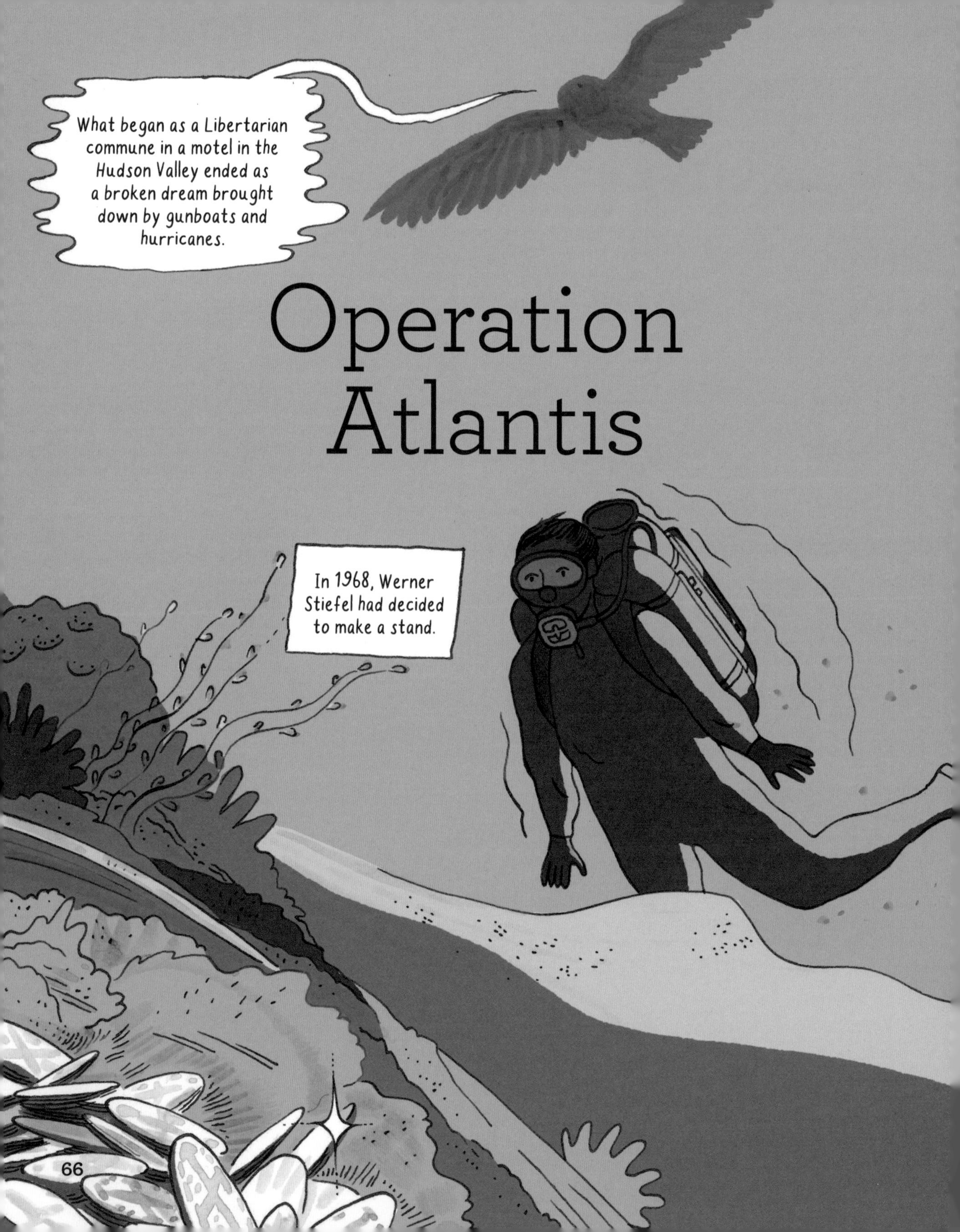
What began as a Libertarian commune in a motel in the Hudson Valley ended as a broken dream brought down by gunboats and hurricanes.
In 1968, Werner Stiefel had decided to make a stand.

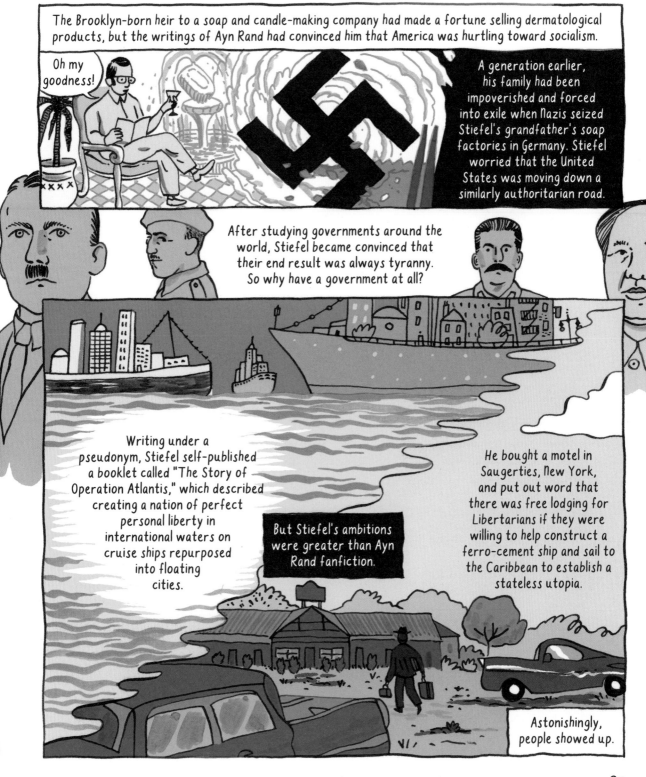

The Brooklyn-born heir to a soap and candle-making company had made a fortune selling dermatological products, but the writings of Ayn Rand had convinced him that America was hurtling toward socialism.

Oh my goodness!

A generation earlier, his family had been impoverished and forced into exile when Nazis seized Stiefel's grandfather's soap factories in Germany. Stiefel worried that the United States was moving down a similarly authoritarian road.

After studying governments around the world, Stiefel became convinced that their end result was always tyranny. So why have a government at all?

Writing under a pseudonym, Stiefel self-published a booklet called "The Story of Operation Atlantis," which described creating a nation of perfect personal liberty in international waters on cruise ships repurposed into floating cities.

But Stiefel's ambitions were greater than Ayn Rand fanfiction.

He bought a motel in Saugerties, New York, and put out word that there was free lodging for Libertarians if they were willing to help construct a ferro-cement ship and sail to the Caribbean to establish a stateless utopia.

Astonishingly, people showed up.

The Atlanteans constructed a 23-foot-high geodesic dome on the hotel grounds and spent two years building a boat inside it.

On a high tide in 1971, the Libertarians launched their vessel into the Hudson River.

The virgin journey of Atlantis II!

It immediately capsized and caught on fire.

Um ...

Undaunted, the Atlanteans righted the boat and repaired it.

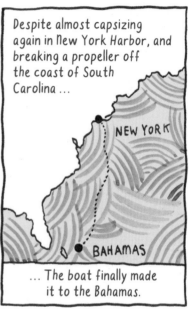

Despite almost capsizing again in New York Harbor, and breaking a propeller off the coast of South Carolina ...

NEW YORK

BAHAMAS

... The boat finally made it to the Bahamas.

It was promptly sunk by a hurricane.

But Werner Stiefel was not a man easily dissuaded.

He bought a second boat and sailed it to Silver Shoals, a disputed territory between Haiti and the Bahamas ...

... that was rumored to be the location of several shipwrecked Spanish galleons.

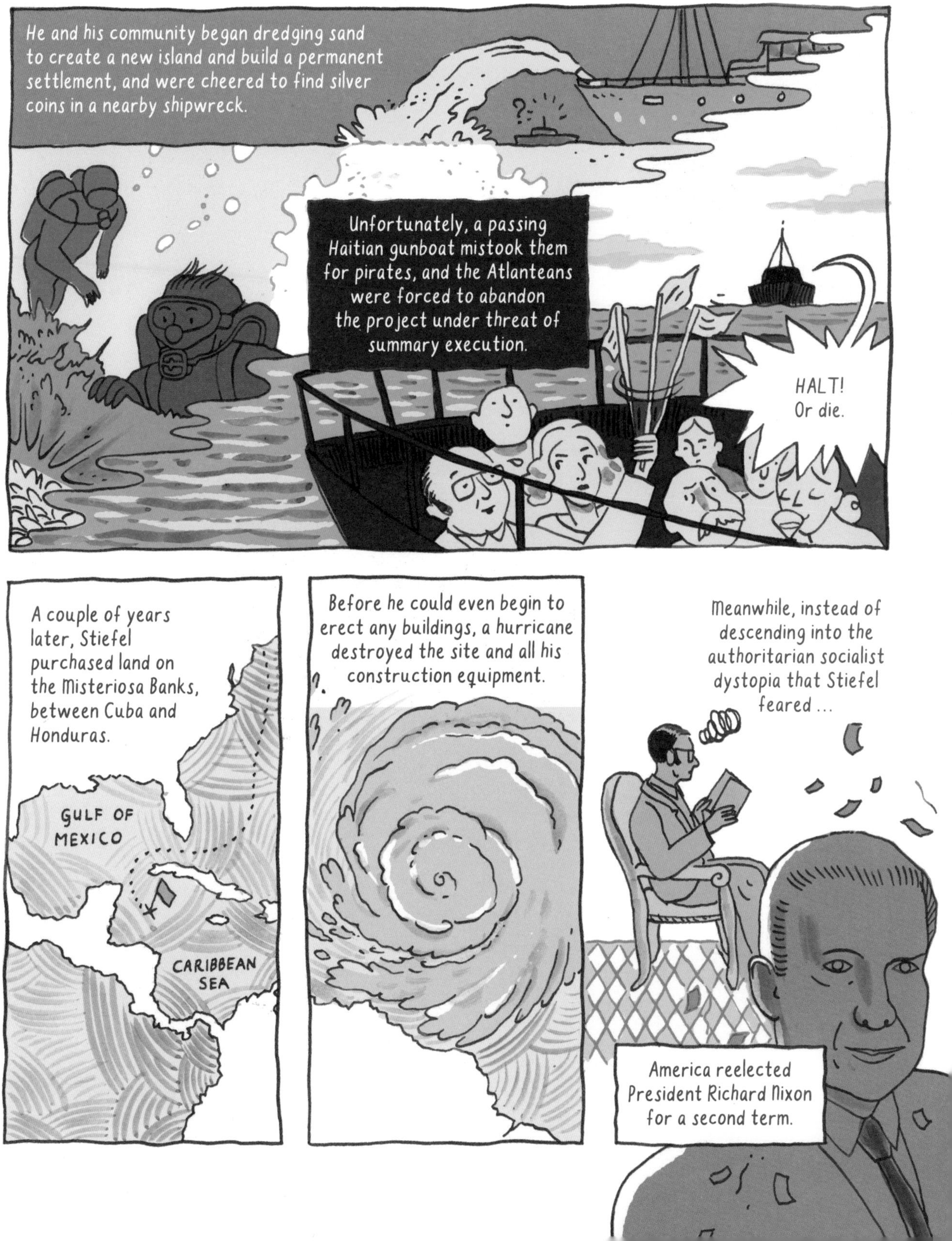
He and his community began dredging sand to create a new island and build a permanent settlement, and were cheered to find silver coins in a nearby shipwreck.
?
Unfortunately, a passing Haitian gunboat mistook them for pirates, and the Atlanteans were forced to abandon the project under threat of summary execution.
HALT! Or die.
A couple of years later, Stiefel purchased land on the Misteriosa Banks, between Cuba and Honduras.
GULF OF MEXICO
CARIBBEAN SEA
Before he could even begin to erect any buildings, a hurricane destroyed the site and all his construction equipment.
Meanwhile, instead of descending into the authoritarian socialist dystopia that Stiefel feared ...
America reelected President Richard Nixon for a second term.

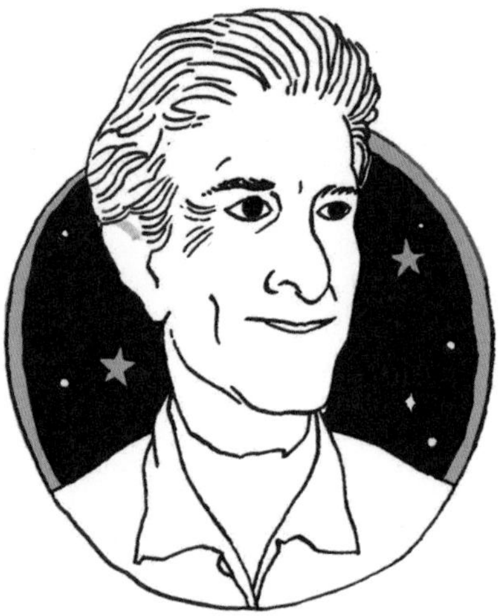

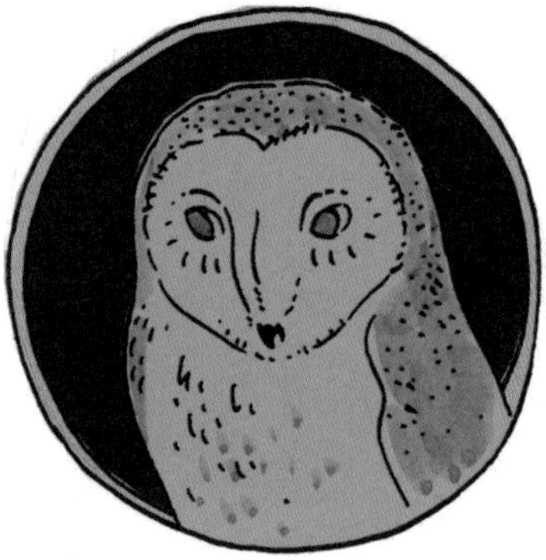
The brilliant and eccentric Lord Dumpling rules over a fantasy island that he built to showcase his earnest belief in energy independence.

North Dumpling Island

Lord Dumpling is also known as Dean Kamen. He invented a wheelchair that stands up on two wheels, a human cannon for shooting first responders onto roofs, a working robotic prosthetic arm (nicknamed "Luke" for Luke Skywalker), and—most famously—the Segway.

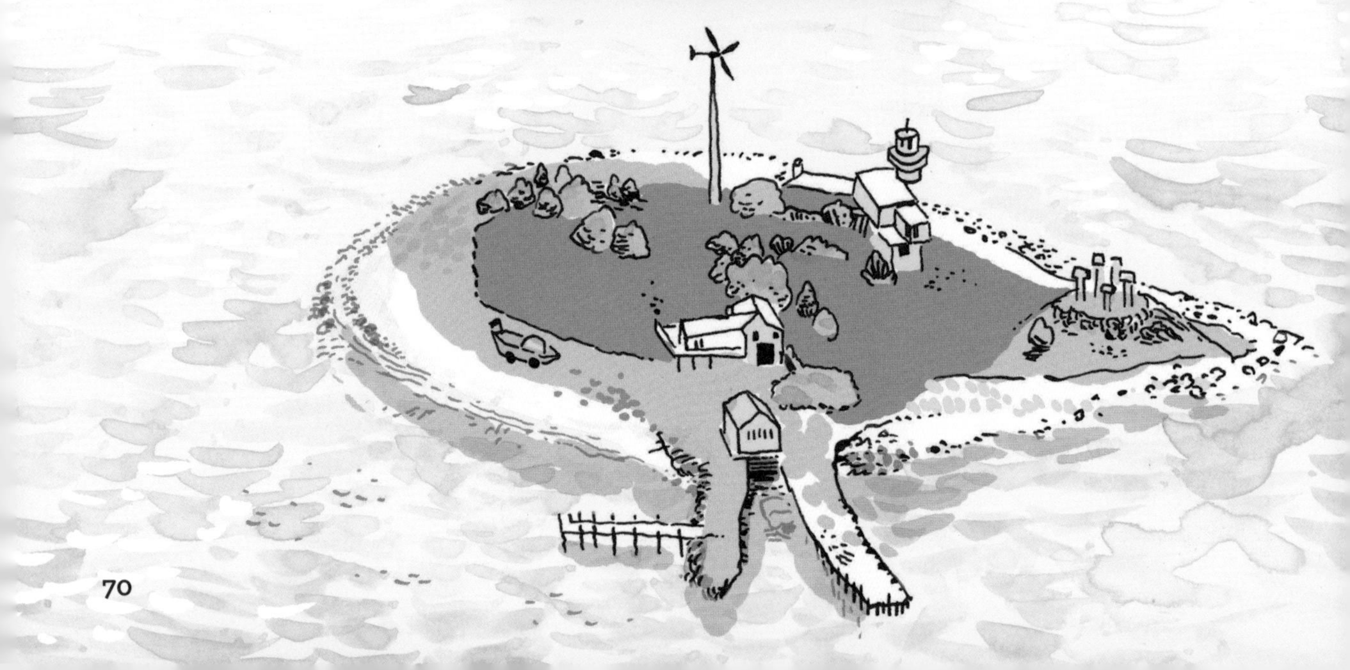

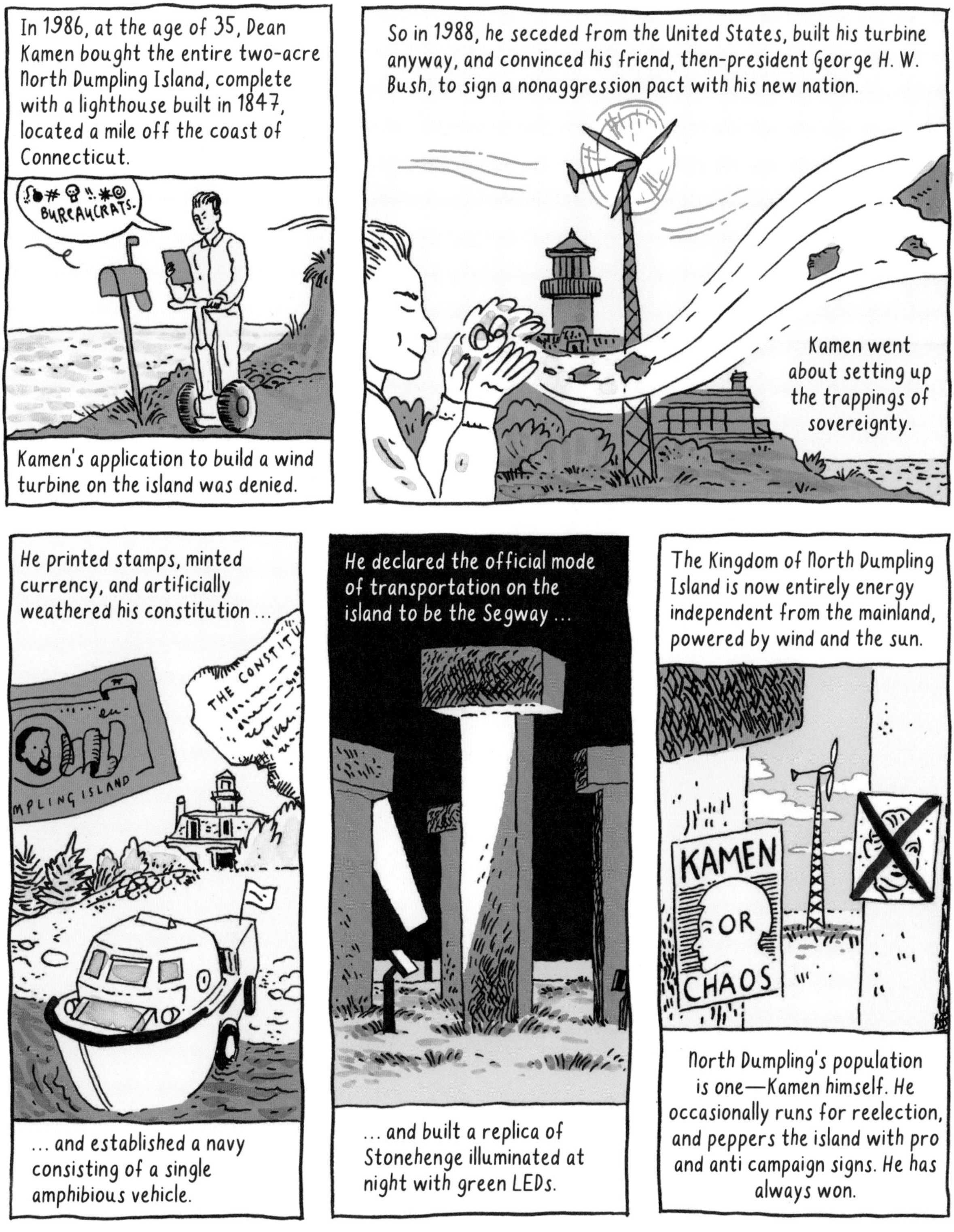
In 1986, at the age of 35, Dean Kamen bought the entire two-acre North Dumpling Island, complete with a lighthouse built in 1847, located a mile off the coast of Connecticut.
BUREAUCRATS.
Kamen's application to build a wind turbine on the island was denied.
So in 1988, he seceded from the United States, built his turbine anyway, and convinced his friend, then-president George H. W. Bush, to sign a nonaggression pact with his new nation.
Kamen went about setting up the trappings of sovereignty.
He printed stamps, minted currency, and artificially weathered his constitution ...
... and established a navy consisting of a single amphibious vehicle.
He declared the official mode of transportation on the island to be the Segway ...
... and built a replica of Stonehenge illuminated at night with green LEDs.
The Kingdom of North Dumpling Island is now entirely energy independent from the mainland, powered by wind and the sun.
KAMEN
OR
CHAOS
North Dumpling's population is one—Kamen himself. He occasionally runs for reelection, and peppers the island with pro and anti campaign signs. He has always won.

Ladonia

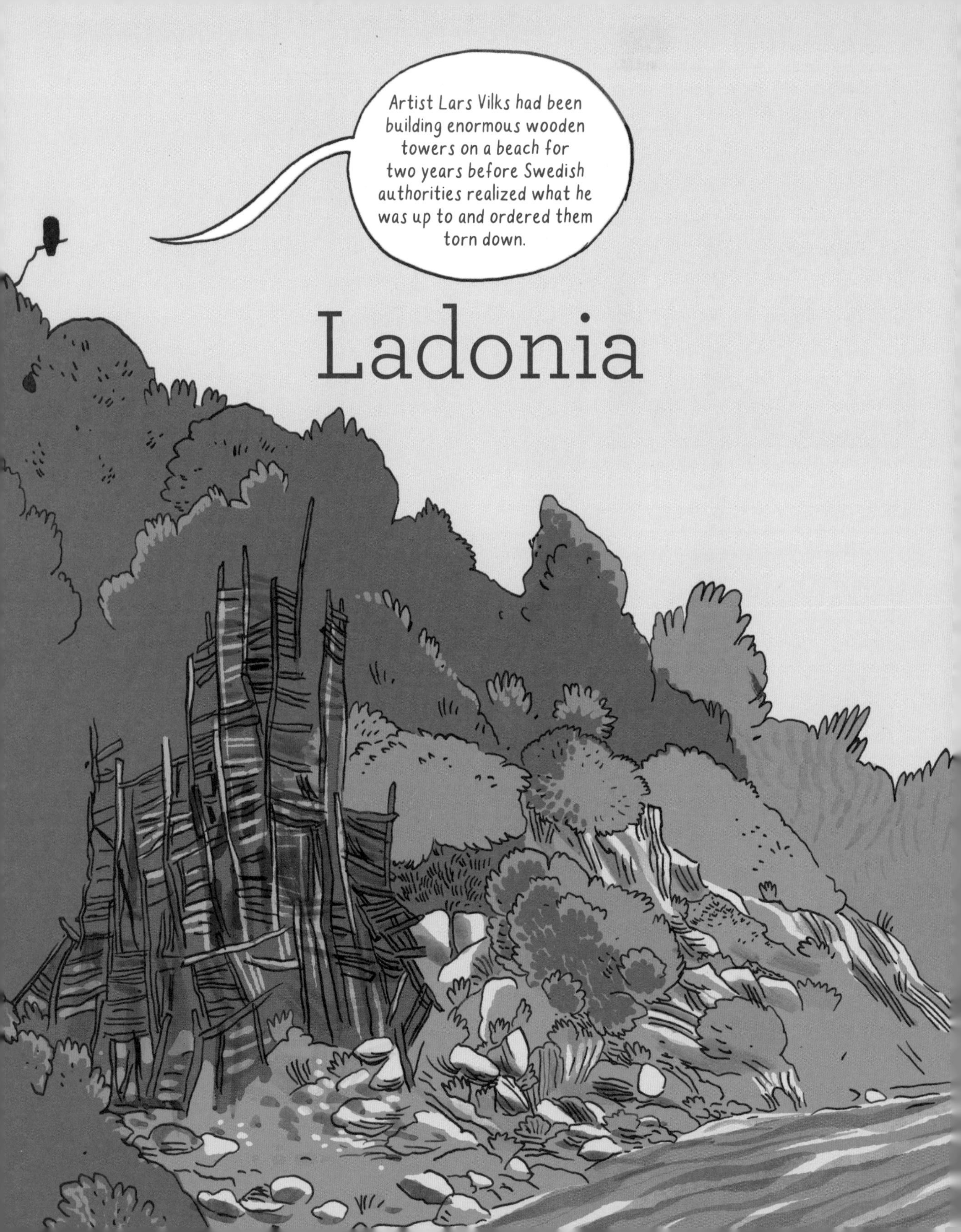
Artist Lars Vilks had been building enormous wooden towers on a beach for two years before Swedish authorities realized what he was up to and ordered them torn down.

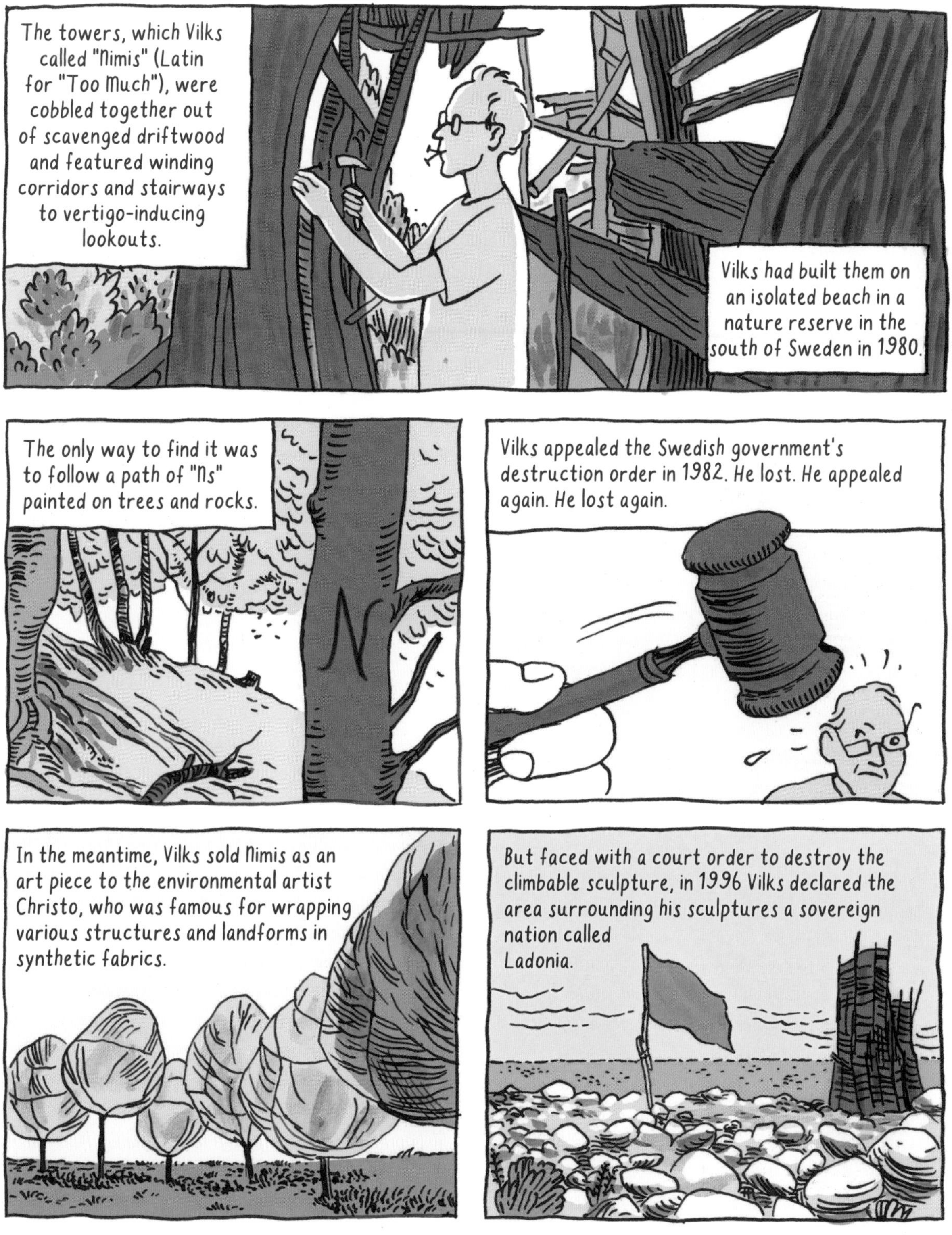
The towers, which Vilks called "Nimis" (Latin for "Too Much"), were cobbled together out of scavenged driftwood and featured winding corridors and stairways to vertigo-inducing lookouts.
Vilks had built them on an isolated beach in a nature reserve in the south of Sweden in 1980.
The only way to find it was to follow a path of "Ns" painted on trees and rocks.
N
Vilks appealed the Swedish government's destruction order in 1982. He lost. He appealed again. He lost again.
In the meantime, Vilks sold Nimis as an art piece to the environmental artist Christo, who was famous for wrapping various structures and landforms in synthetic fabrics.
But faced with a court order to destroy the climbable sculpture, in 1996 Vilks declared the area surrounding his sculptures a sovereign nation called Ladonia.

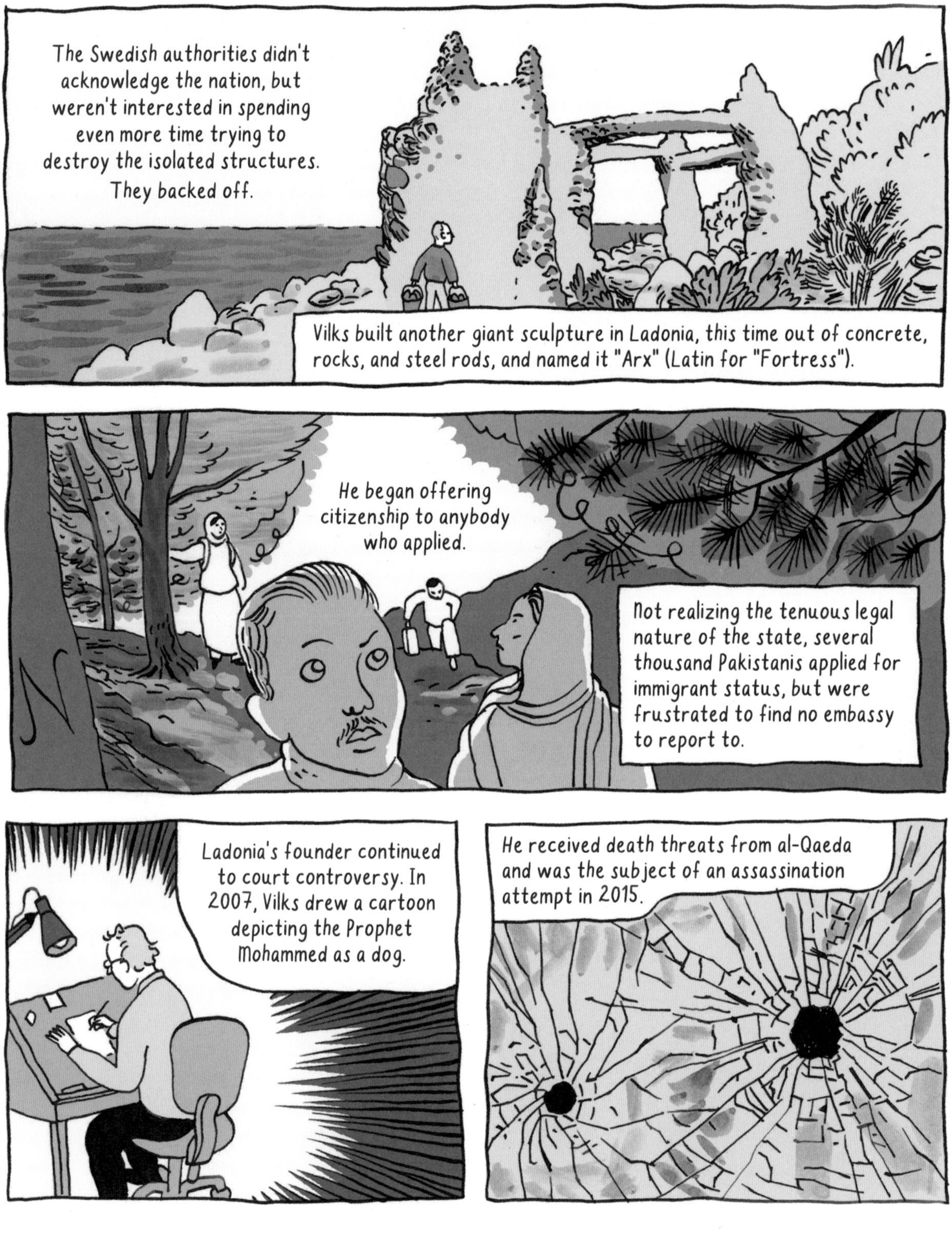

The Swedish authorities didn't acknowledge the nation, but weren't interested in spending even more time trying to destroy the isolated structures. They backed off.
Vilks built another giant sculpture in Ladonia, this time out of concrete, rocks, and steel rods, and named it "Arx" (Latin for "Fortress").
He began offering citizenship to anybody who applied.
Not realizing the tenuous legal nature of the state, several thousand Pakistanis applied for immigrant status, but were frustrated to find no embassy to report to.
Ladonia's founder continued to court controversy. In 2007, Vilks drew a cartoon depicting the Prophet Mohammed as a dog.
He received death threats from al-Qaeda and was the subject of an assassination attempt in 2015.

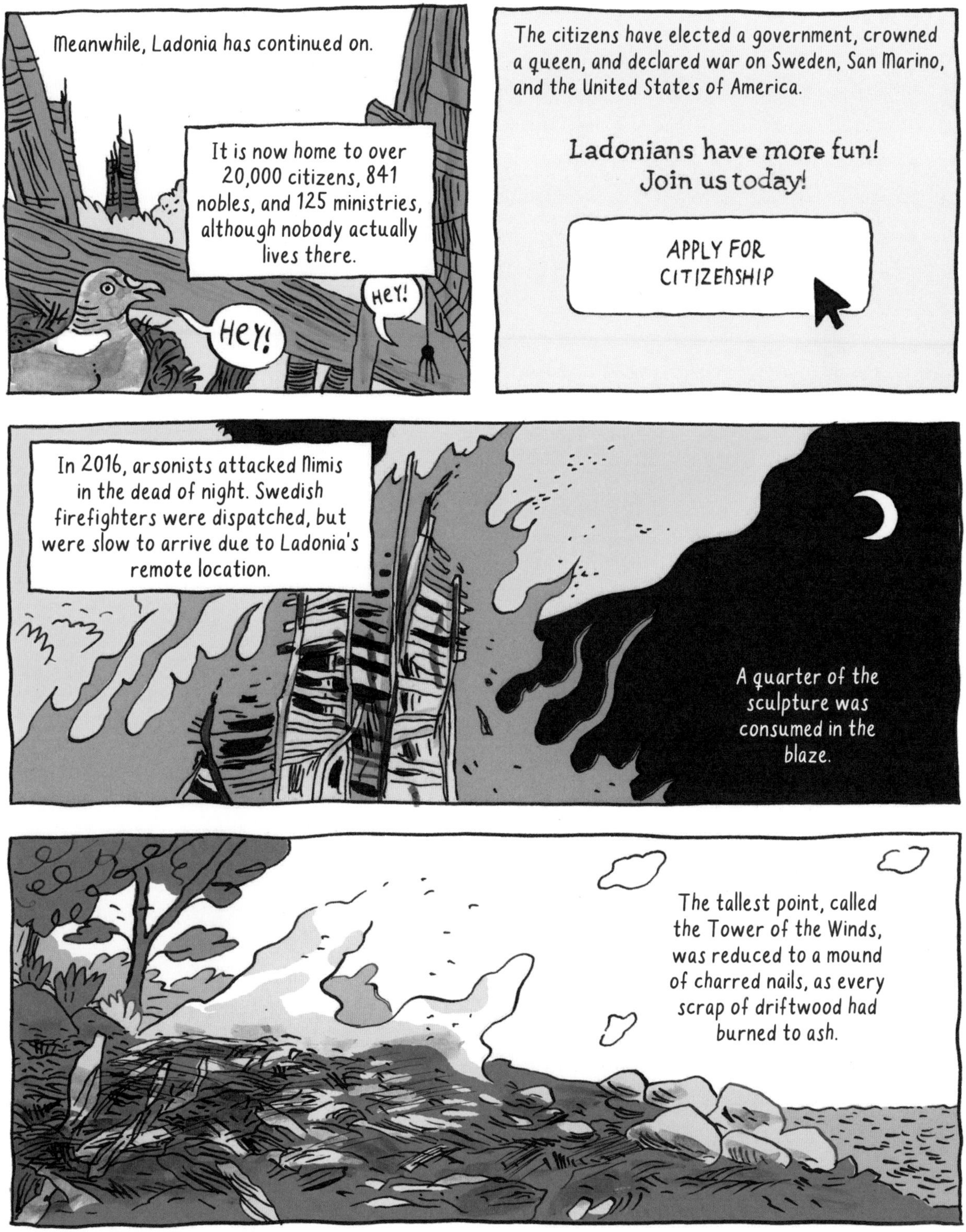
Meanwhile, Ladonia has continued on.
It is now home to over 20,000 citizens, 841 nobles, and 125 ministries, although nobody actually lives there.
HEY!
HEY!
The citizens have elected a government, crowned a queen, and declared war on Sweden, San Marino, and the United States of America.
Ladonians have more fun! Join us today!
APPLY FOR CITIZENSHIP
In 2016, arsonists attacked Nimis in the dead of night. Swedish firefighters were dispatched, but were slow to arrive due to Ladonia's remote location.
A quarter of the sculpture was consumed in the blaze.
The tallest point, called the Tower of the Winds, was reduced to a mound of charred nails, as every scrap of driftwood had burned to ash.

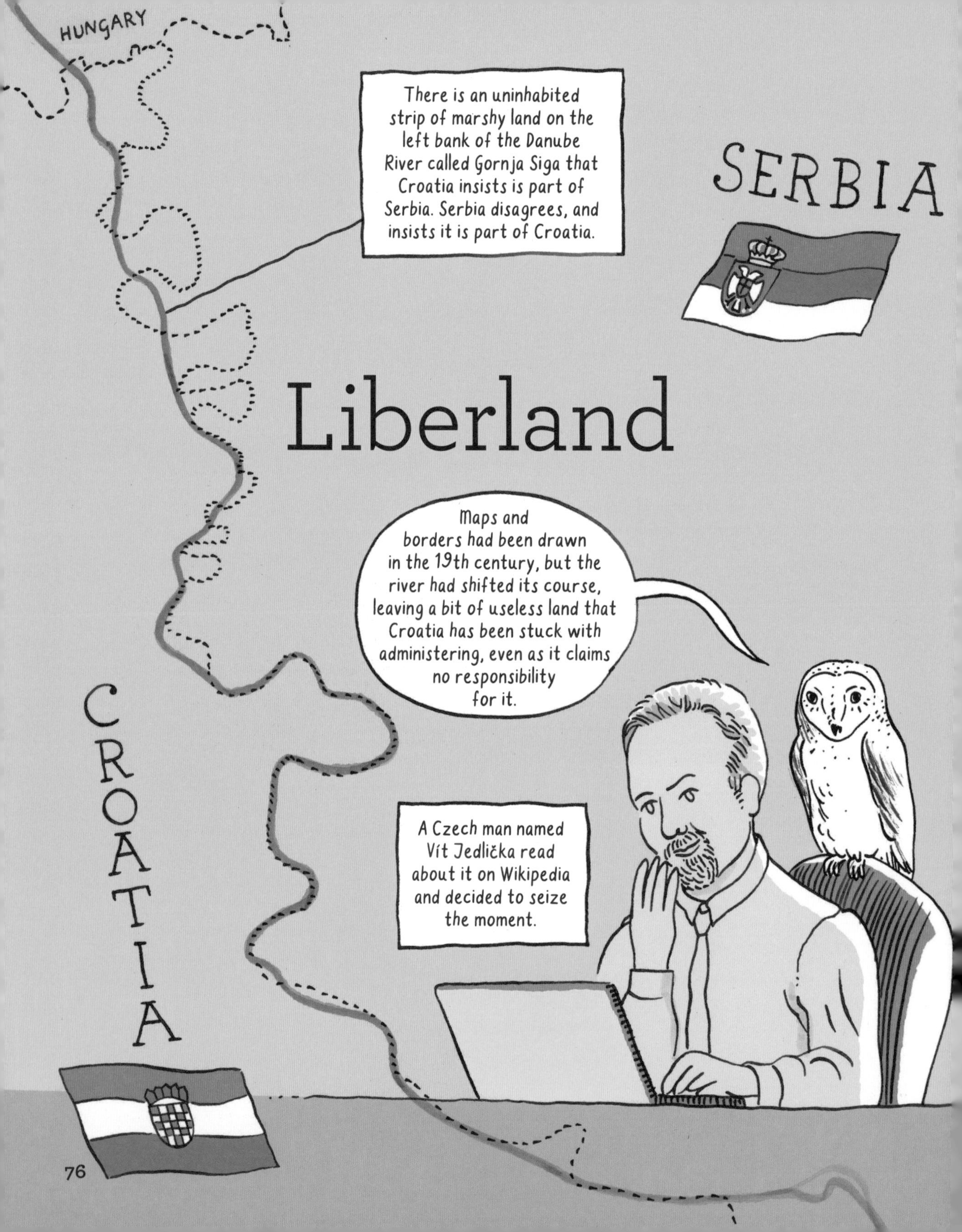
HUNGARY
There is an uninhabited strip of marshy land on the left bank of the Danube River called Gornja Siga that Croatia insists is part of Serbia. Serbia disagrees, and insists it is part of Croatia.
SERBIA
Liberland
Maps and borders had been drawn in the 19th century, but the river had shifted its course, leaving a bit of useless land that Croatia has been stuck with administering, even as it claims no responsibility for it.
CROATIA
A Czech man named Vít Jedlička read about it on Wikipedia and decided to seize the moment.

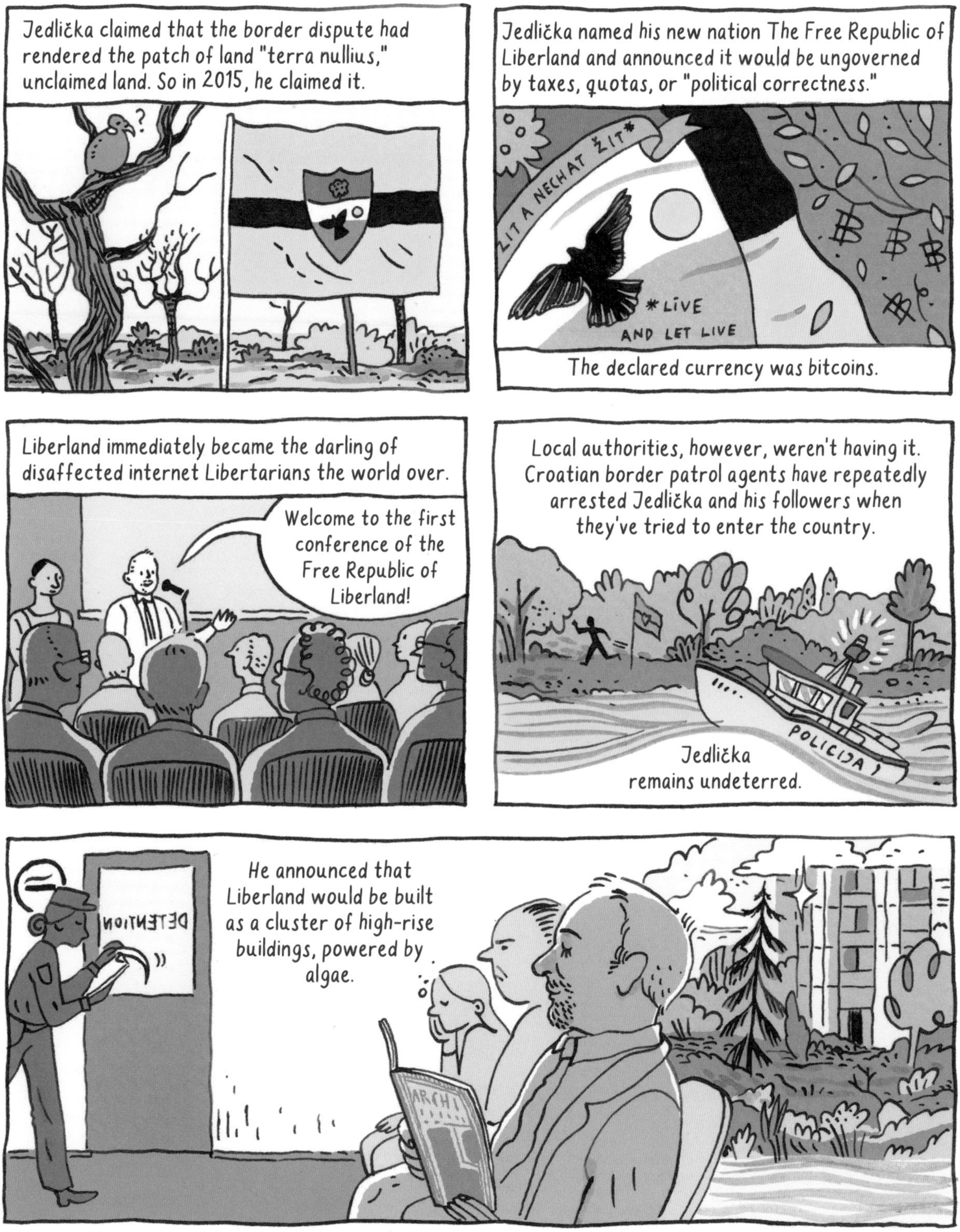
Jedlička claimed that the border dispute had rendered the patch of land "terra nullius," unclaimed land. So in 2015, he claimed it.
?
Jedlička named his new nation The Free Republic of Liberland and announced it would be ungoverned by taxes, quotas, or "political correctness."
ŽIT A NECHAT ŽIT*
*LIVE AND LET LIVE
The declared currency was bitcoins.
Liberland immediately became the darling of disaffected internet Libertarians the world over.
Welcome to the first conference of the Free Republic of Liberland!
Local authorities, however, weren't having it. Croatian border patrol agents have repeatedly arrested Jedlička and his followers when they've tried to enter the country.
POLICIJA
Jedlička remains undeterred.
DETENTION
He announced that Liberland would be built as a cluster of high-rise buildings, powered by algae.
ARCHI

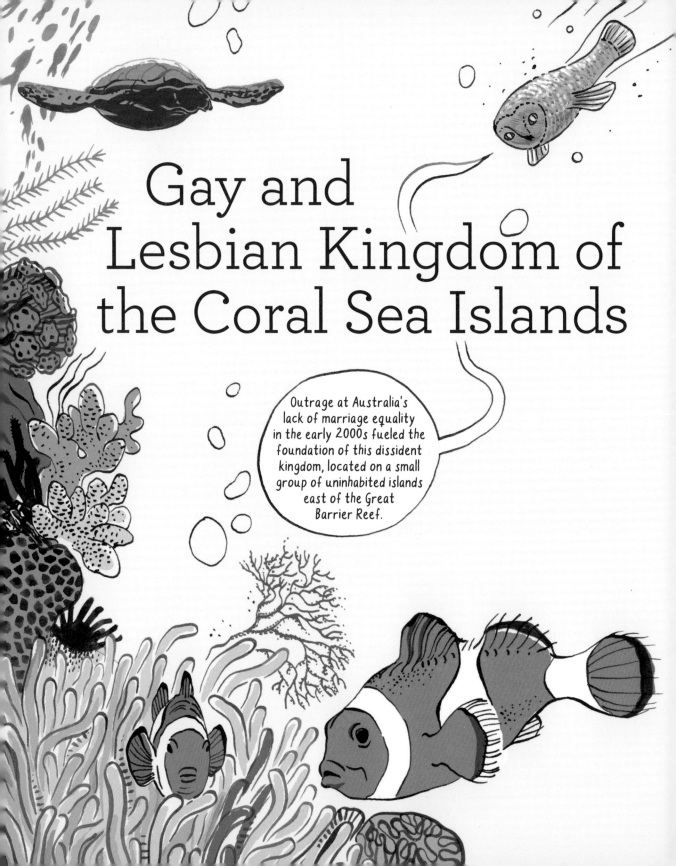

Gay and Lesbian Kingdom of the Coral Sea Islands

Outrage at Australia's lack of marriage equality in the early 2000s fueled the foundation of this dissident kingdom, located on a small group of uninhabited islands east of the Great Barrier Reef.

After a Gay Pride festival in Brisbane in 2004, a group of friends was fuming that the Australian government not only refused to legalize gay marriage, but also denied recognition to unions performed in other countries that allowed it.

Faced with a state intent on a policy of discrimination, the activists decided to secede.

They sailed a ship called the "Gayflower" to an uninhabited atoll off the northeast coast of Australia, claimed it for all the LGBT people of the world, and founded a monarchy, exploiting a legal loophole involving foreign kings that prevented the Australian government from trying them for treason.

Coral Sea

The kingdom declared war on Australia immediately upon its founding. As with hostilities from the Principality of Hutt River, Australia did not respond.

Why does this keep happening …

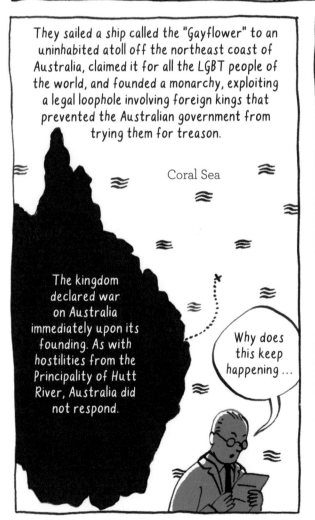

Dale Parker Anderson was enthroned as emperor and claimed descent from King Edward II of England, a 14th-century monarch who was rumored to have been gay.

The kingdom adopted the rainbow pride flag as their national flag.

Its capital, a barebones campsite on the beach, was named "Heaven" after a famous gay nightclub in London that has existed since 1979.

All LGBT people of the world were granted automatic citizenship should they apply, a law modeled on Israel's Law of Return.

• INTRODUCTION
• ABOUT US
• HISTORY
• FUTURE
• DECLARATION

A website was set up to promote tourism to the island.

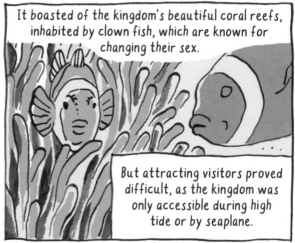

It boasted of the kingdom's beautiful coral reefs, inhabited by clown fish, which are known for changing their sex.

But attracting visitors proved difficult, as the kingdom was only accessible during high tide or by seaplane.

The kingdom's founders gradually lost interest in the project.

VRₐRRRᴿᴿR

Emperor Anderson abdicated without fanfare in 2014.

RₖRRₐₐ

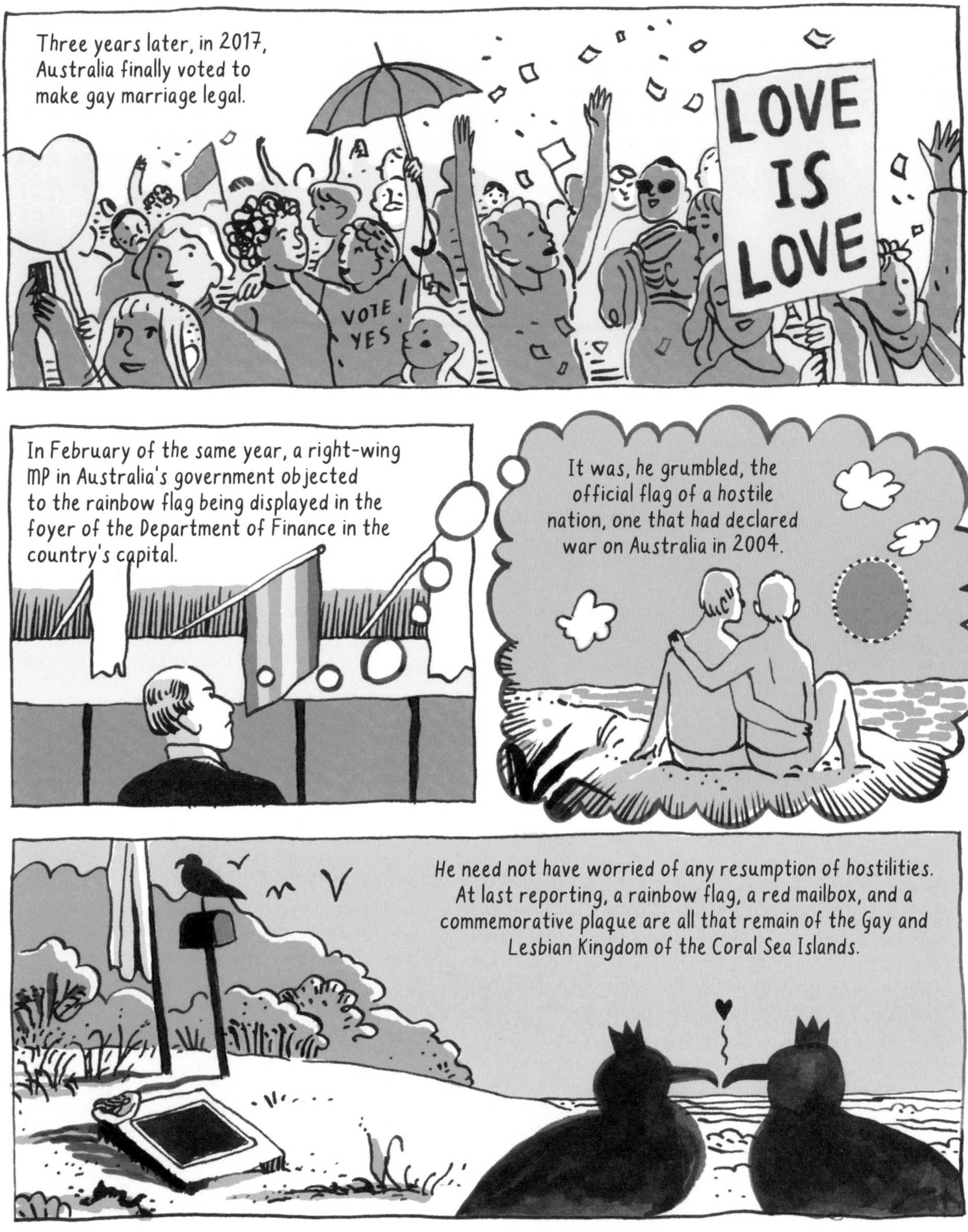
Three years later, in 2017, Australia finally voted to make gay marriage legal.
LOVE IS LOVE
VOTE YES
In February of the same year, a right-wing MP in Australia's government objected to the rainbow flag being displayed in the foyer of the Department of Finance in the country's capital.
It was, he grumbled, the official flag of a hostile nation, one that had declared war on Australia in 2004.
He need not have worried of any resumption of hostilities. At last reporting, a rainbow flag, a red mailbox, and a commemorative plaque are all that remain of the Gay and Lesbian Kingdom of the Coral Sea Islands.

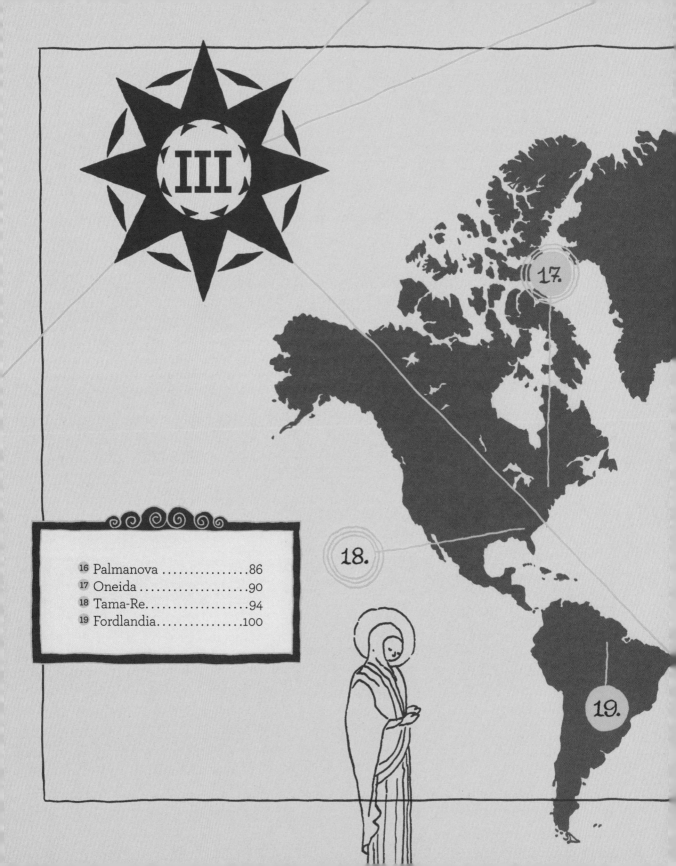

III

17.

18.

19.

FAILED UTOPIAS

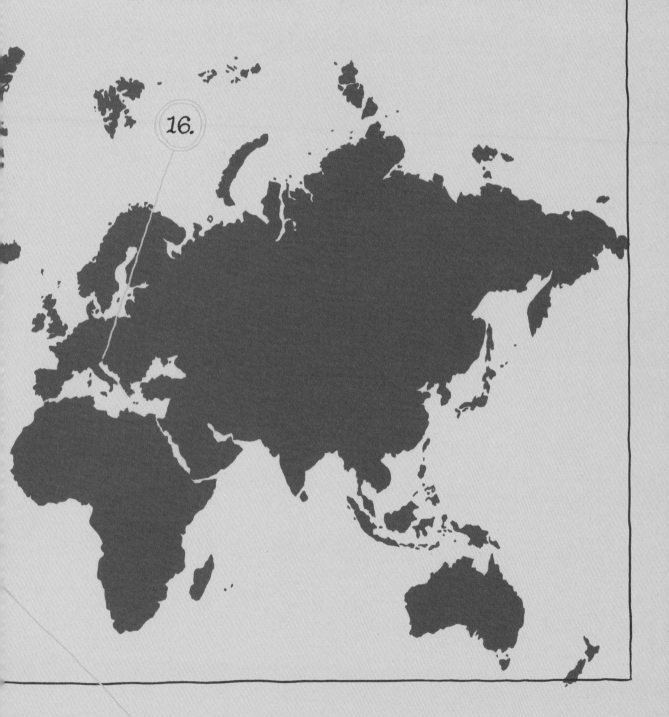

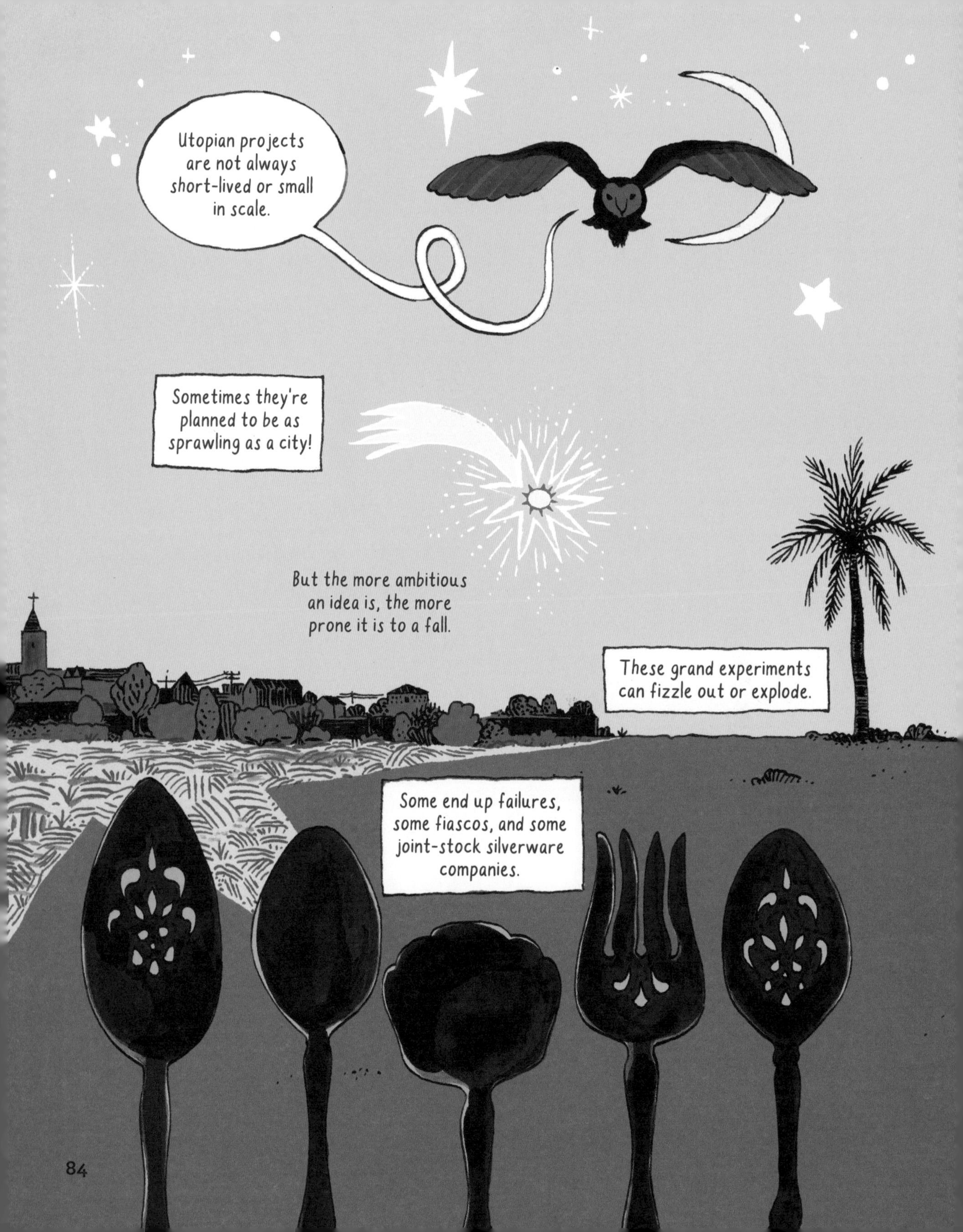
Utopian projects are not always short-lived or small in scale.
Sometimes they're planned to be as sprawling as a city!
But the more ambitious an idea is, the more prone it is to a fall.
These grand experiments can fizzle out or explode.
Some end up failures, some fiascos, and some joint-stock silverware companies.

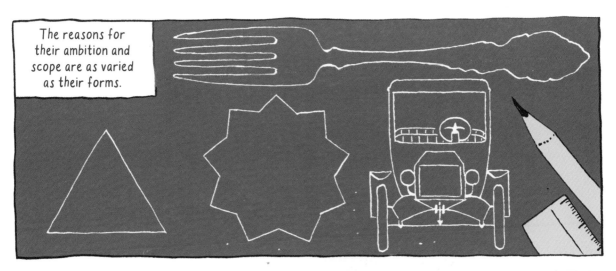

The reasons for their ambition and scope are as varied as their forms.

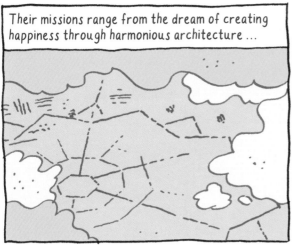

Their missions range from the dream of creating happiness through harmonious architecture ...

... to reshaping South America into the American Midwest.

And their downfalls are just as varied, from the hubris of a titan of industry ...

... to not obeying building codes.

Ahem ...

If you find yourself in a plane flying over the northeast of Italy, near the Slovenian border, look down.

Palmanova

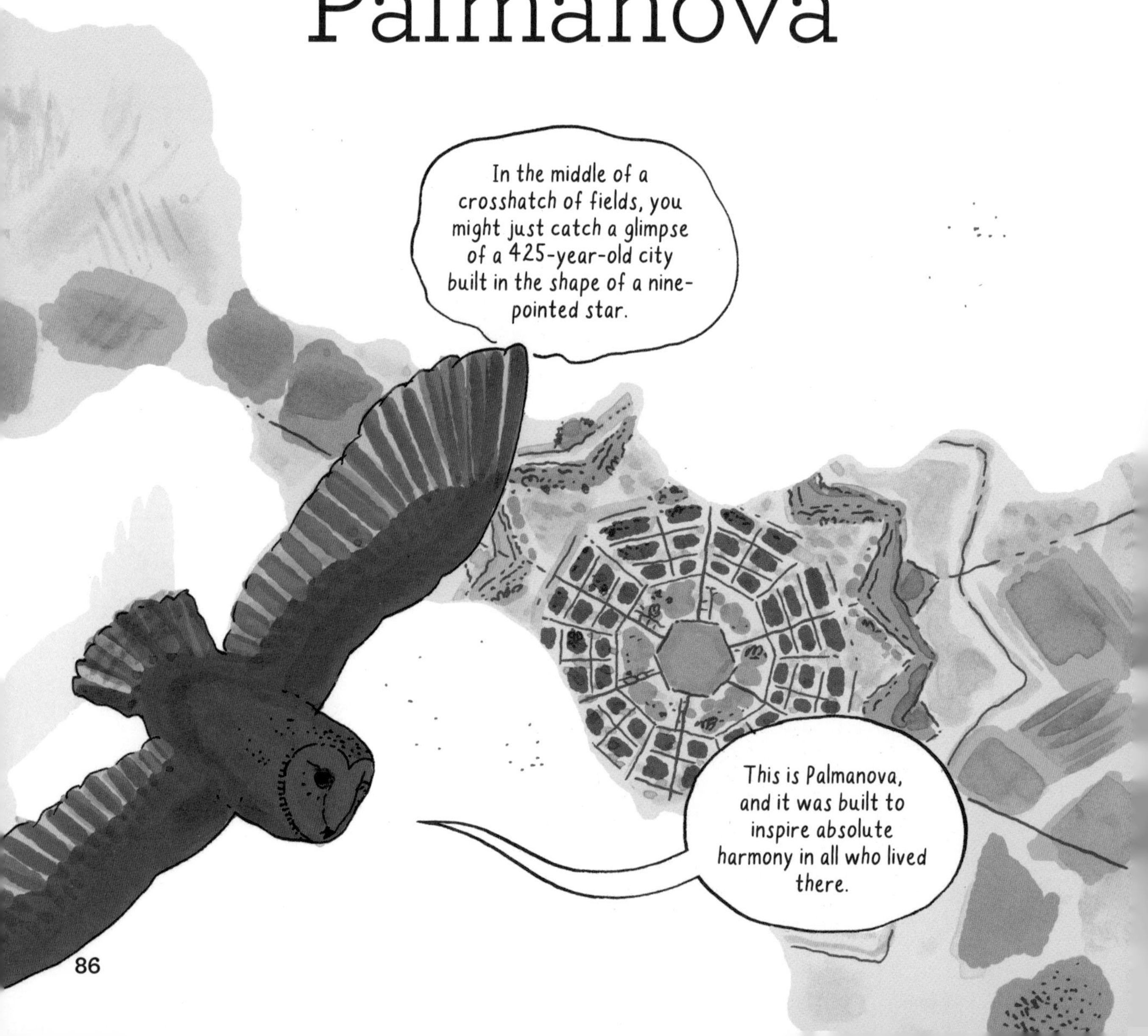
In the middle of a crosshatch of fields, you might just catch a glimpse of a 425-year-old city built in the shape of a nine-pointed star.
This is Palmanova, and it was built to inspire absolute harmony in all who lived there.

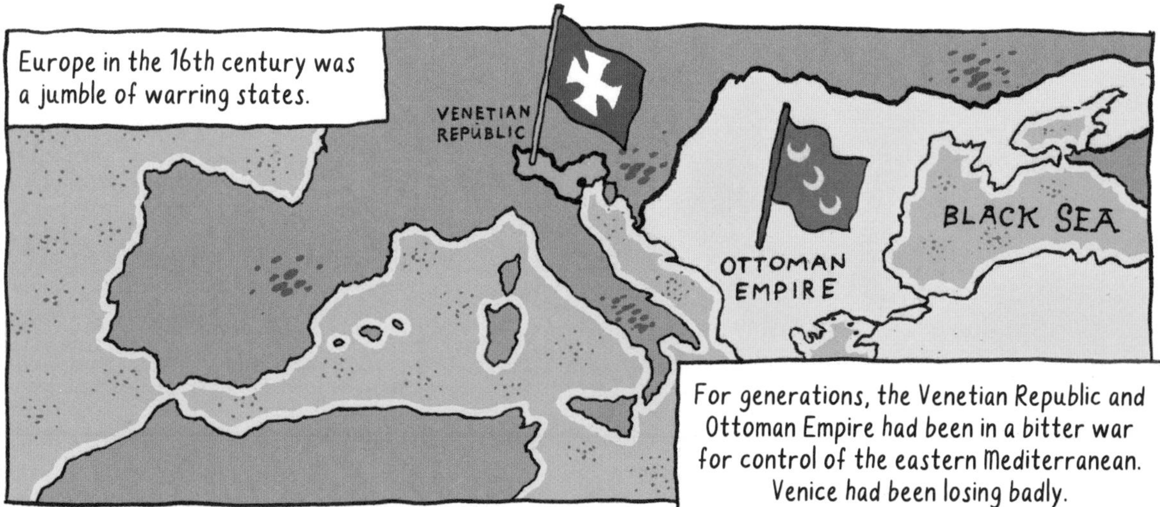
Europe in the 16th century was a jumble of warring states.
VENETIAN REPUBLIC
OTTOMAN EMPIRE
BLACK SEA
For generations, the Venetian Republic and Ottoman Empire had been in a bitter war for control of the eastern Mediterranean. Venice had been losing badly.

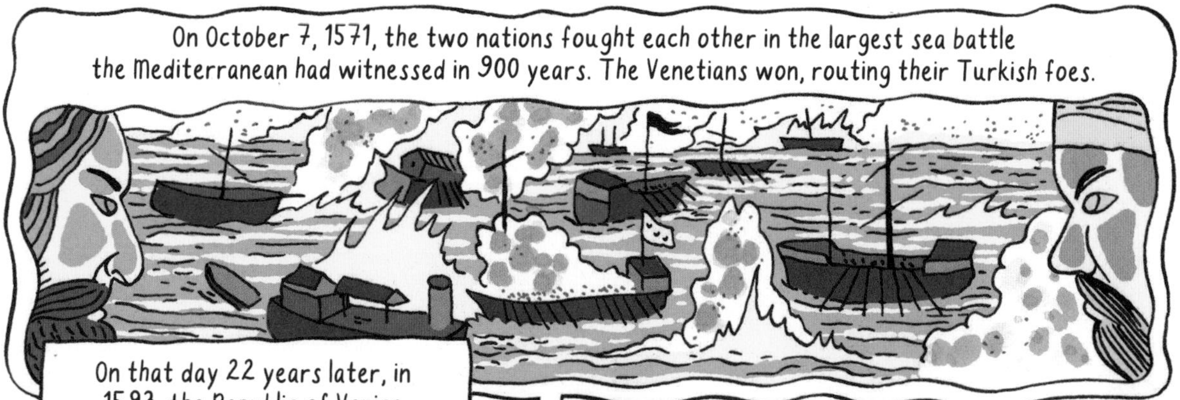
On October 7, 1571, the two nations fought each other in the largest sea battle the Mediterranean had witnessed in 900 years. The Venetians won, routing their Turkish foes.

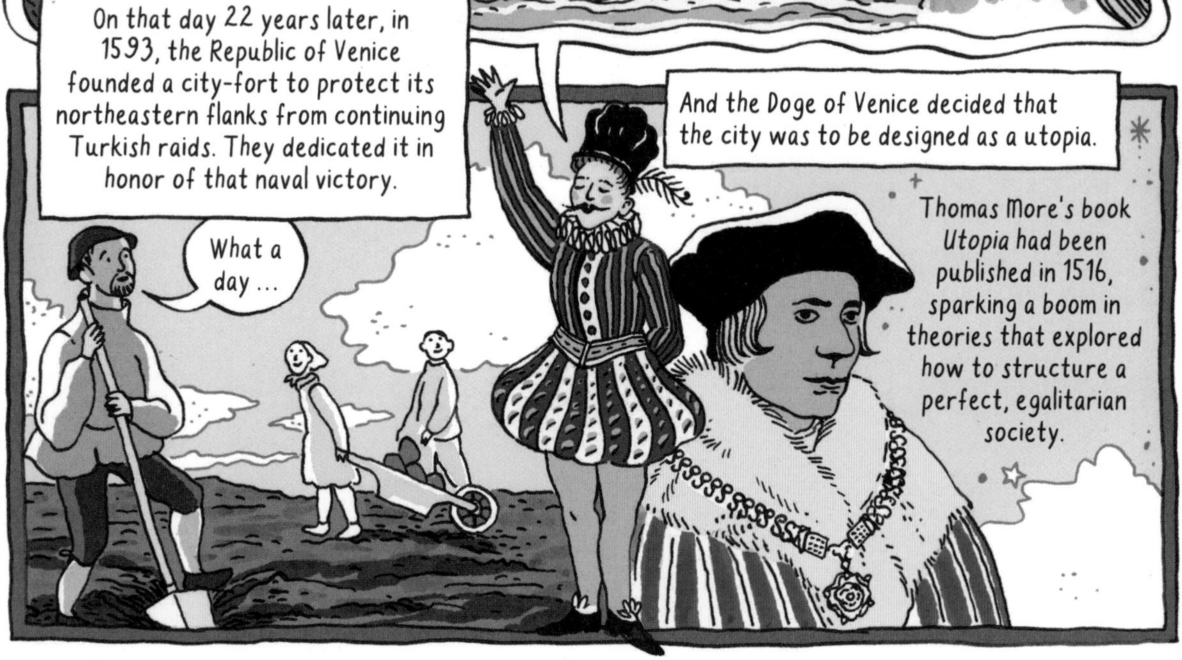
On that day 22 years later, in 1593, the Republic of Venice founded a city-fort to protect its northeastern flanks from continuing Turkish raids. They dedicated it in honor of that naval victory.
And the Doge of Venice decided that the city was to be designed as a utopia.
What a day ...
Thomas More's book *Utopia* had been published in 1516, sparking a boom in theories that explored how to structure a perfect, egalitarian society.

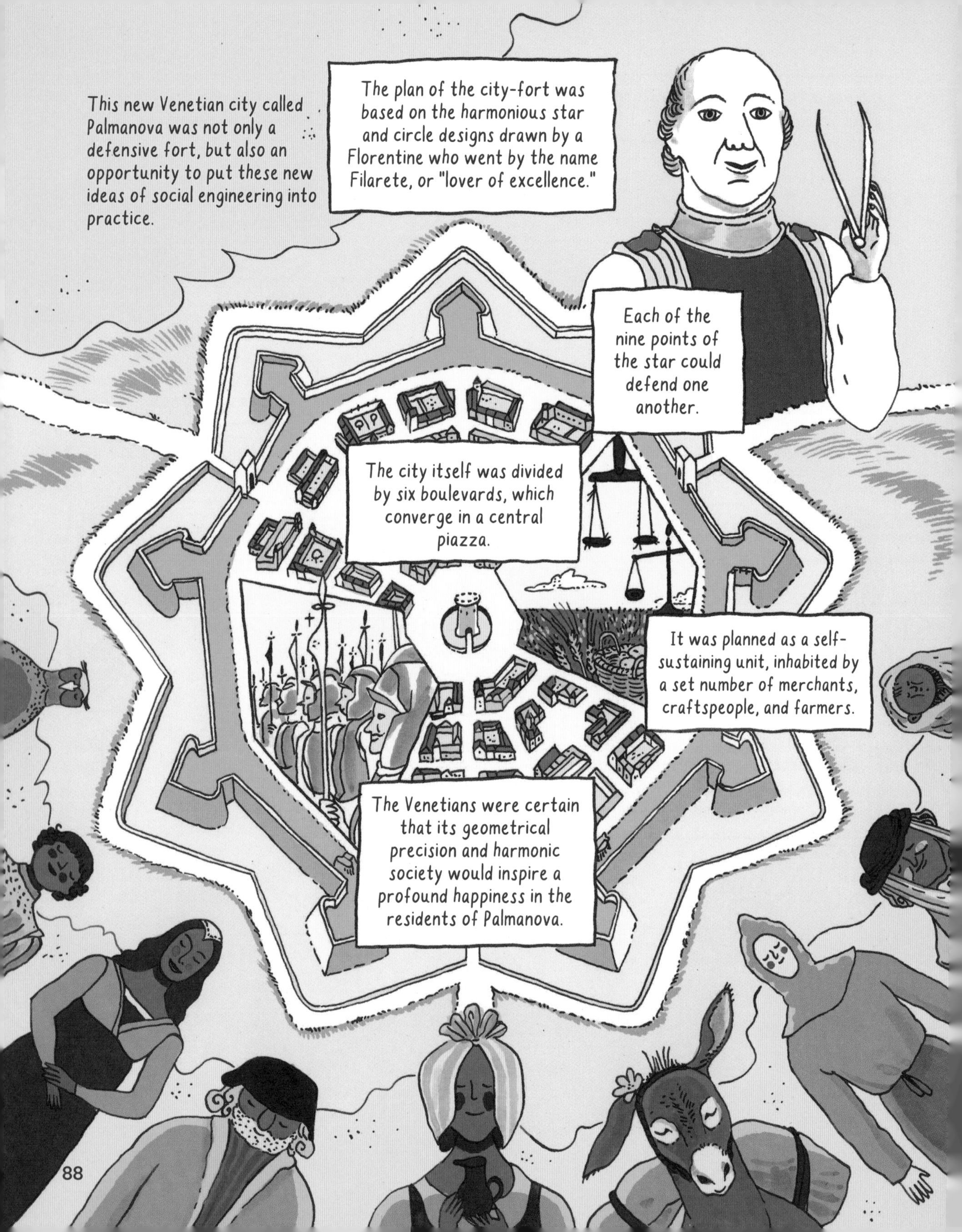

This new Venetian city called Palmanova was not only a defensive fort, but also an opportunity to put these new ideas of social engineering into practice.
The plan of the city-fort was based on the harmonious star and circle designs drawn by a Florentine who went by the name Filarete, or "lover of excellence."
Each of the nine points of the star could defend one another.
The city itself was divided by six boulevards, which converge in a central piazza.
It was planned as a self-sustaining unit, inhabited by a set number of merchants, craftspeople, and farmers.
The Venetians were certain that its geometrical precision and harmonic society would inspire a profound happiness in the residents of Palmanova.

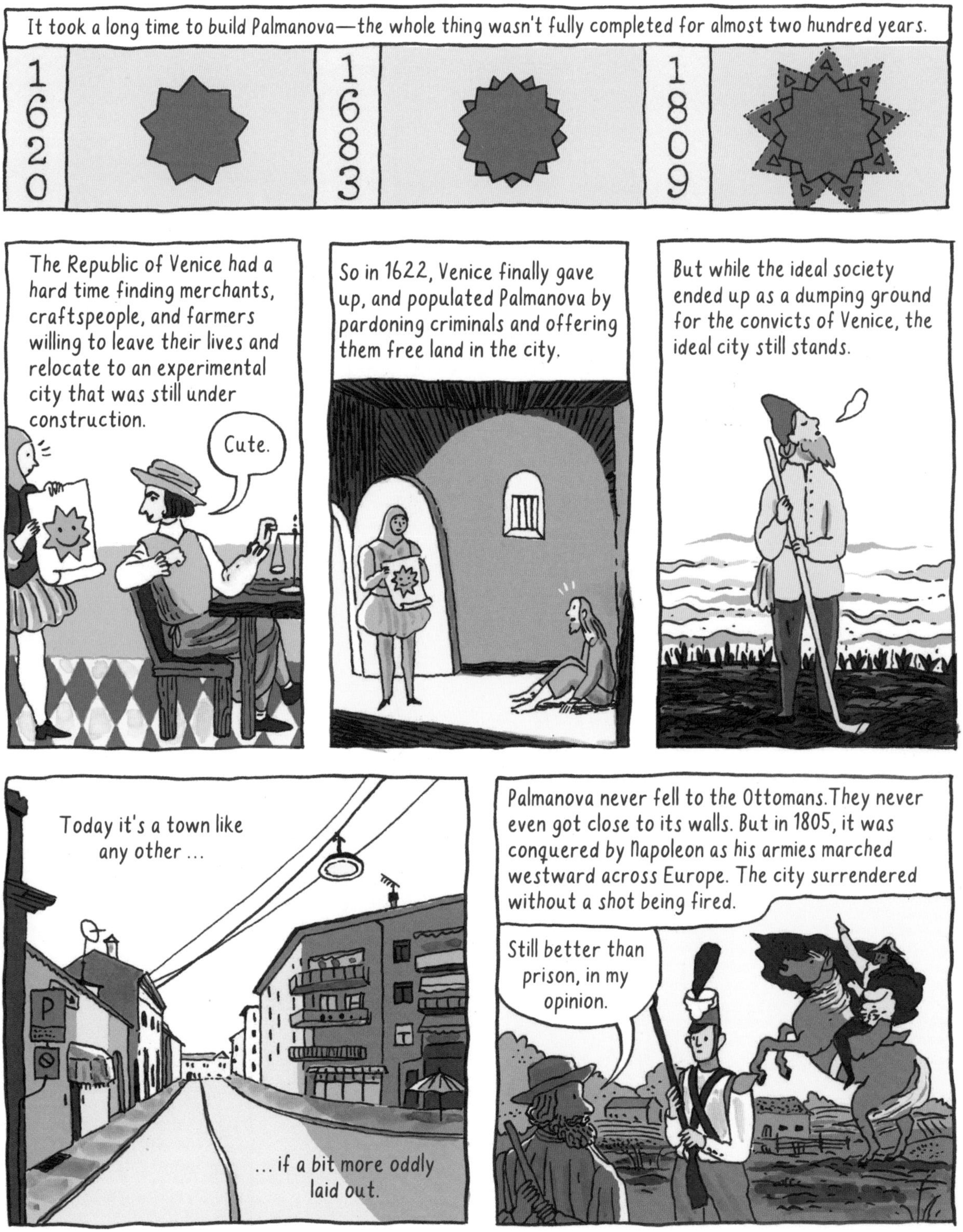
It took a long time to build Palmanova—the whole thing wasn't fully completed for almost two hundred years.
1620
1683
1809
The Republic of Venice had a hard time finding merchants, craftspeople, and farmers willing to leave their lives and relocate to an experimental city that was still under construction.
Cute.
So in 1622, Venice finally gave up, and populated Palmanova by pardoning criminals and offering them free land in the city.
But while the ideal society ended up as a dumping ground for the convicts of Venice, the ideal city still stands.
Today it's a town like any other ...
... if a bit more oddly laid out.
Palmanova never fell to the Ottomans. They never even got close to its walls. But in 1805, it was conquered by Napoleon as his armies marched westward across Europe. The city surrendered without a shot being fired.
Still better than prison, in my opinion.

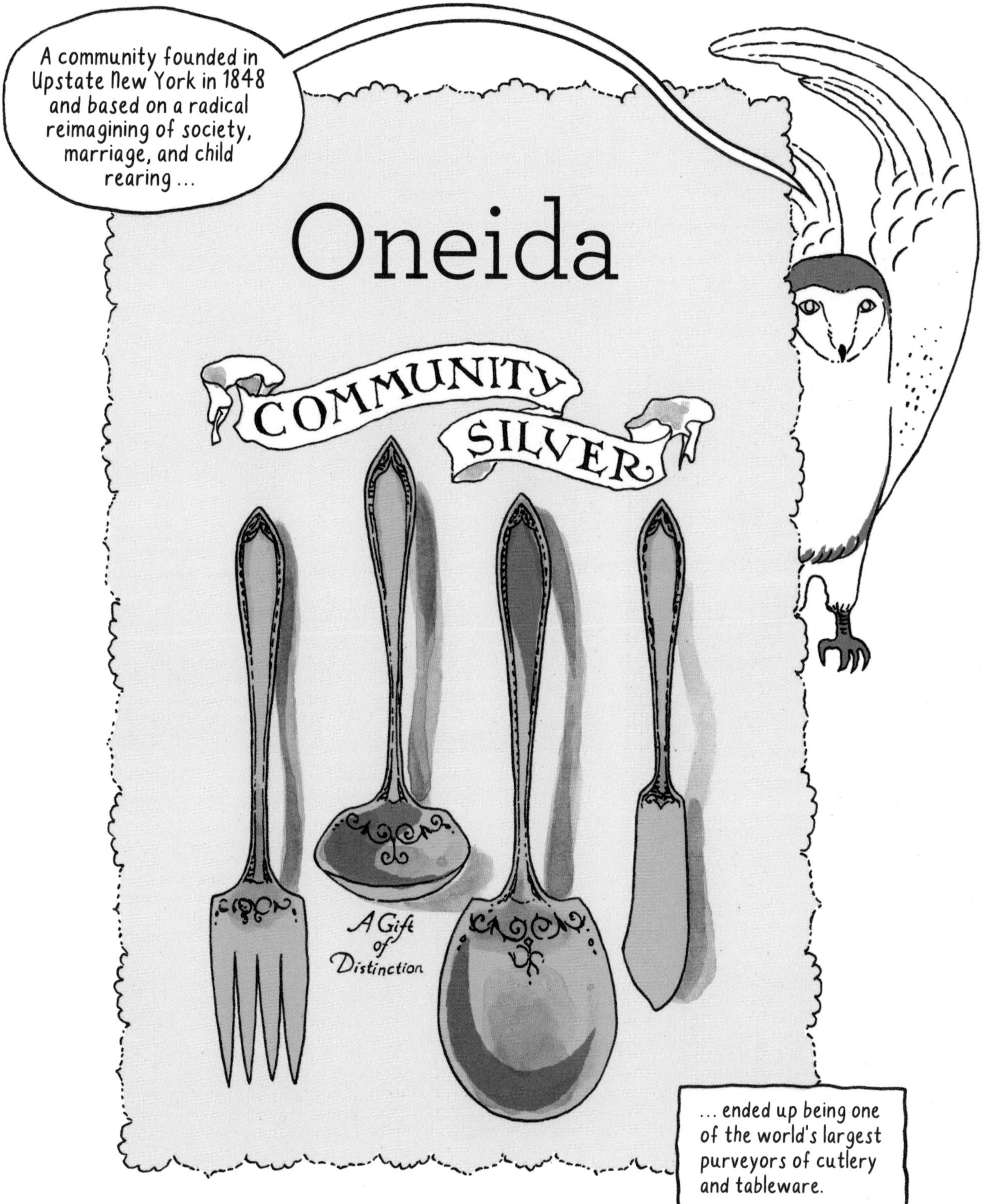
A community founded in Upstate New York in 1848 and based on a radical reimagining of society, marriage, and child rearing ...
Oneida
COMMUNITY SILVER
A Gift of Distinction
... ended up being one of the world's largest purveyors of cutlery and tableware.

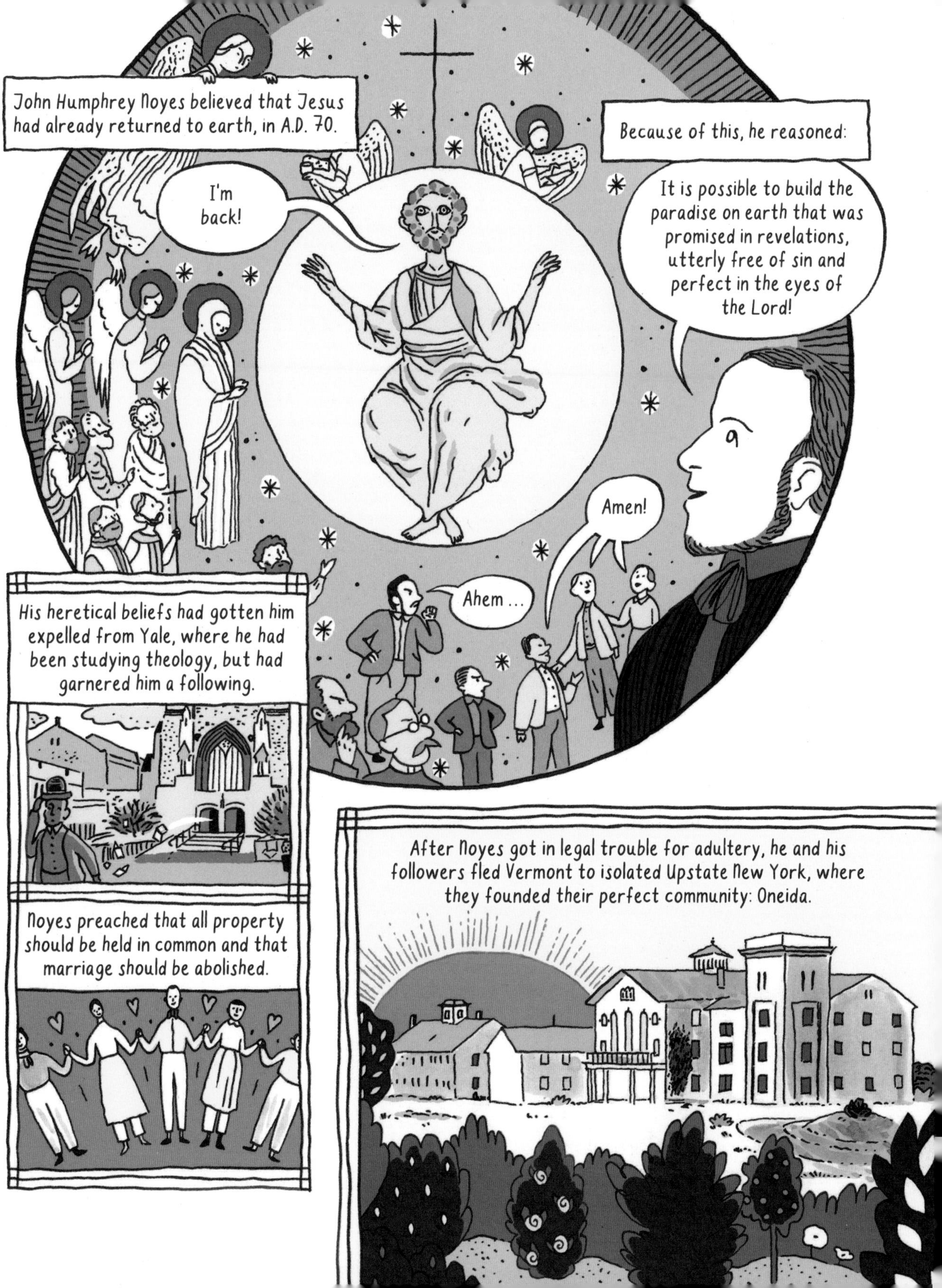
John Humphrey Noyes believed that Jesus had already returned to earth, in A.D. 70.
I'm back!
Because of this, he reasoned:
It is possible to build the paradise on earth that was promised in revelations, utterly free of sin and perfect in the eyes of the Lord!
Amen!
Ahem ...
His heretical beliefs had gotten him expelled from Yale, where he had been studying theology, but had garnered him a following.
Noyes preached that all property should be held in common and that marriage should be abolished.
After Noyes got in legal trouble for adultery, he and his followers fled Vermont to isolated Upstate New York, where they founded their perfect community: Oneida.

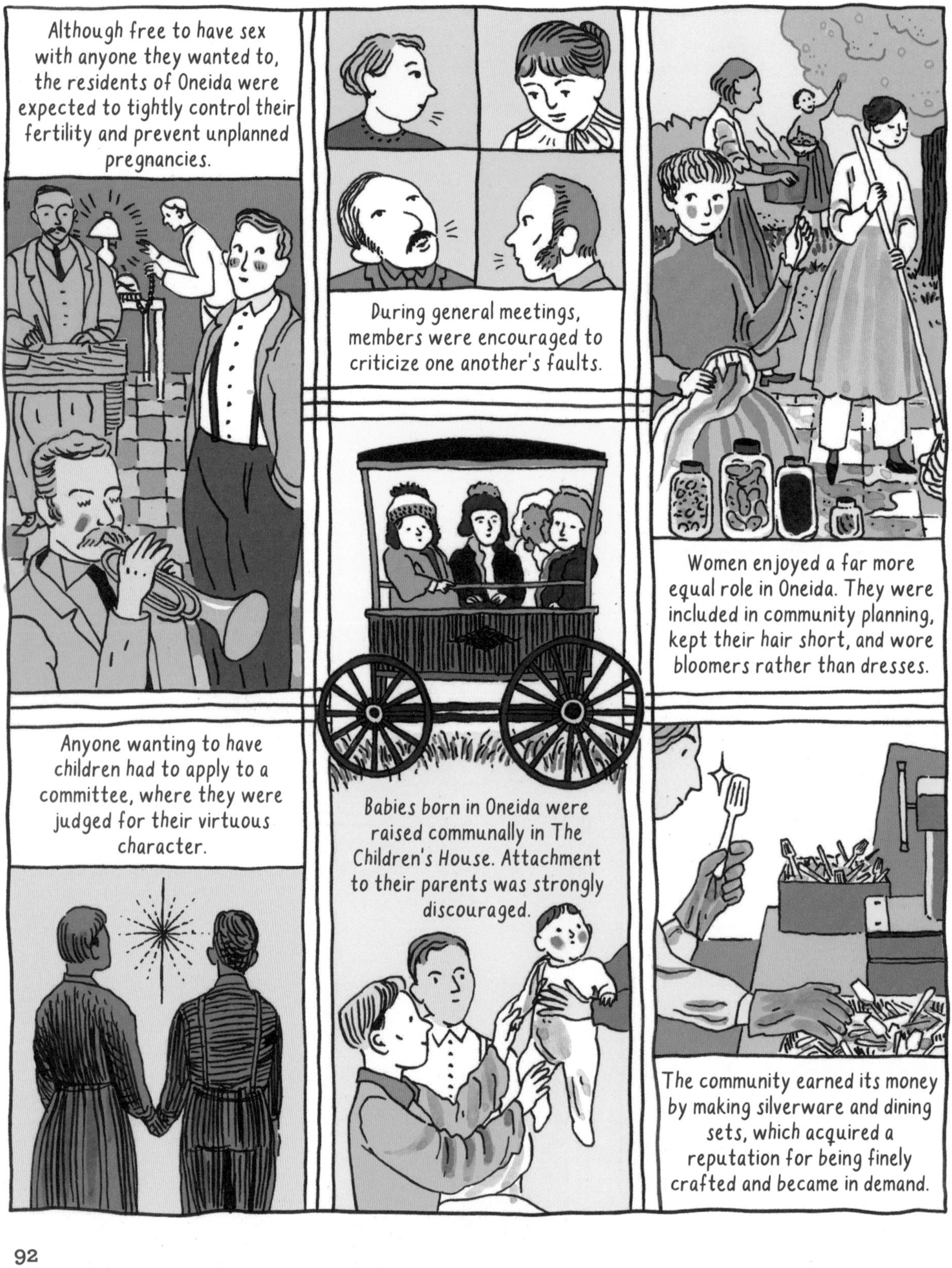
Although free to have sex with anyone they wanted to, the residents of Oneida were expected to tightly control their fertility and prevent unplanned pregnancies.
During general meetings, members were encouraged to criticize one another's faults.
Women enjoyed a far more equal role in Oneida. They were included in community planning, kept their hair short, and wore bloomers rather than dresses.
Anyone wanting to have children had to apply to a committee, where they were judged for their virtuous character.
Babies born in Oneida were raised communally in The Children's House. Attachment to their parents was strongly discouraged.
The community earned its money by making silverware and dining sets, which acquired a reputation for being finely crafted and became in demand.

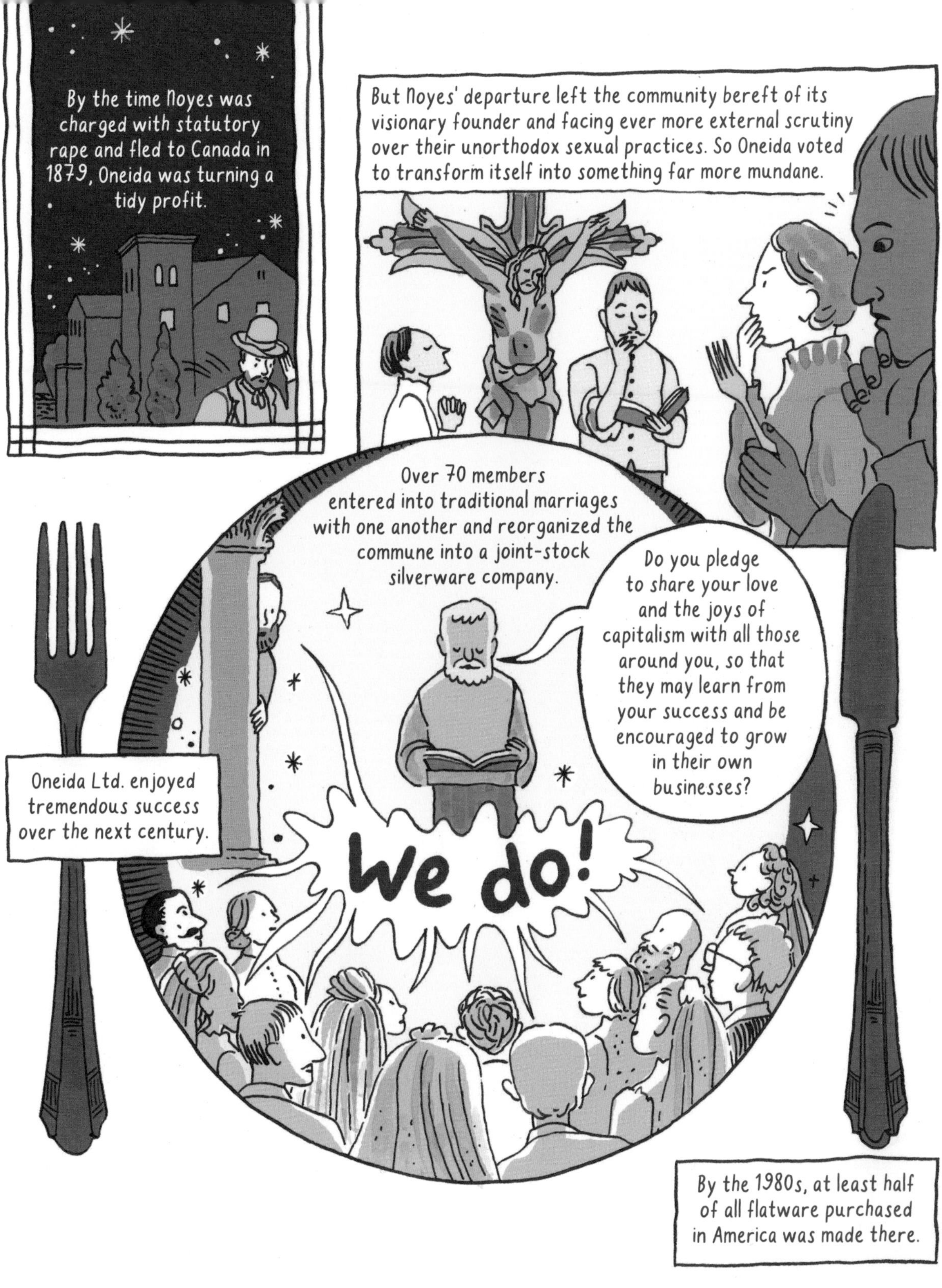
By the time Noyes was charged with statutory rape and fled to Canada in 1879, Oneida was turning a tidy profit.
But Noyes' departure left the community bereft of its visionary founder and facing ever more external scrutiny over their unorthodox sexual practices. So Oneida voted to transform itself into something far more mundane.
Over 70 members entered into traditional marriages with one another and reorganized the commune into a joint-stock silverware company.
Do you pledge to share your love and the joys of capitalism with all those around you, so that they may learn from your success and be encouraged to grow in their own businesses?
We do!
Oneida Ltd. enjoyed tremendous success over the next century.
By the 1980s, at least half of all flatware purchased in America was made there.

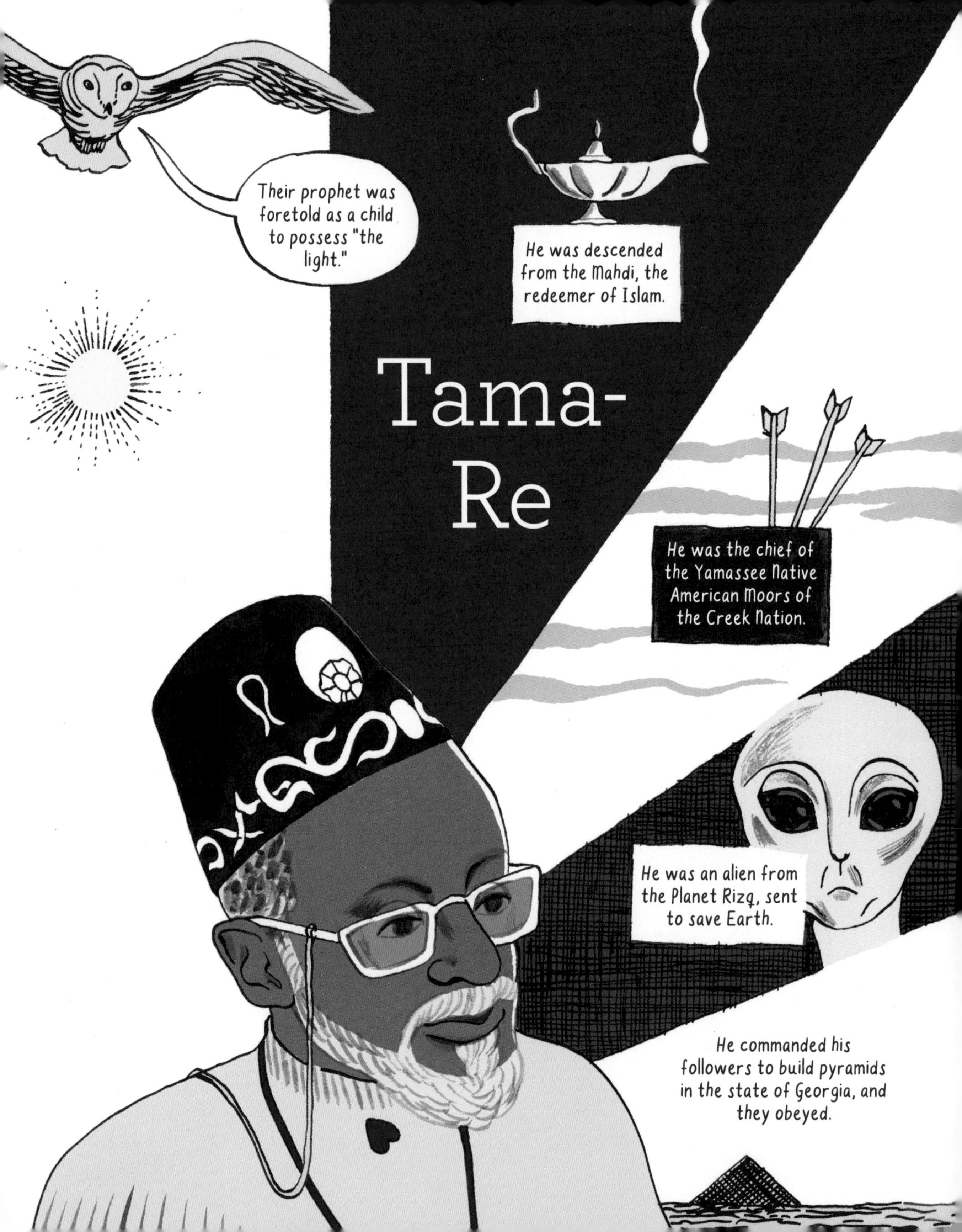
Their prophet was foretold as a child to possess "the light."
He was descended from the Mahdi, the redeemer of Islam.
Tama-Re
He was the chief of the Yamassee Native American Moors of the Creek Nation.
He was an alien from the Planet Rizq, sent to save Earth.
He commanded his followers to build pyramids in the state of Georgia, and they obeyed.

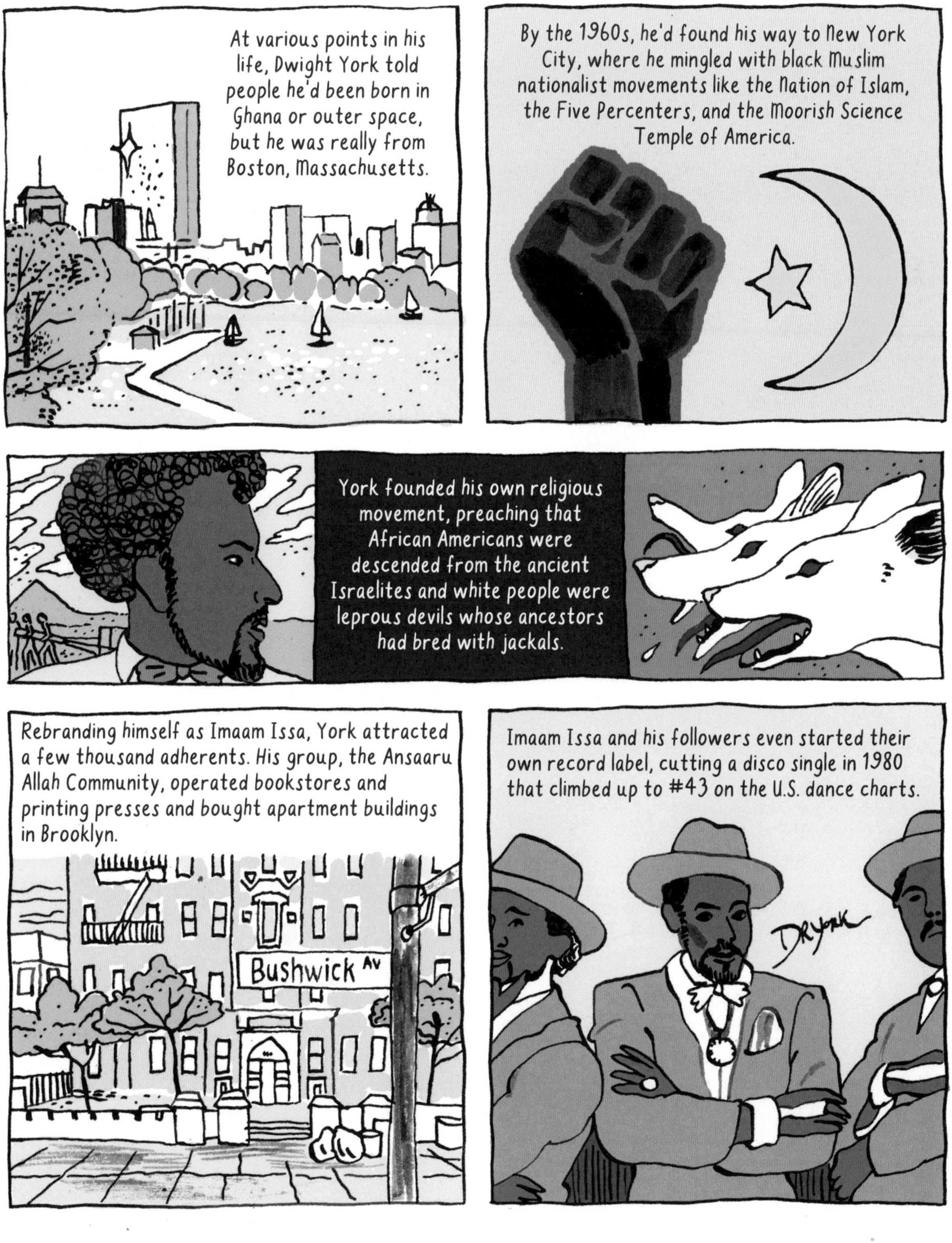
At various points in his life, Dwight York told people he'd been born in Ghana or outer space, but he was really from Boston, Massachusetts.
By the 1960s, he'd found his way to New York City, where he mingled with black Muslim nationalist movements like the Nation of Islam, the Five Percenters, and the Moorish Science Temple of America.
York founded his own religious movement, preaching that African Americans were descended from the ancient Israelites and white people were leprous devils whose ancestors had bred with jackals.
Rebranding himself as Imaam Issa, York attracted a few thousand adherents. His group, the Ansaaru Allah Community, operated bookstores and printing presses and bought apartment buildings in Brooklyn.
Bushwick AV
Imaam Issa and his followers even started their own record label, cutting a disco single in 1980 that climbed up to #43 on the U.S. dance charts.

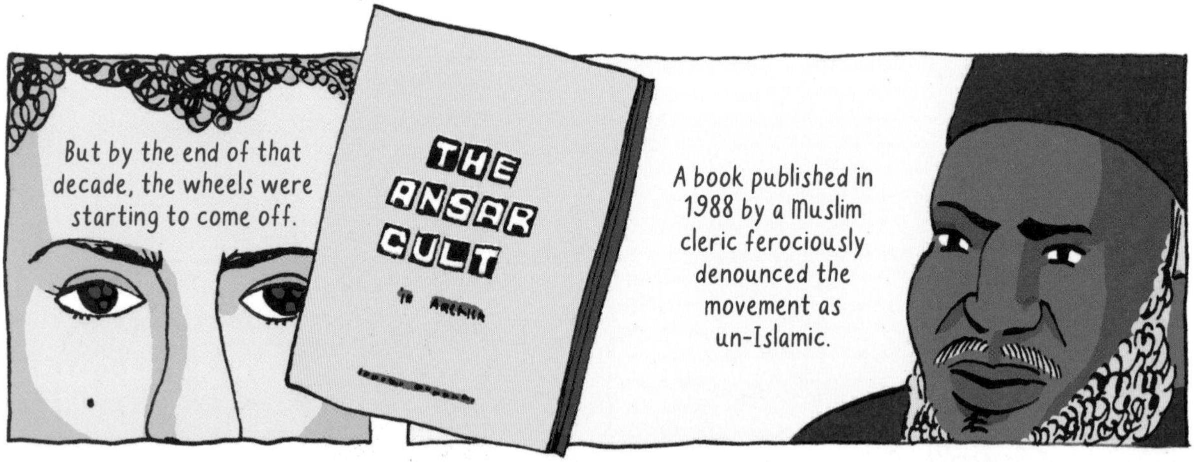
But by the end of that decade, the wheels were starting to come off.
THE ANSAR CULT
A book published in 1988 by a Muslim cleric ferociously denounced the movement as un-Islamic.

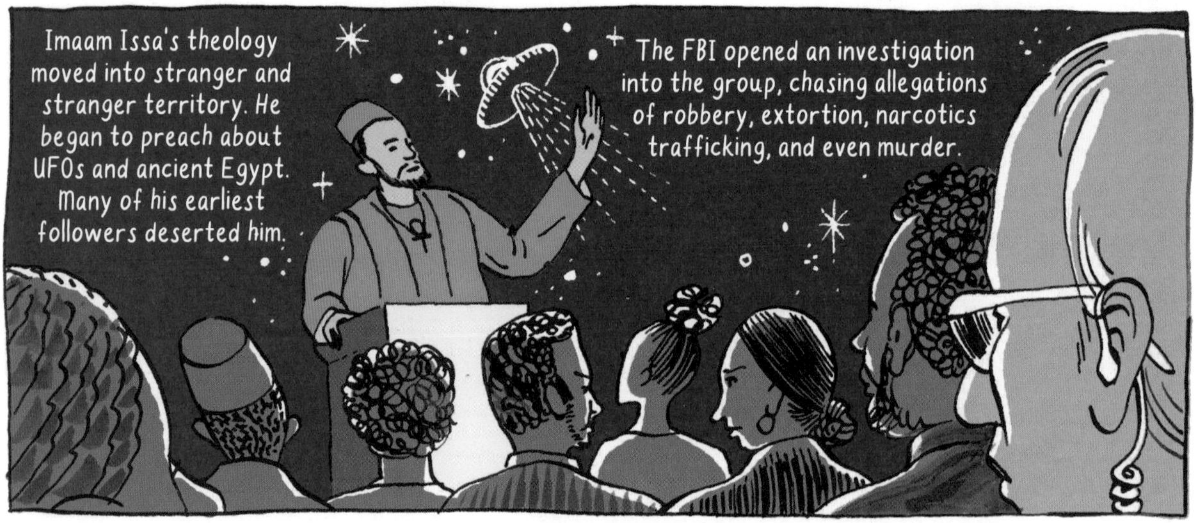
Imaam Issa's theology moved into stranger and stranger territory. He began to preach about UFOs and ancient Egypt. Many of his earliest followers deserted him.
The FBI opened an investigation into the group, chasing allegations of robbery, extortion, narcotics trafficking, and even murder.

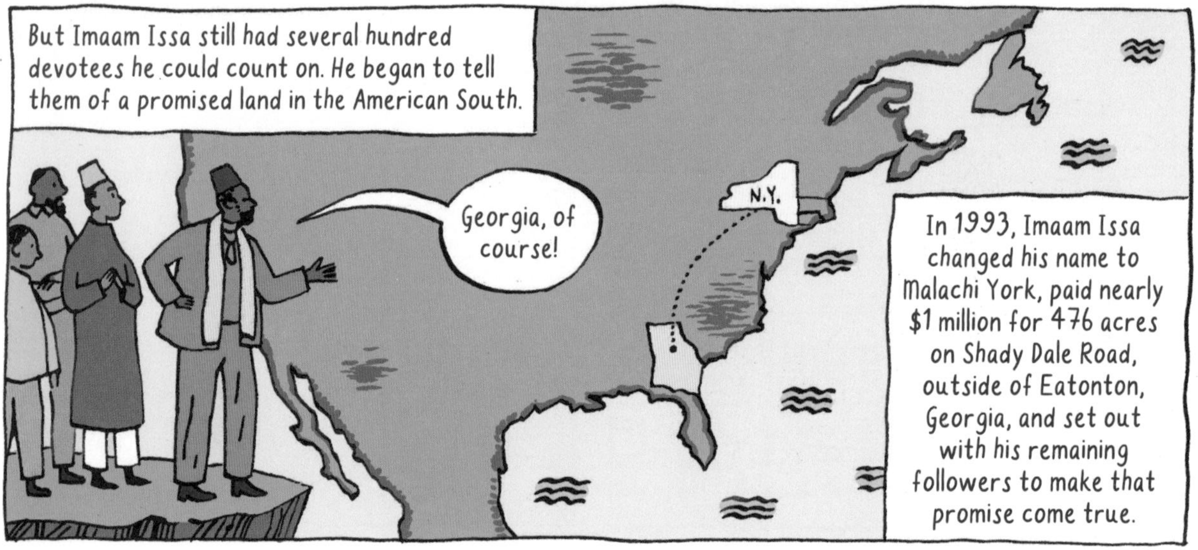
But Imaam Issa still had several hundred devotees he could count on. He began to tell them of a promised land in the American South.
Georgia, of course!
N.Y.
In 1993, Imaam Issa changed his name to Malachi York, paid nearly $1 million for 476 acres on Shady Dale Road, outside of Eatonton, Georgia, and set out with his remaining followers to make that promise come true.

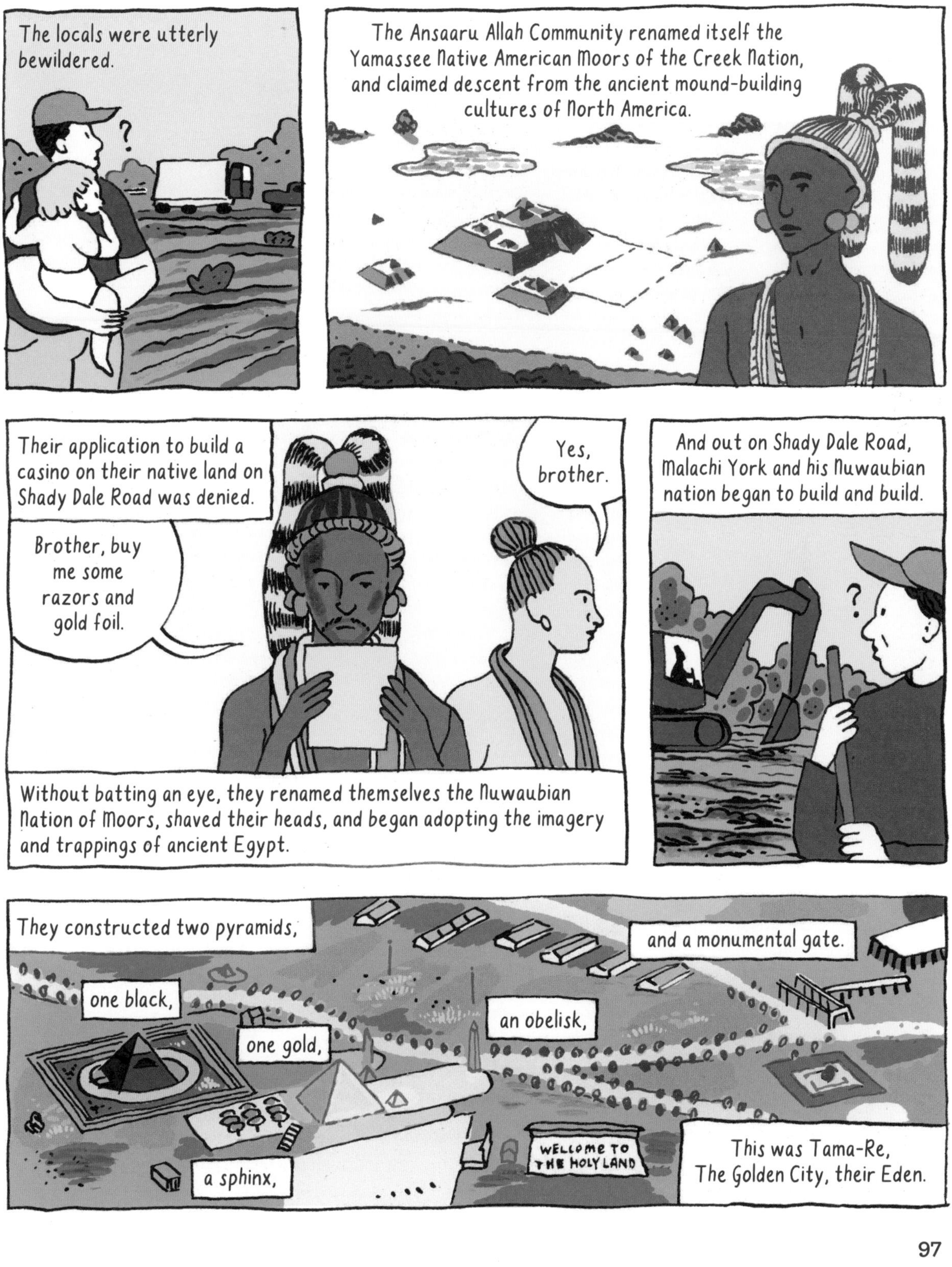
The locals were utterly bewildered.
The Ansaaru Allah Community renamed itself the Yamassee Native American Moors of the Creek Nation, and claimed descent from the ancient mound-building cultures of North America.
Their application to build a casino on their native land on Shady Dale Road was denied.
Brother, buy me some razors and gold foil.
Yes, brother.
Without batting an eye, they renamed themselves the Nuwaubian Nation of Moors, shaved their heads, and began adopting the imagery and trappings of ancient Egypt.
And out on Shady Dale Road, Malachi York and his Nuwaubian nation began to build and build.
They constructed two pyramids,
one black,
one gold,
an obelisk,
a sphinx,
and a monumental gate.
WELCOME TO THE HOLY LAND
This was Tama-Re, The Golden City, their Eden.

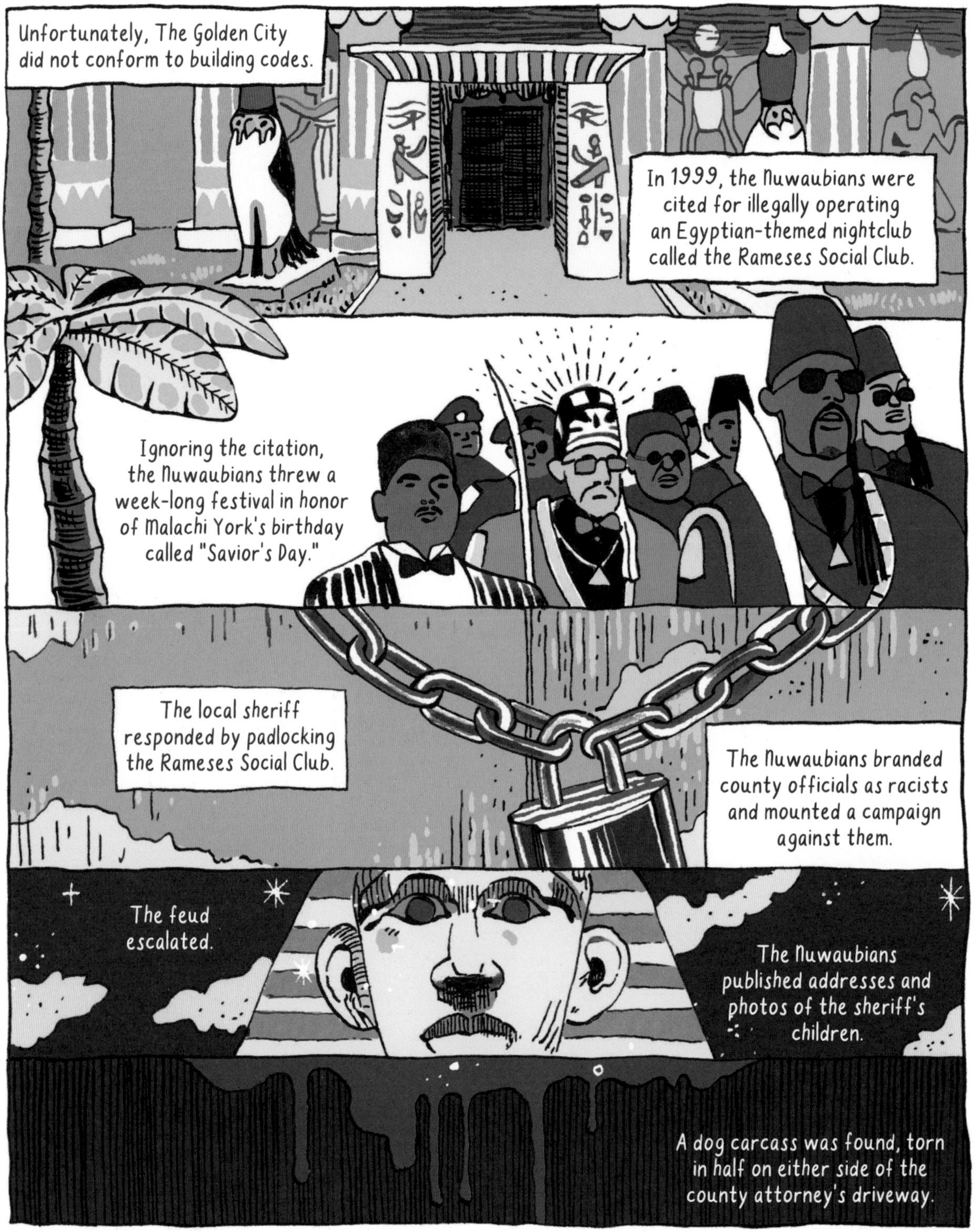
Unfortunately, The Golden City did not conform to building codes.
In 1999, the Nuwaubians were cited for illegally operating an Egyptian-themed nightclub called the Rameses Social Club.
Ignoring the citation, the Nuwaubians threw a week-long festival in honor of Malachi York's birthday called "Savior's Day."
The local sheriff responded by padlocking the Rameses Social Club.
The Nuwaubians branded county officials as racists and mounted a campaign against them.
The feud escalated.
The Nuwaubians published addresses and photos of the sheriff's children.
A dog carcass was found, torn in half on either side of the county attorney's driveway.

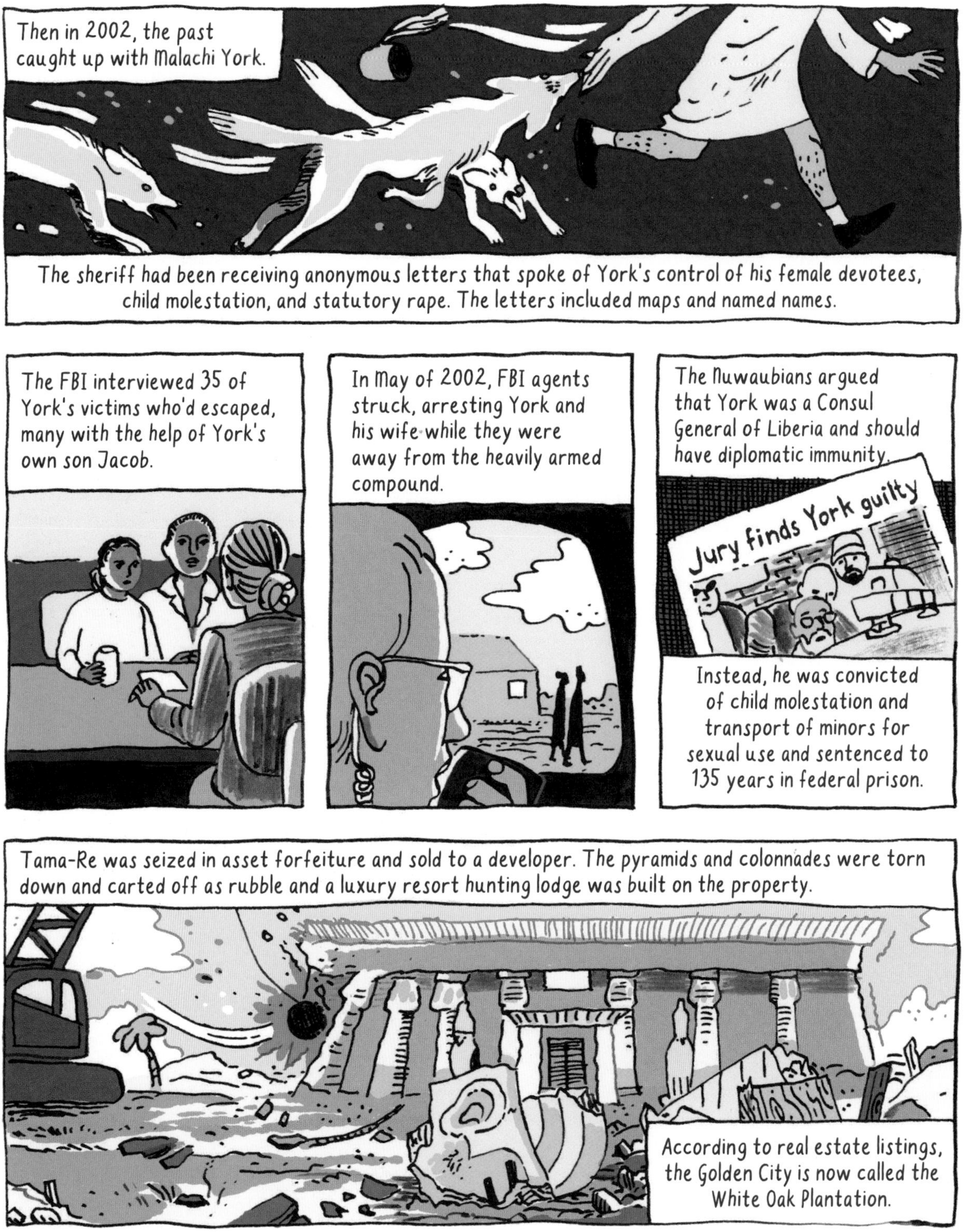
Then in 2002, the past caught up with Malachi York.
The sheriff had been receiving anonymous letters that spoke of York's control of his female devotees, child molestation, and statutory rape. The letters included maps and named names.
The FBI interviewed 35 of York's victims who'd escaped, many with the help of York's own son Jacob.
In May of 2002, FBI agents struck, arresting York and his wife while they were away from the heavily armed compound.
The Nuwaubians argued that York was a Consul General of Liberia and should have diplomatic immunity.
Jury finds York guilty
Instead, he was convicted of child molestation and transport of minors for sexual use and sentenced to 135 years in federal prison.
Tama-Re was seized in asset forfeiture and sold to a developer. The pyramids and colonnades were torn down and carted off as rubble and a luxury resort hunting lodge was built on the property.
According to real estate listings, the Golden City is now called the White Oak Plantation.

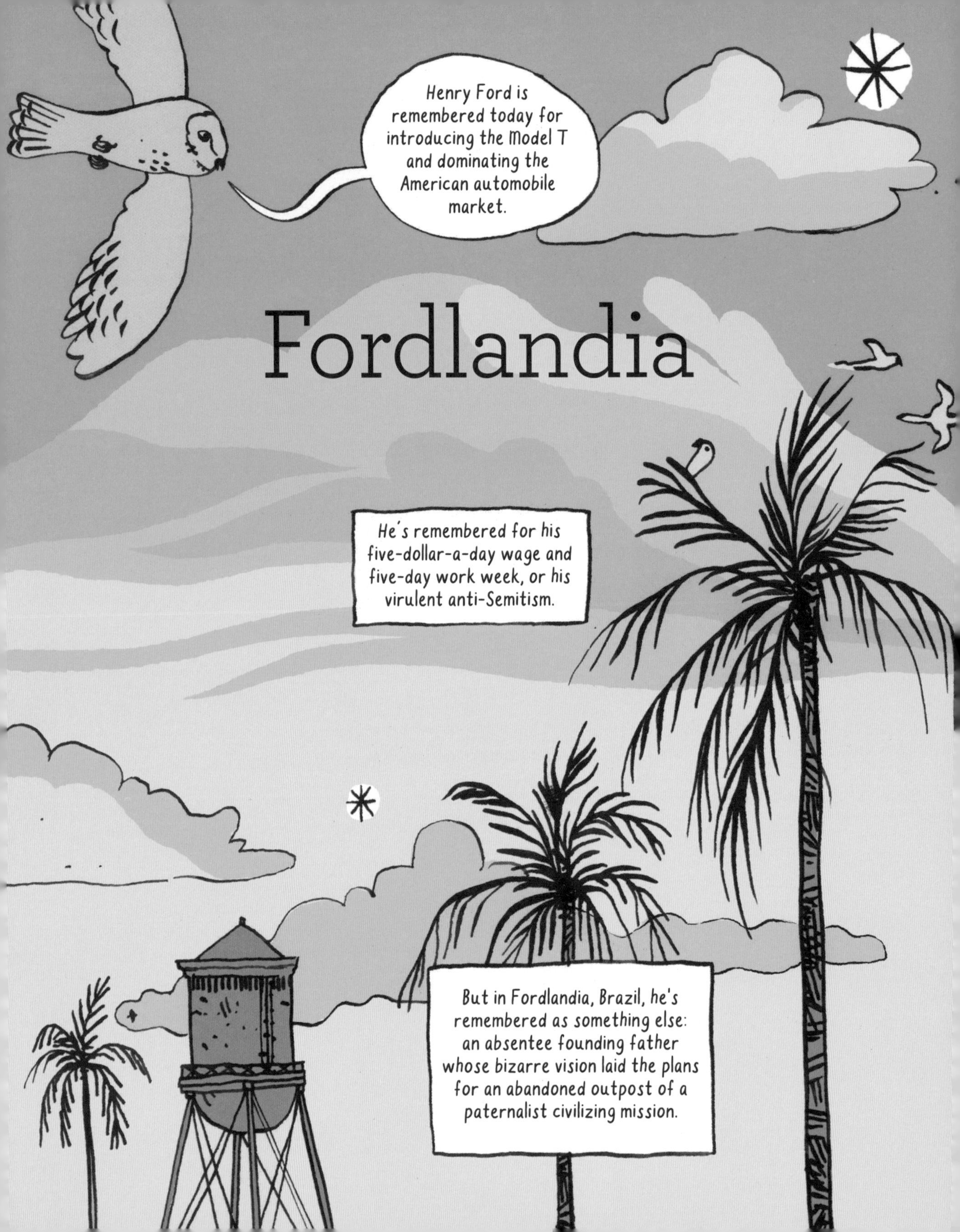
Henry Ford is remembered today for introducing the Model T and dominating the American automobile market.
Fordlandia
He's remembered for his five-dollar-a-day wage and five-day work week, or his virulent anti-Semitism.
But in Fordlandia, Brazil, he's remembered as something else: an absentee founding father whose bizarre vision laid the plans for an abandoned outpost of a paternalist civilizing mission.

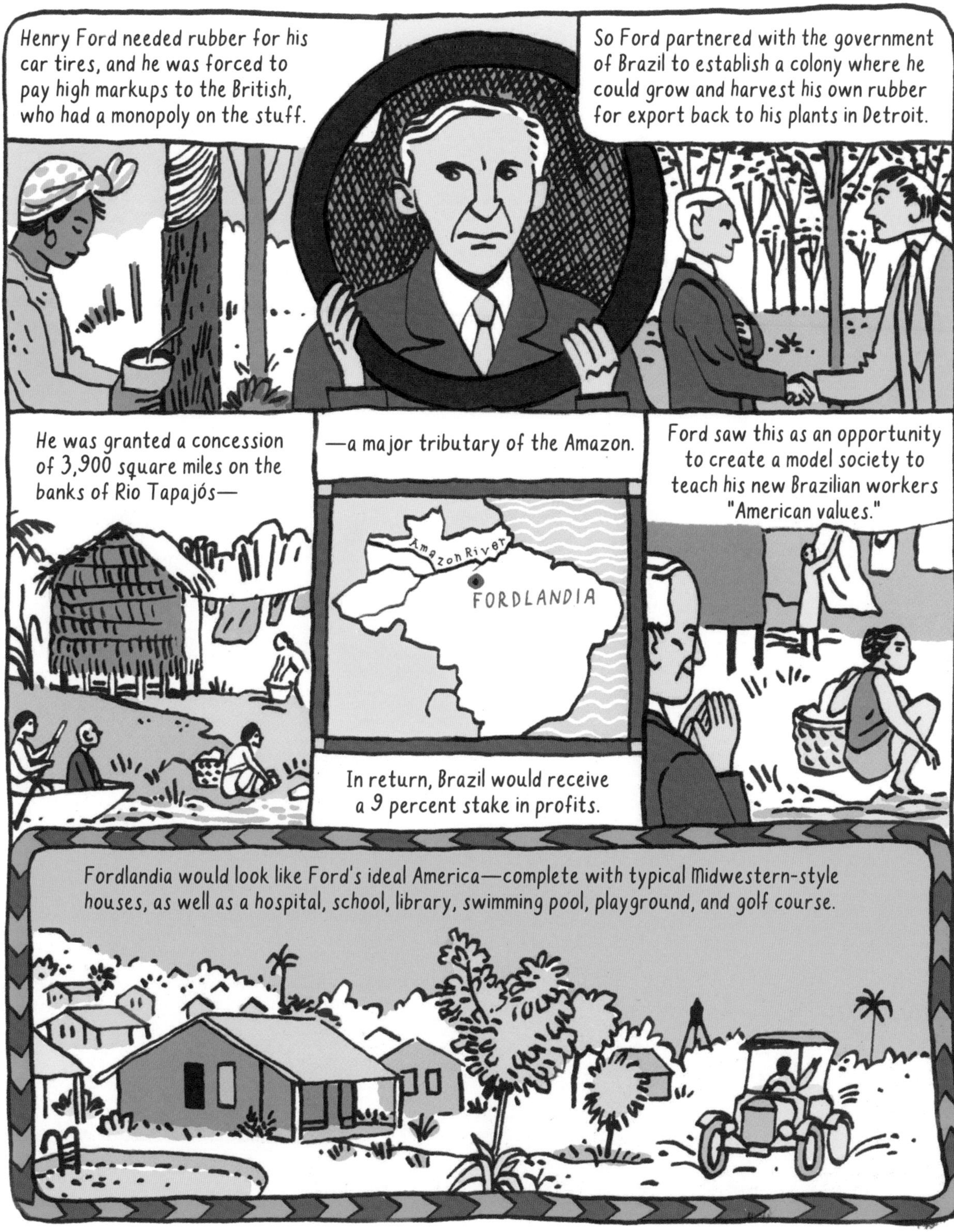
Henry Ford needed rubber for his car tires, and he was forced to pay high markups to the British, who had a monopoly on the stuff.
So Ford partnered with the government of Brazil to establish a colony where he could grow and harvest his own rubber for export back to his plants in Detroit.
He was granted a concession of 3,900 square miles on the banks of Rio Tapajós—
—a major tributary of the Amazon.
Amazon River
FORDLANDIA
In return, Brazil would receive a 9 percent stake in profits.
Ford saw this as an opportunity to create a model society to teach his new Brazilian workers "American values."
Fordlandia would look like Ford's ideal America—complete with typical Midwestern-style houses, as well as a hospital, school, library, swimming pool, playground, and golf course.

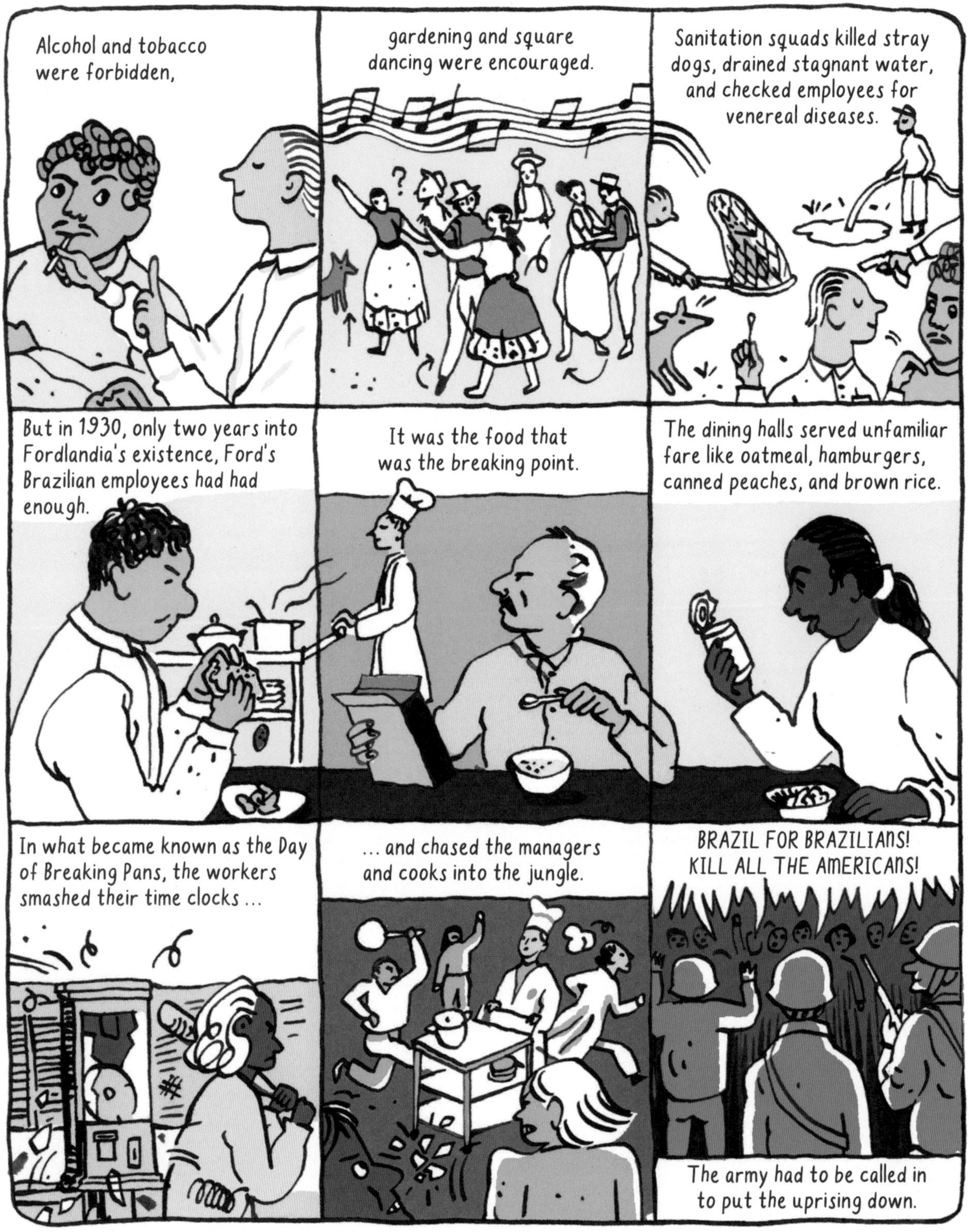
Alcohol and tobacco were forbidden,
gardening and square dancing were encouraged.
Sanitation squads killed stray dogs, drained stagnant water, and checked employees for venereal diseases.
But in 1930, only two years into Fordlandia's existence, Ford's Brazilian employees had had enough.
It was the food that was the breaking point.
The dining halls served unfamiliar fare like oatmeal, hamburgers, canned peaches, and brown rice.
In what became known as the Day of Breaking Pans, the workers smashed their time clocks ...
... and chased the managers and cooks into the jungle.
BRAZIL FOR BRAZILIANS! KILL ALL THE AMERICANS!
The army had to be called in to put the uprising down.

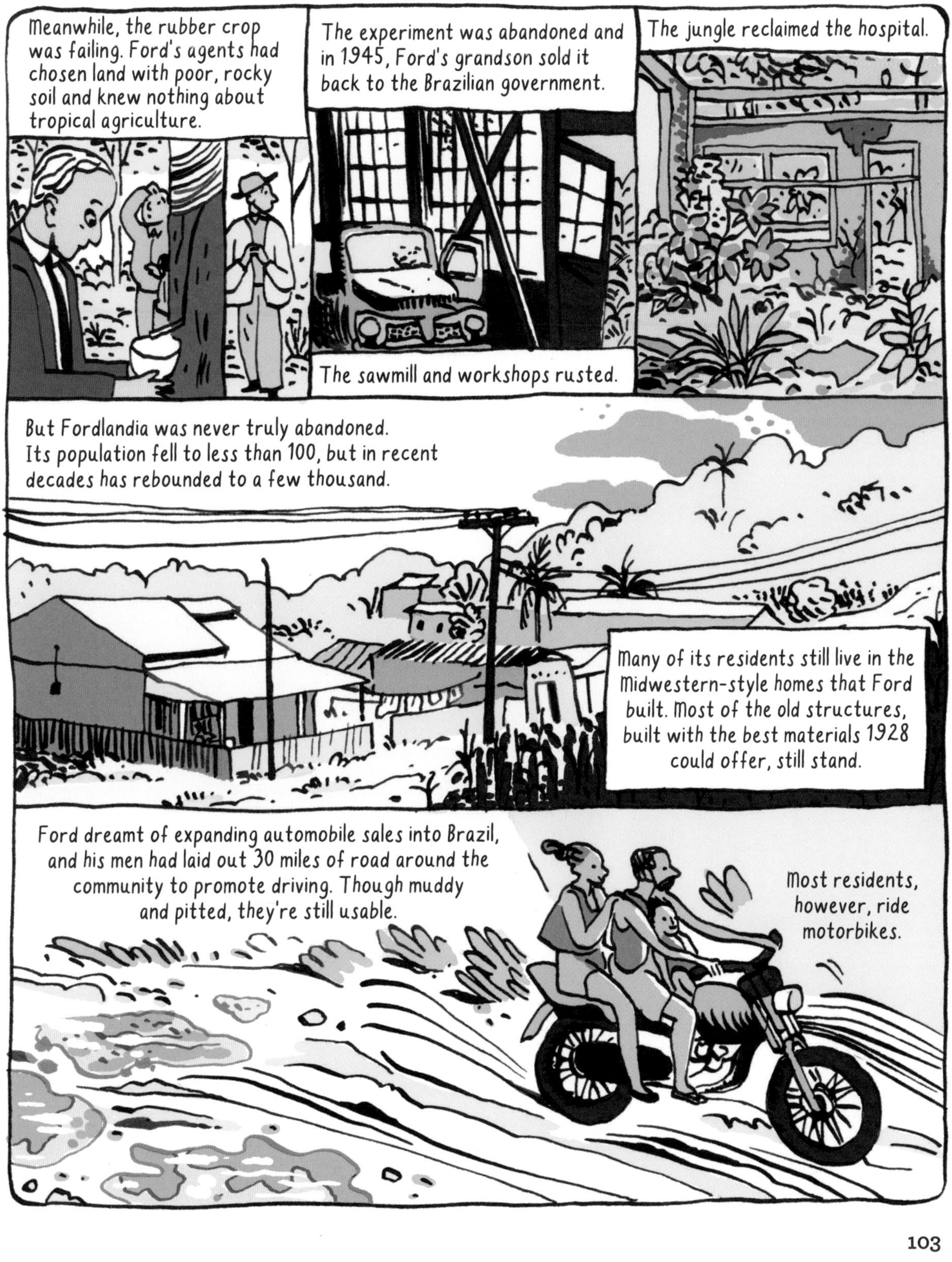
Meanwhile, the rubber crop was failing. Ford's agents had chosen land with poor, rocky soil and knew nothing about tropical agriculture.
The experiment was abandoned and in 1945, Ford's grandson sold it back to the Brazilian government.
The sawmill and workshops rusted.
The jungle reclaimed the hospital.
But Fordlandia was never truly abandoned. Its population fell to less than 100, but in recent decades has rebounded to a few thousand.
Many of its residents still live in the Midwestern-style homes that Ford built. Most of the old structures, built with the best materials 1928 could offer, still stand.
Ford dreamt of expanding automobile sales into Brazil, and his men had laid out 30 miles of road around the community to promote driving. Though muddy and pitted, they're still usable.
Most residents, however, ride motorbikes.

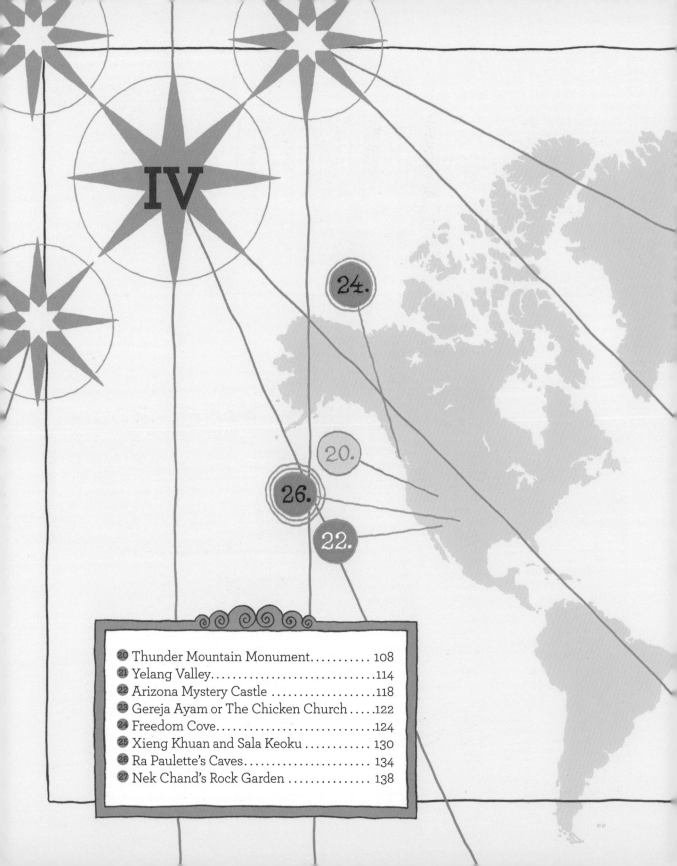

IV

VISIONARY ENVIRONMENTS

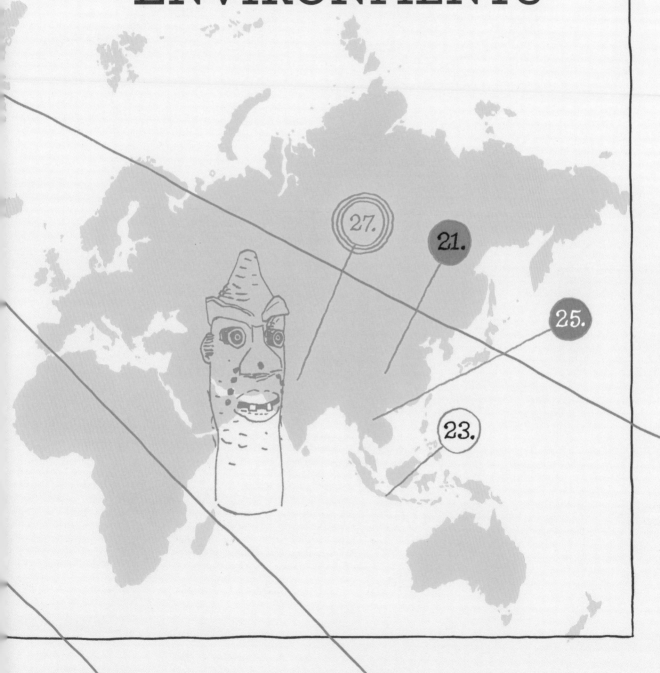

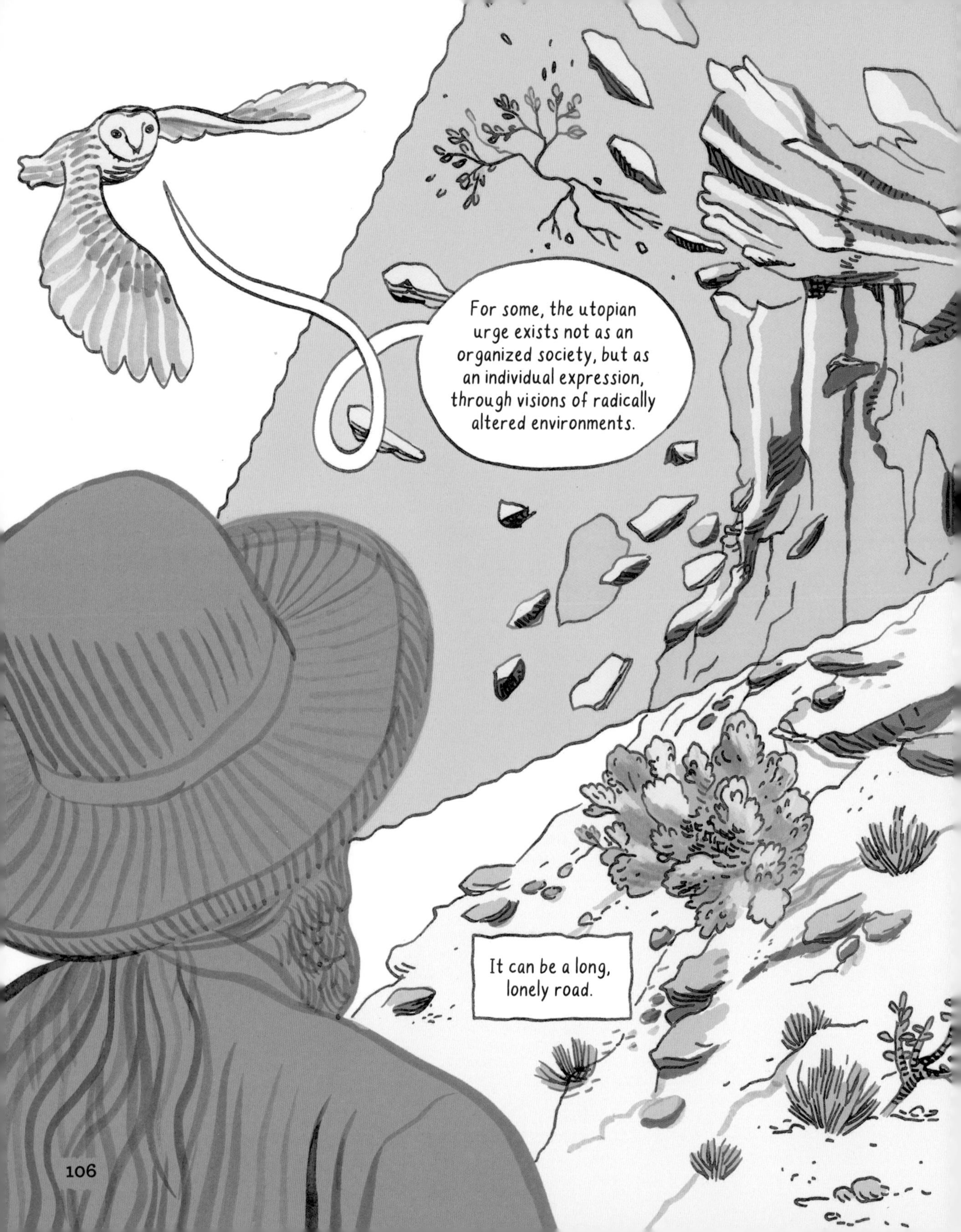
For some, the utopian urge exists not as an organized society, but as an individual expression, through visions of radically altered environments.
It can be a long, lonely road.

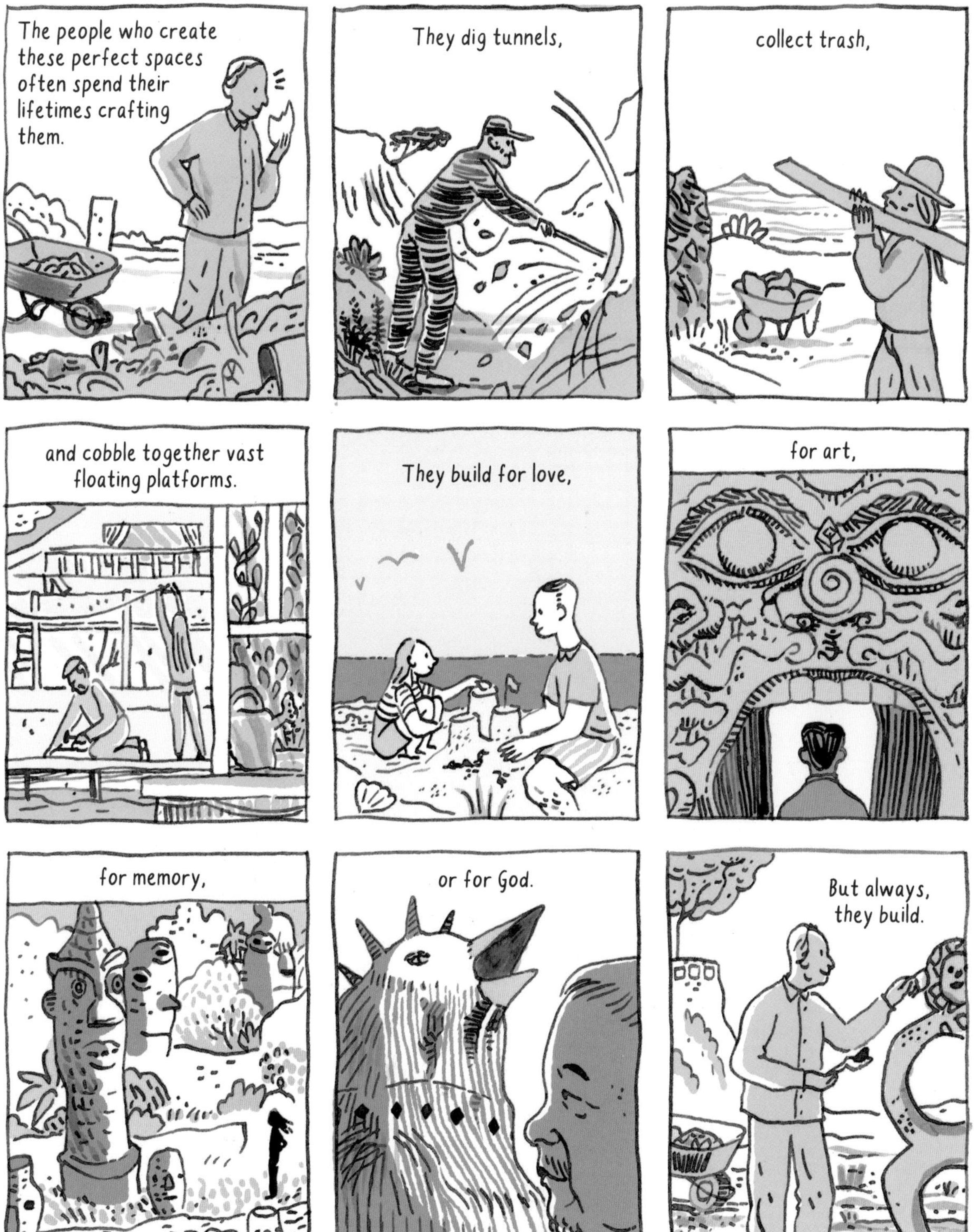

The people who create these perfect spaces often spend their lifetimes crafting them.
They dig tunnels,
collect trash,
and cobble together vast floating platforms.
They build for love,
for art,
for memory,
or for God.
But always, they build.

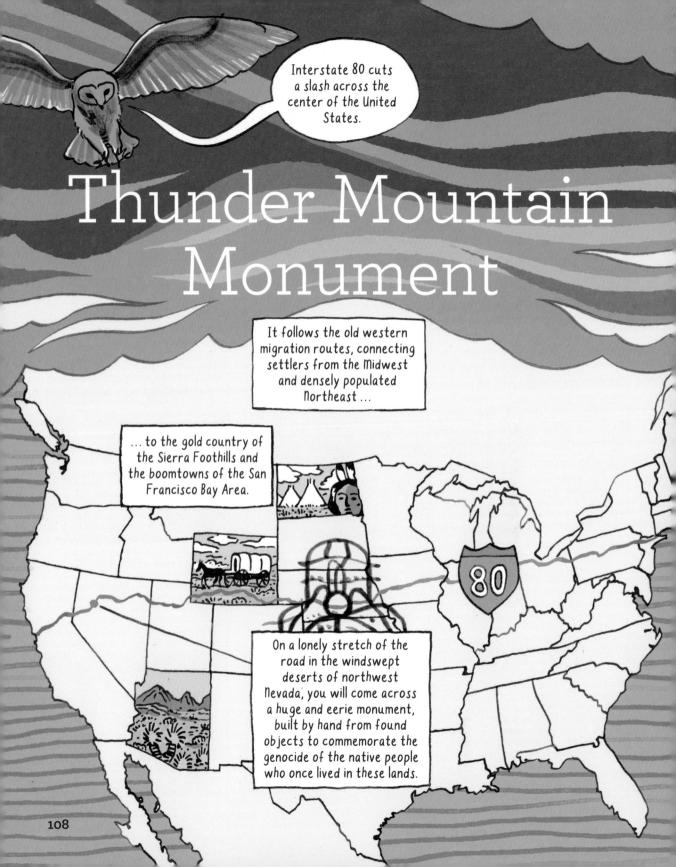

Thunder Mountain Monument

Interstate 80 cuts a slash across the center of the United States.

It follows the old western migration routes, connecting settlers from the Midwest and densely populated Northeast ...

... to the gold country of the Sierra Foothills and the boomtowns of the San Francisco Bay Area.

On a lonely stretch of the road in the windswept deserts of northwest Nevada, you will come across a huge and eerie monument, built by hand from found objects to commemorate the genocide of the native people who once lived in these lands.

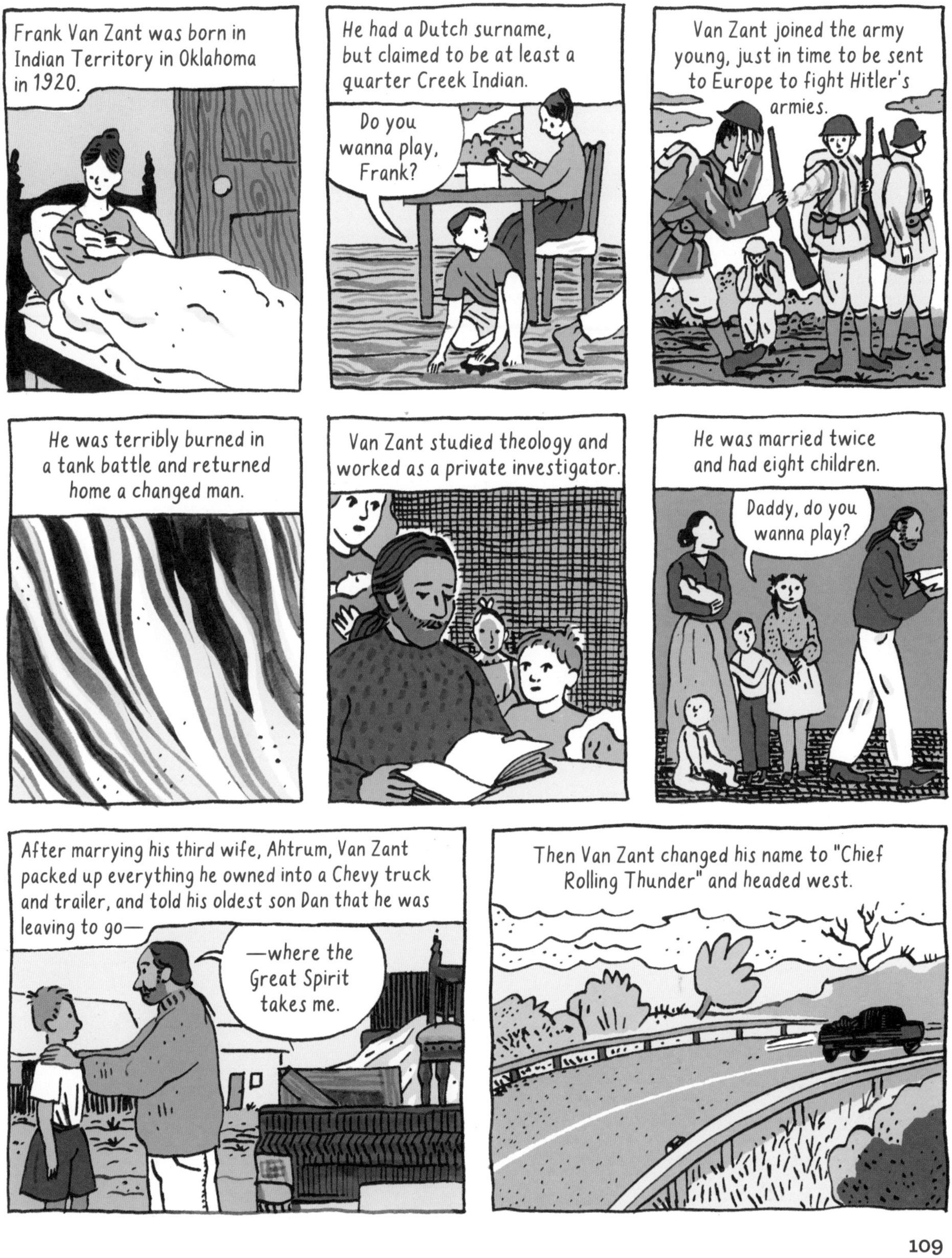
Frank Van Zant was born in Indian Territory in Oklahoma in 1920.
He had a Dutch surname, but claimed to be at least a quarter Creek Indian.
Do you wanna play, Frank?
Van Zant joined the army young, just in time to be sent to Europe to fight Hitler's armies.
He was terribly burned in a tank battle and returned home a changed man.
Van Zant studied theology and worked as a private investigator.
He was married twice and had eight children.
Daddy, do you wanna play?
After marrying his third wife, Ahtrum, Van Zant packed up everything he owned into a Chevy truck and trailer, and told his oldest son Dan that he was leaving to go—
—where the Great Spirit takes me.
Then Van Zant changed his name to "Chief Rolling Thunder" and headed west.

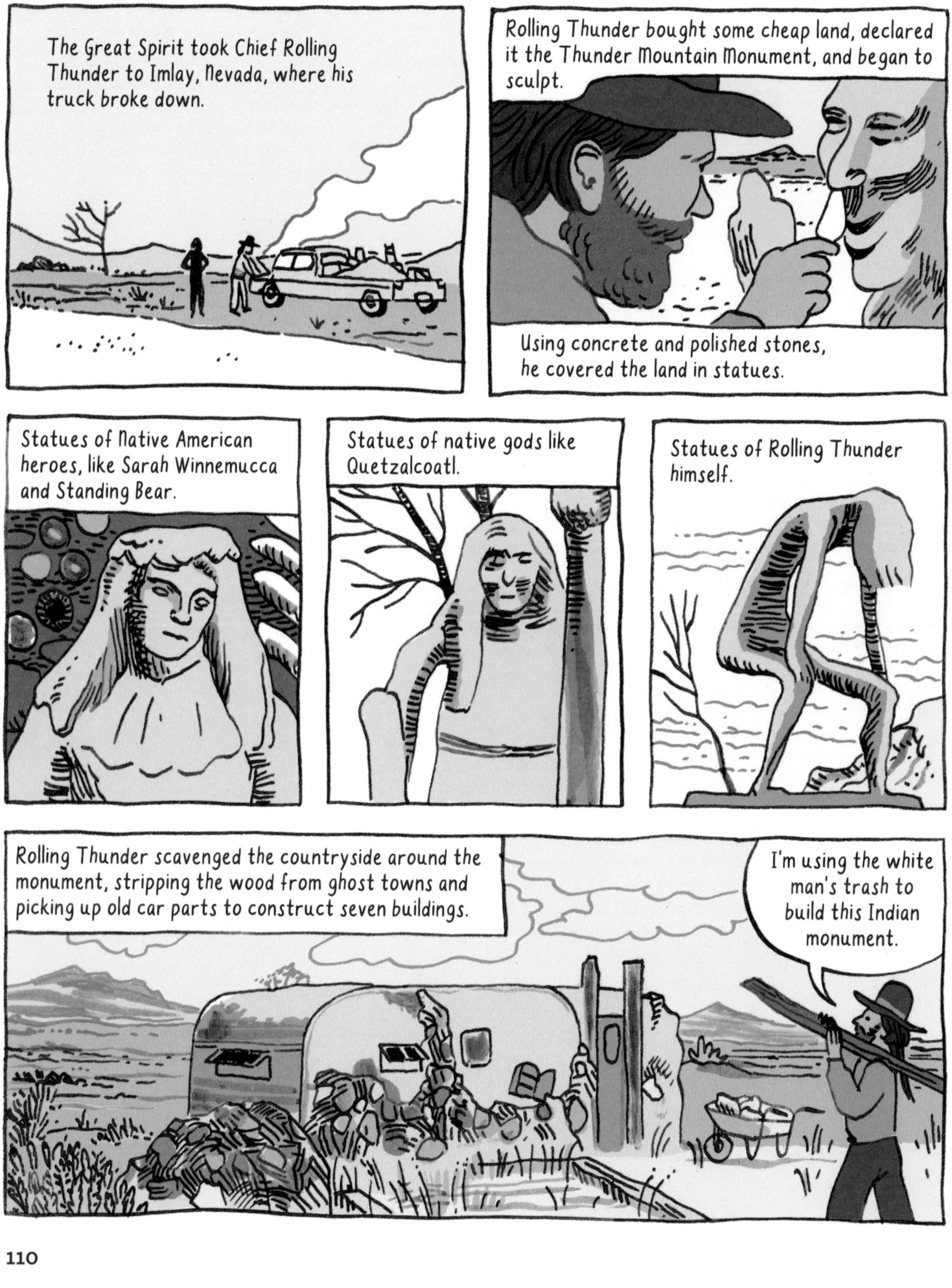
The Great Spirit took Chief Rolling Thunder to Imlay, Nevada, where his truck broke down.
Rolling Thunder bought some cheap land, declared it the Thunder Mountain Monument, and began to sculpt.
Using concrete and polished stones, he covered the land in statues.
Statues of Native American heroes, like Sarah Winnemucca and Standing Bear.
Statues of native gods like Quetzalcoatl.
Statues of Rolling Thunder himself.
Rolling Thunder scavenged the countryside around the monument, stripping the wood from ghost towns and picking up old car parts to construct seven buildings.
I'm using the white man's trash to build this Indian monument.

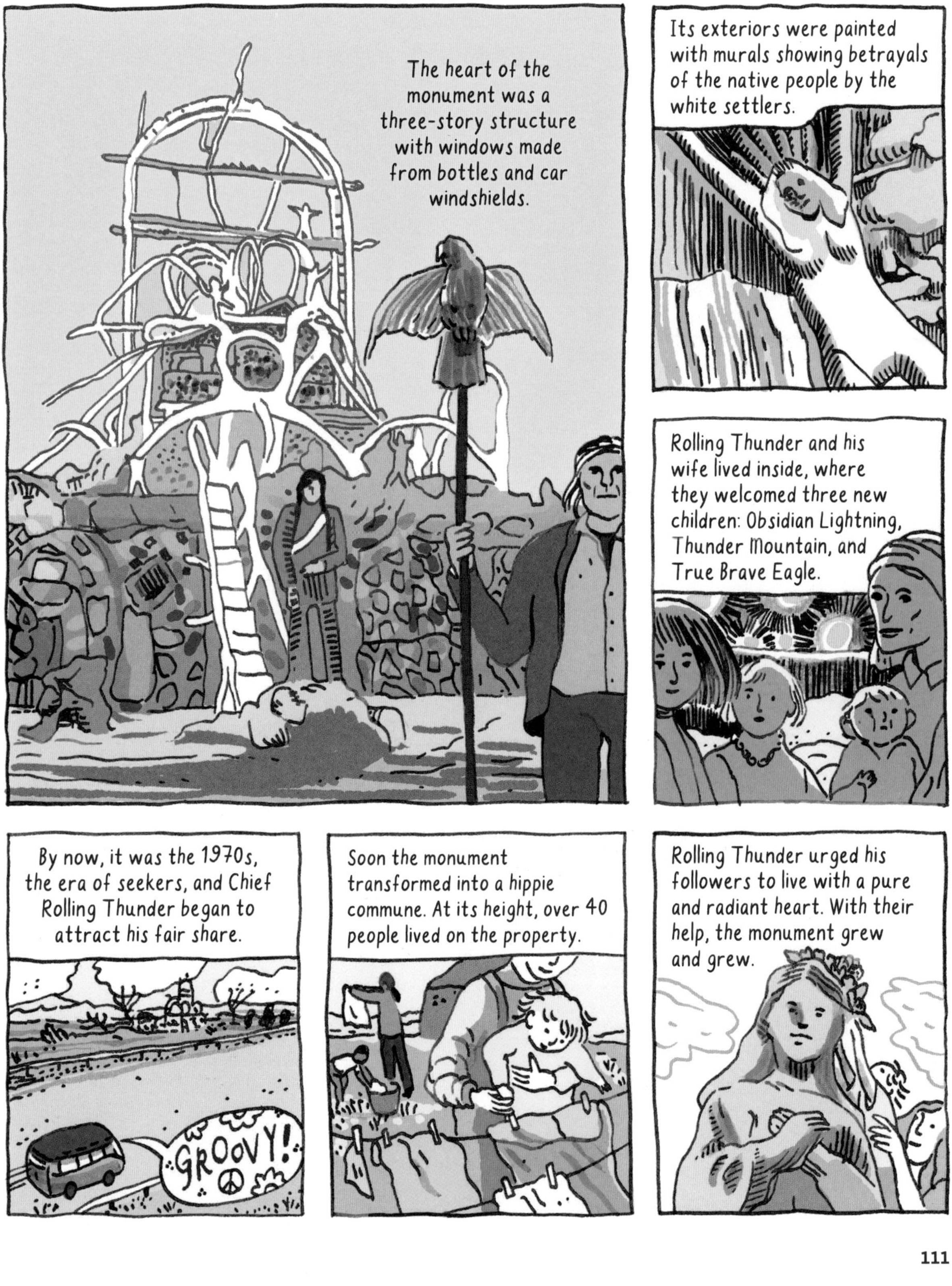
The heart of the monument was a three-story structure with windows made from bottles and car windshields.
Its exteriors were painted with murals showing betrayals of the native people by the white settlers.
Rolling Thunder and his wife lived inside, where they welcomed three new children: Obsidian Lightning, Thunder Mountain, and True Brave Eagle.
By now, it was the 1970s, the era of seekers, and Chief Rolling Thunder began to attract his fair share.
GROOVY!
Soon the monument transformed into a hippie commune. At its height, over 40 people lived on the property.
Rolling Thunder urged his followers to live with a pure and radiant heart. With their help, the monument grew and grew.

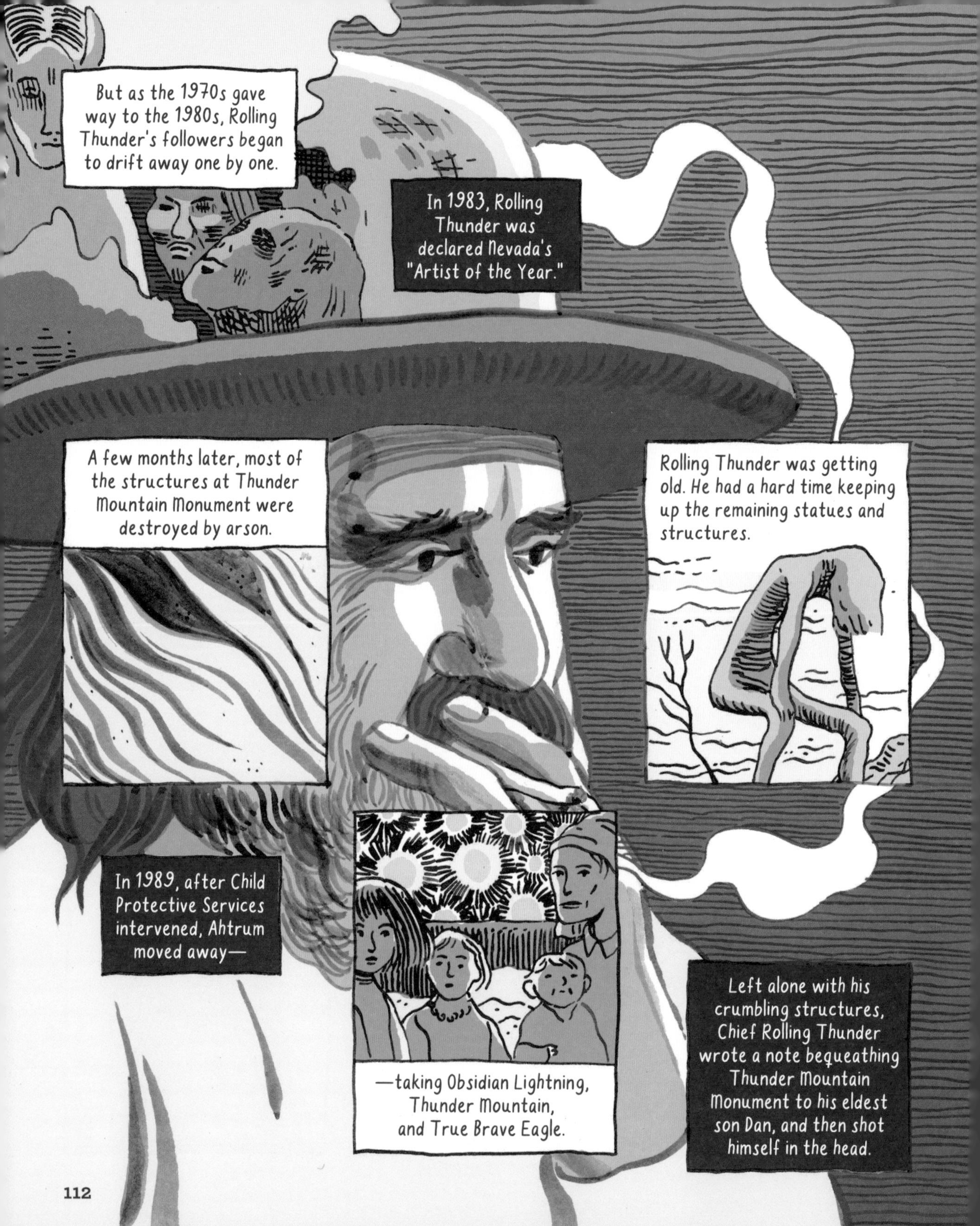
But as the 1970s gave way to the 1980s, Rolling Thunder's followers began to drift away one by one.
In 1983, Rolling Thunder was declared Nevada's "Artist of the Year."
A few months later, most of the structures at Thunder Mountain Monument were destroyed by arson.
Rolling Thunder was getting old. He had a hard time keeping up the remaining statues and structures.
In 1989, after Child Protective Services intervened, Ahtrum moved away—
—taking Obsidian Lightning, Thunder Mountain, and True Brave Eagle.
Left alone with his crumbling structures, Chief Rolling Thunder wrote a note bequeathing Thunder Mountain Monument to his eldest son Dan, and then shot himself in the head.

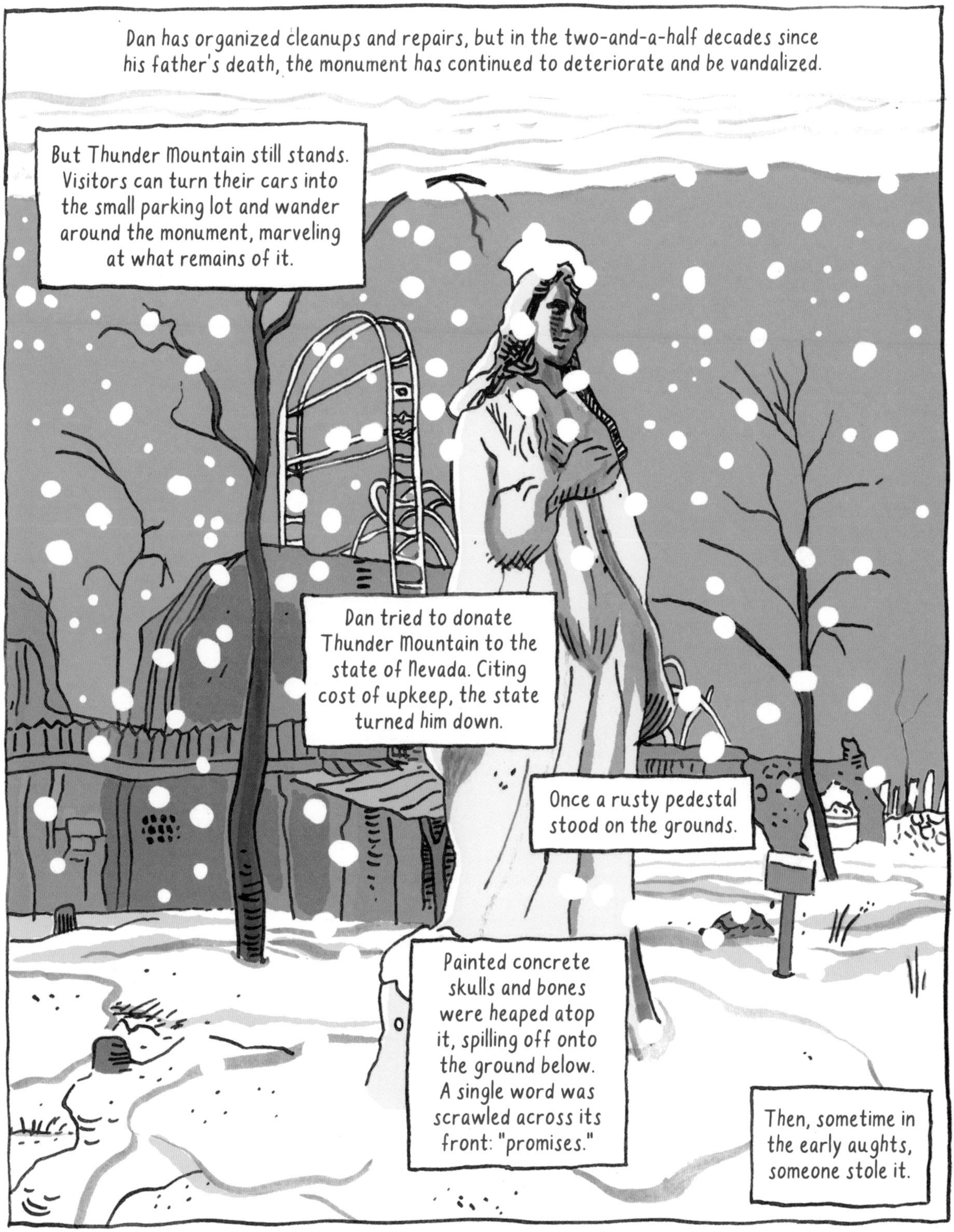
Dan has organized cleanups and repairs, but in the two-and-a-half decades since his father's death, the monument has continued to deteriorate and be vandalized.
But Thunder Mountain still stands. Visitors can turn their cars into the small parking lot and wander around the monument, marveling at what remains of it.
Dan tried to donate Thunder Mountain to the state of Nevada. Citing cost of upkeep, the state turned him down.
Once a rusty pedestal stood on the grounds.
Painted concrete skulls and bones were heaped atop it, spilling off onto the ground below. A single word was scrawled across its front: "promises."
Then, sometime in the early aughts, someone stole it.

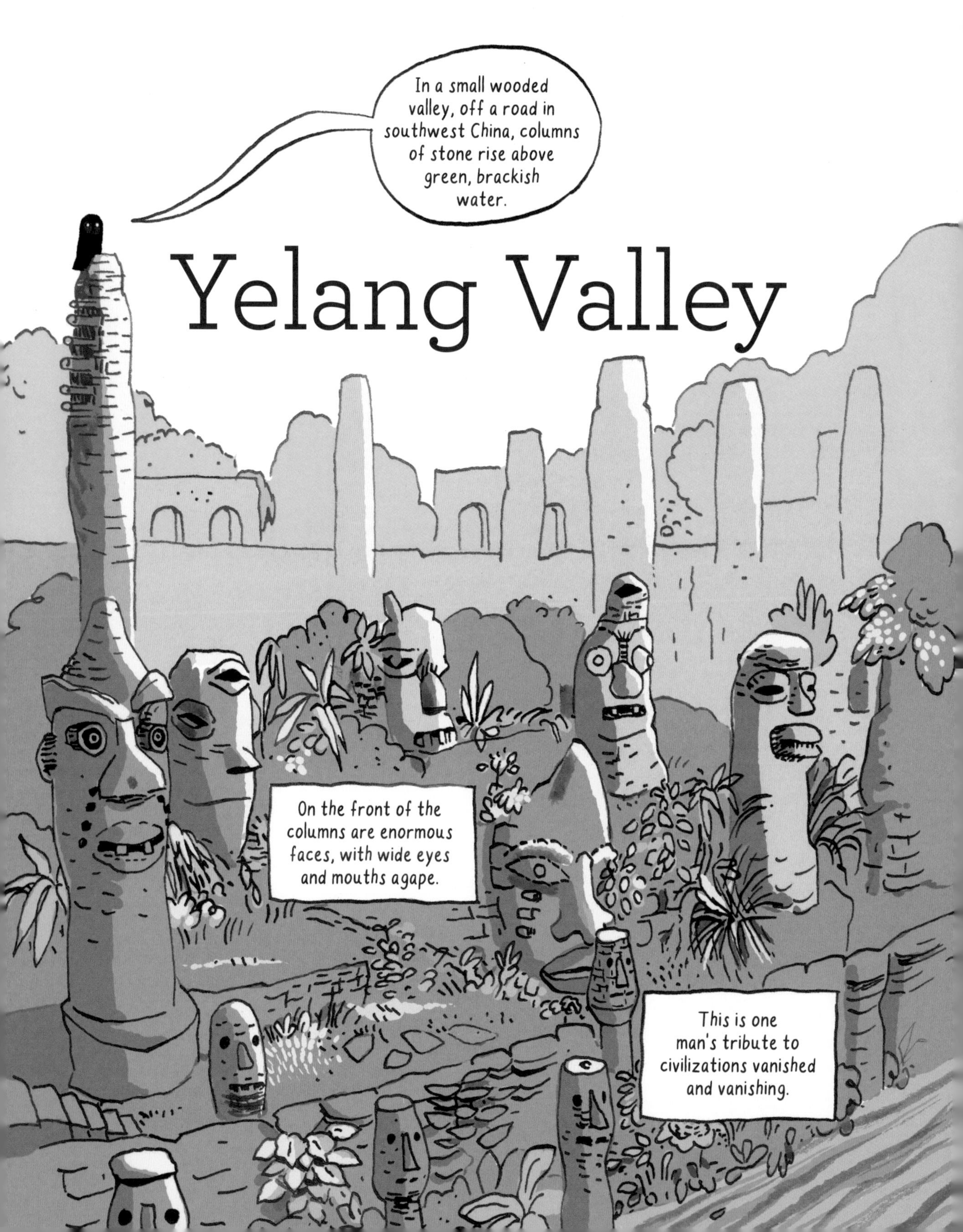
In a small wooded valley, off a road in southwest China, columns of stone rise above green, brackish water.
Yelang Valley
On the front of the columns are enormous faces, with wide eyes and mouths agape.
This is one man's tribute to civilizations vanished and vanishing.

Guizhou province, in southwest China, is very culturally diverse.

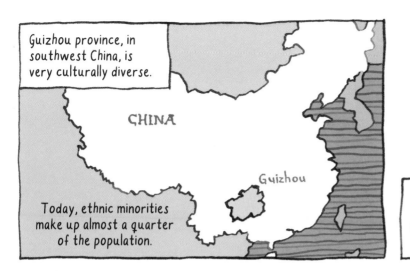

CHINA

Guizhou

Today, ethnic minorities make up almost a quarter of the population.

Guizhou is the cradle of the Nuo religion, which represents its gods with wooden masks.

It is traditionally believed that the masks have the power to ward off diseases and evil spirits.

But like any nation, as China has modernized and industrialized, it has also homogenized.

As young people move to the cities, and old people die, the region's unique traditions have been vanishing.

Song Peilun, born in Guizhou in 1941, saw this firsthand.

115

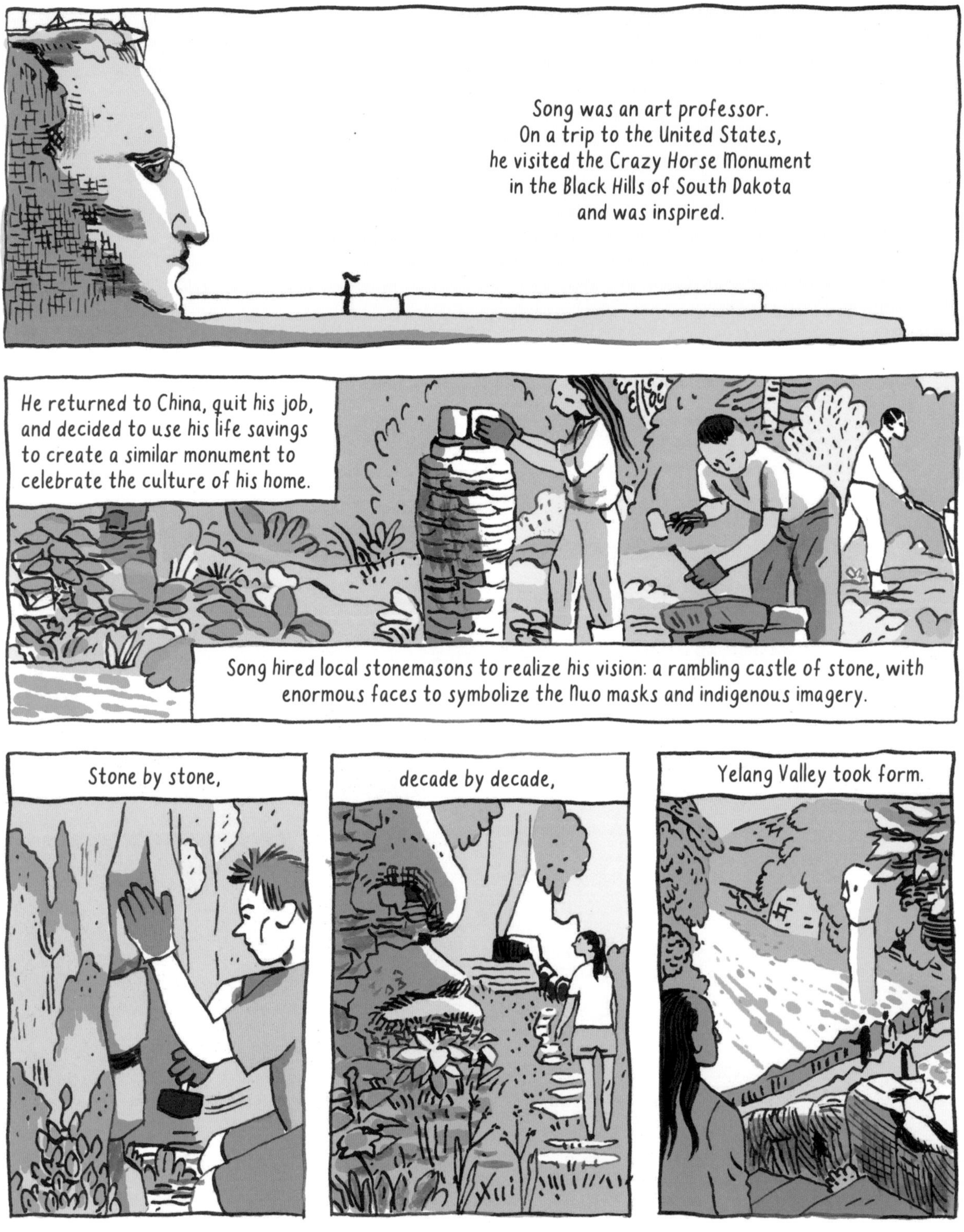
Song was an art professor. On a trip to the United States, he visited the Crazy Horse Monument in the Black Hills of South Dakota and was inspired.
He returned to China, quit his job, and decided to use his life savings to create a similar monument to celebrate the culture of his home.
Song hired local stonemasons to realize his vision: a rambling castle of stone, with enormous faces to symbolize the Nuo masks and indigenous imagery.
Stone by stone,
decade by decade,
Yelang Valley took form.

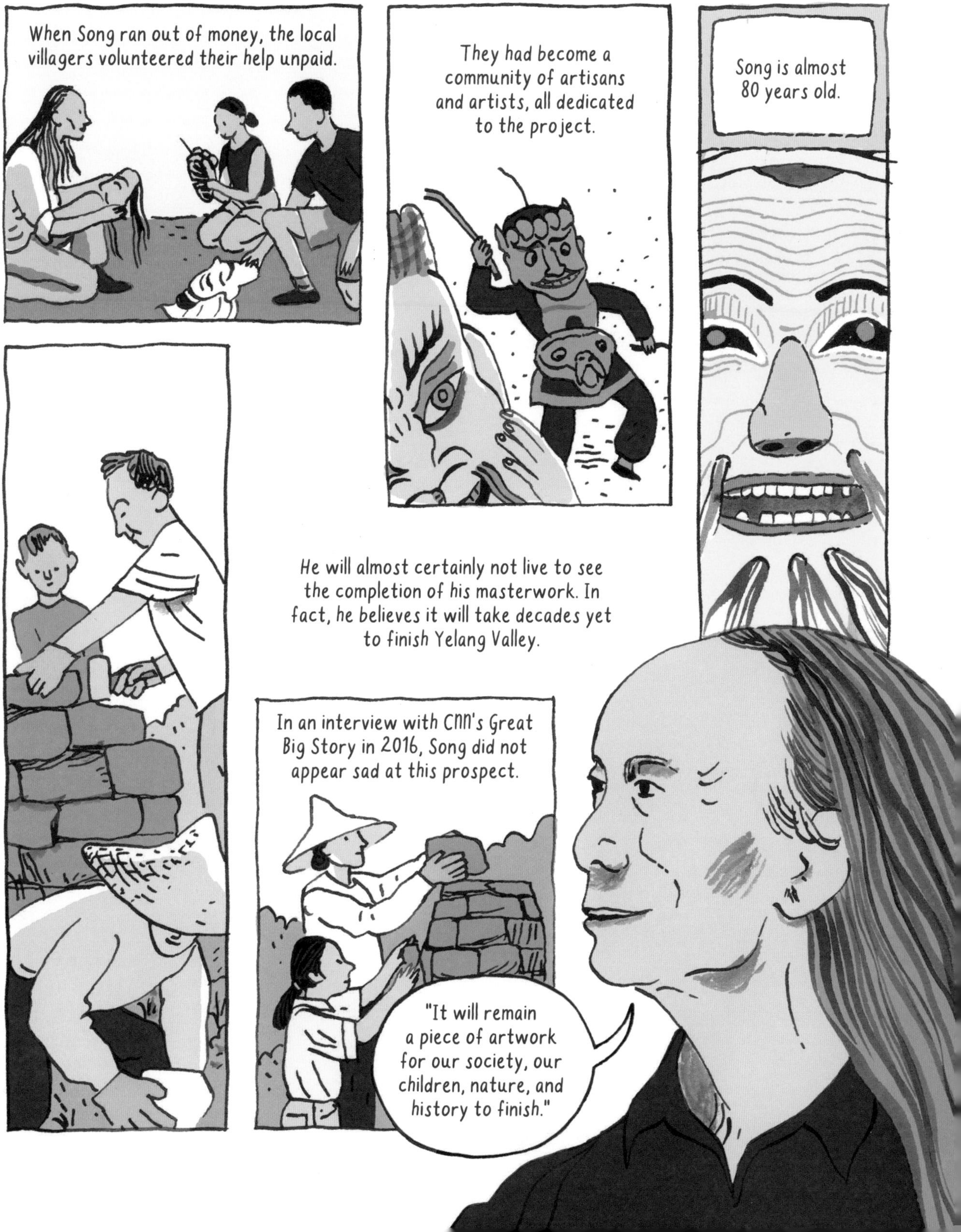
When Song ran out of money, the local villagers volunteered their help unpaid.
They had become a community of artisans and artists, all dedicated to the project.
Song is almost 80 years old.
He will almost certainly not live to see the completion of his masterwork. In fact, he believes it will take decades yet to finish Yelang Valley.
In an interview with CNN's Great Big Story in 2016, Song did not appear sad at this prospect.
"It will remain a piece of artwork for our society, our children, nature, and history to finish."

Arizona Mystery Castle

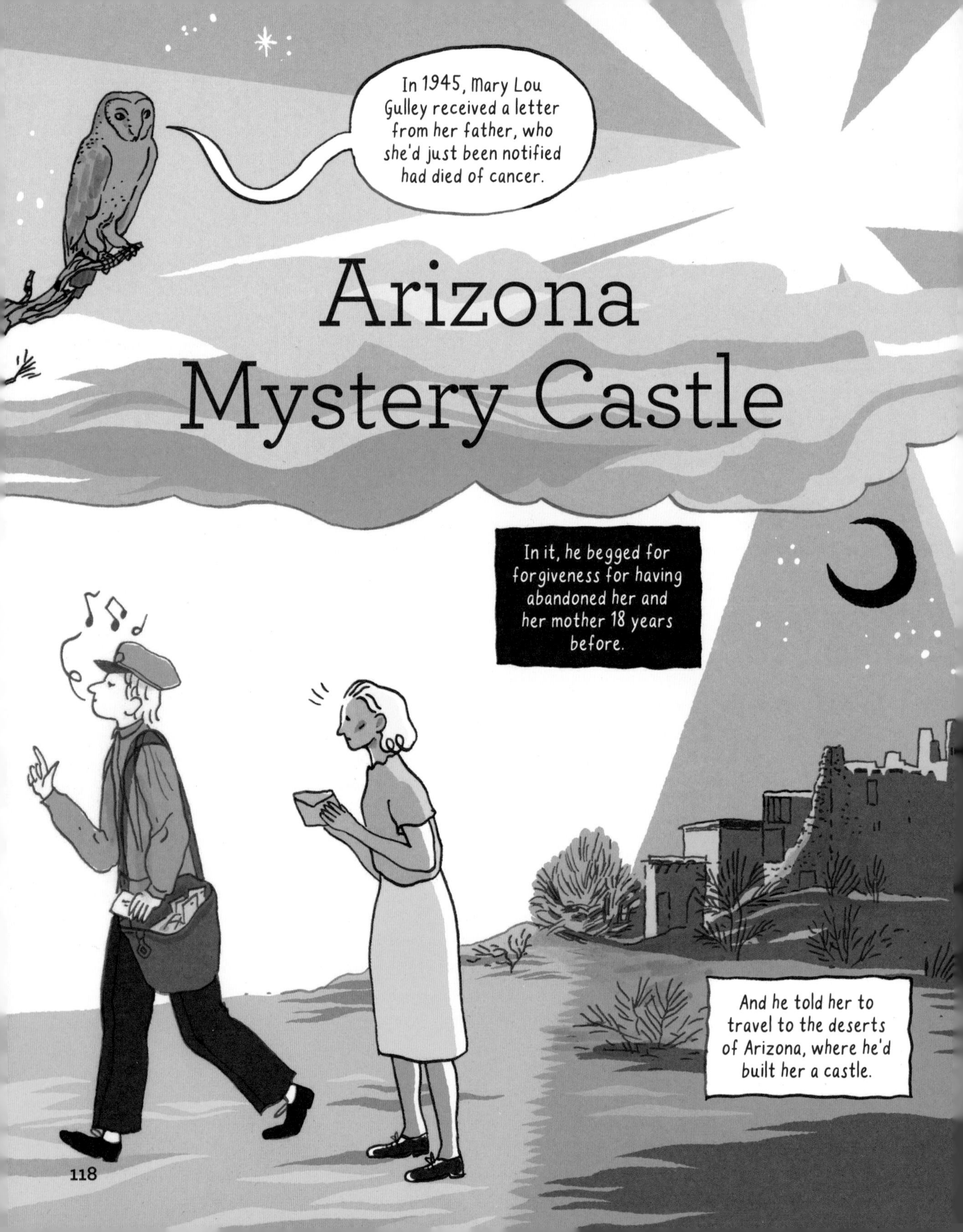
In 1945, Mary Lou Gulley received a letter from her father, who she'd just been notified had died of cancer.
In it, he begged for forgiveness for having abandoned her and her mother 18 years before.
And he told her to travel to the deserts of Arizona, where he'd built her a castle.

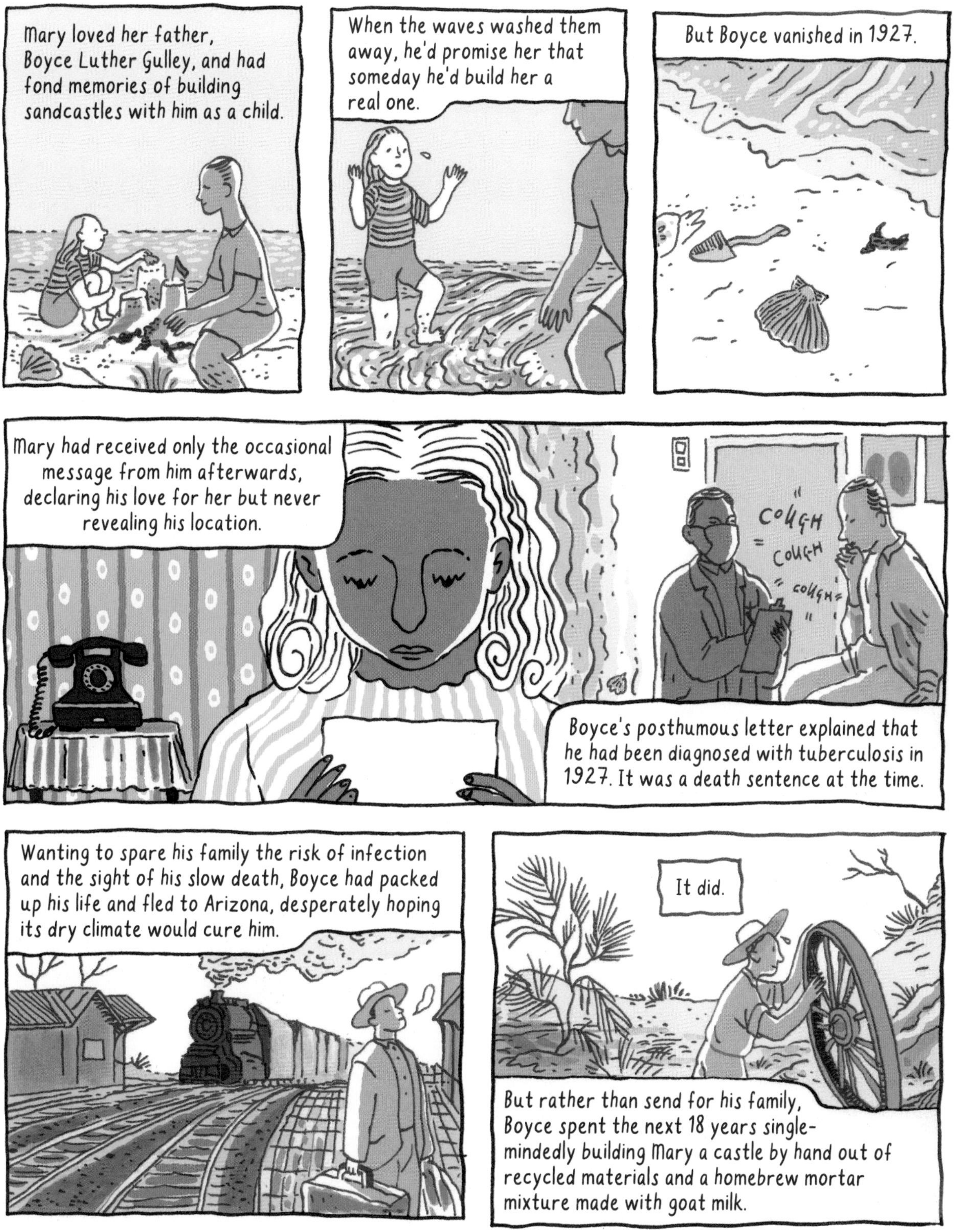
Mary loved her father, Boyce Luther Gulley, and had fond memories of building sandcastles with him as a child.
When the waves washed them away, he'd promise her that someday he'd build her a real one.
But Boyce vanished in 1927.
Mary had received only the occasional message from him afterwards, declaring his love for her but never revealing his location.
COUGH
COUGH
COUGH
Boyce's posthumous letter explained that he had been diagnosed with tuberculosis in 1927. It was a death sentence at the time.
Wanting to spare his family the risk of infection and the sight of his slow death, Boyce had packed up his life and fled to Arizona, desperately hoping its dry climate would cure him.
It did.
But rather than send for his family, Boyce spent the next 18 years single-mindedly building Mary a castle by hand out of recycled materials and a homebrew mortar mixture made with goat milk.

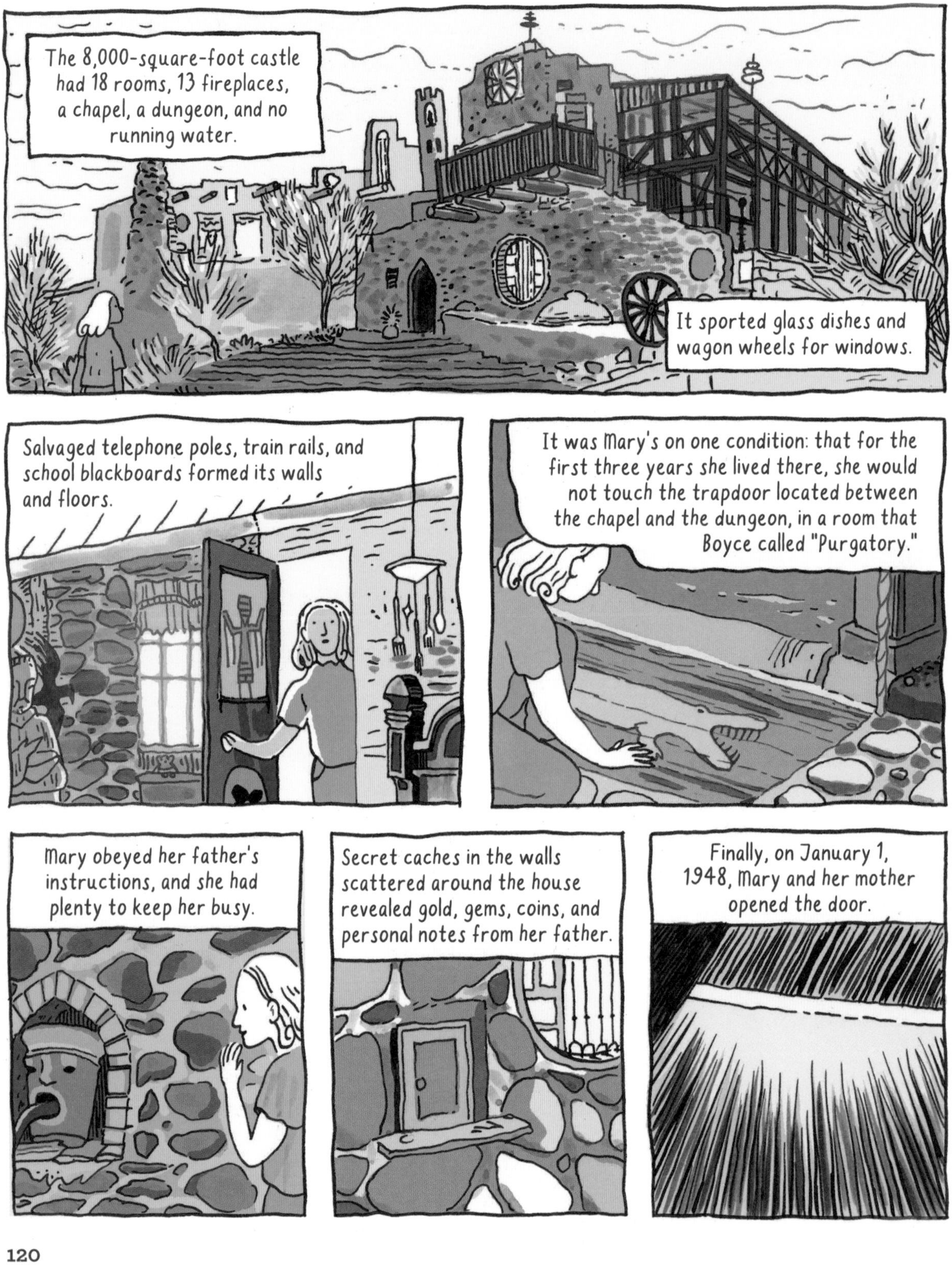
The 8,000-square-foot castle had 18 rooms, 13 fireplaces, a chapel, a dungeon, and no running water.
It sported glass dishes and wagon wheels for windows.
Salvaged telephone poles, train rails, and school blackboards formed its walls and floors.
It was Mary's on one condition: that for the first three years she lived there, she would not touch the trapdoor located between the chapel and the dungeon, in a room that Boyce called "Purgatory."
Mary obeyed her father's instructions, and she had plenty to keep her busy.
Secret caches in the walls scattered around the house revealed gold, gems, coins, and personal notes from her father.
Finally, on January 1, 1948, Mary and her mother opened the door.

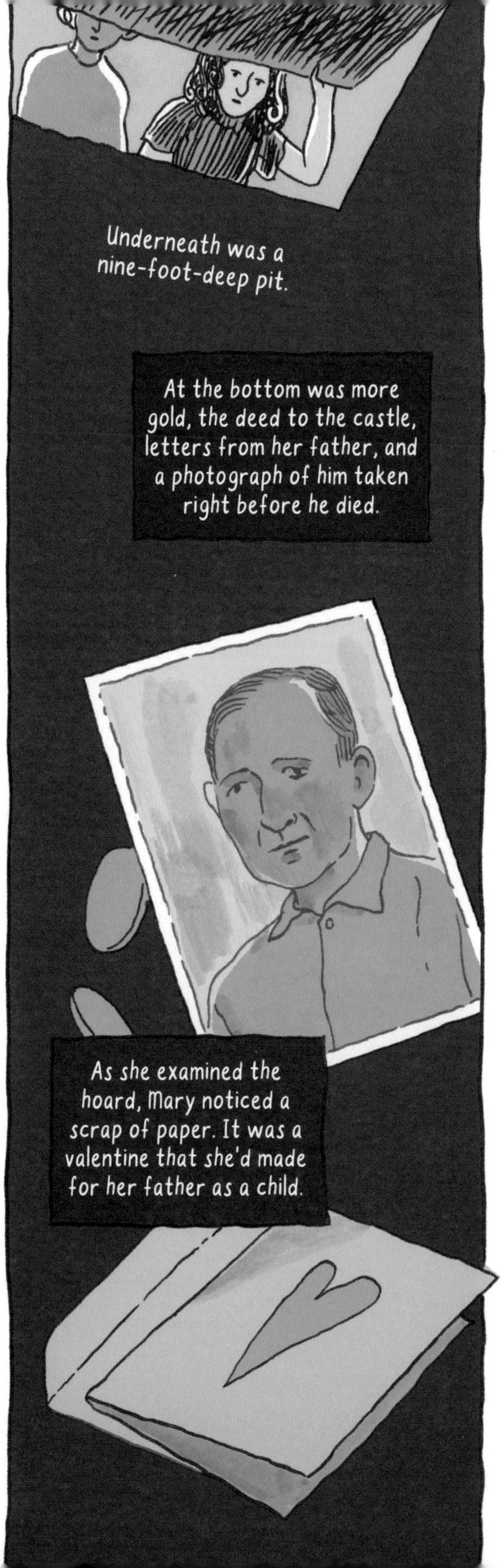
Underneath was a nine-foot-deep pit.
At the bottom was more gold, the deed to the castle, letters from her father, and a photograph of him taken right before he died.
As she examined the hoard, Mary noticed a scrap of paper. It was a valentine that she'd made for her father as a child.

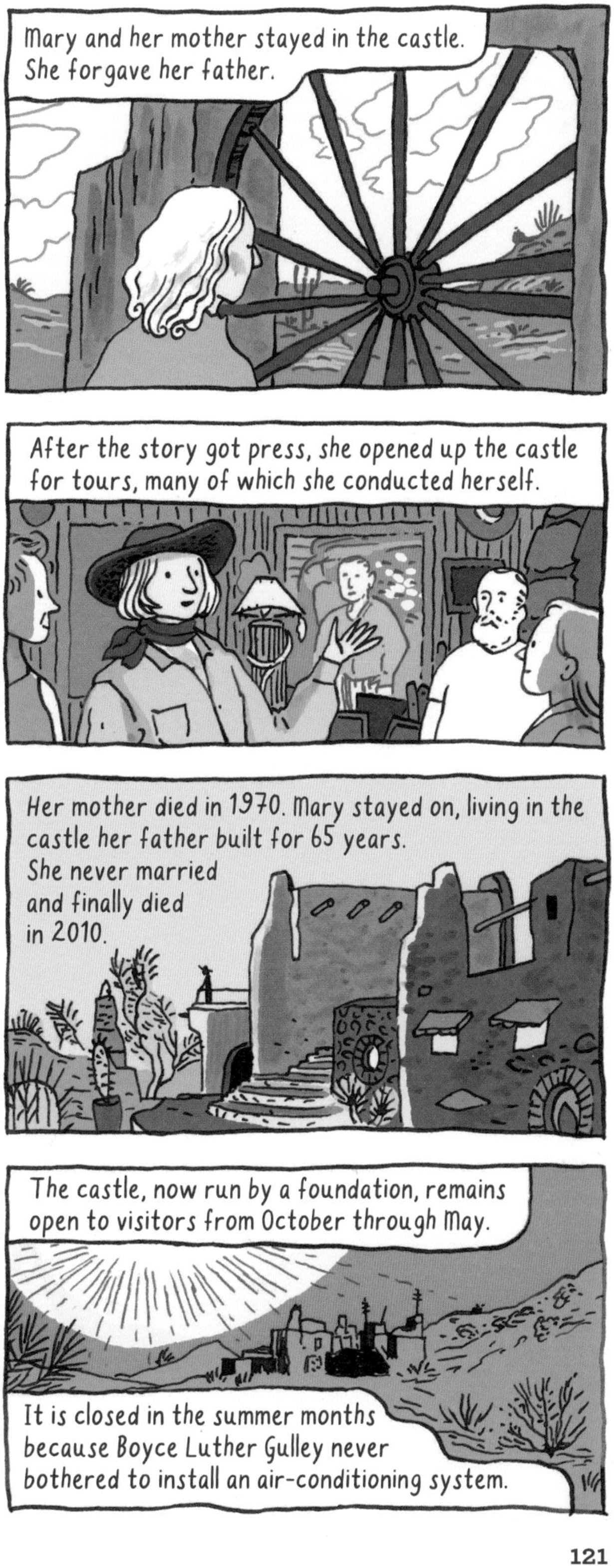
Mary and her mother stayed in the castle. She forgave her father.
After the story got press, she opened up the castle for tours, many of which she conducted herself.
Her mother died in 1970. Mary stayed on, living in the castle her father built for 65 years. She never married and finally died in 2010.
The castle, now run by a foundation, remains open to visitors from October through May.
It is closed in the summer months because Boyce Luther Gulley never bothered to install an air-conditioning system.

Gereja Ayam or The Chicken Church

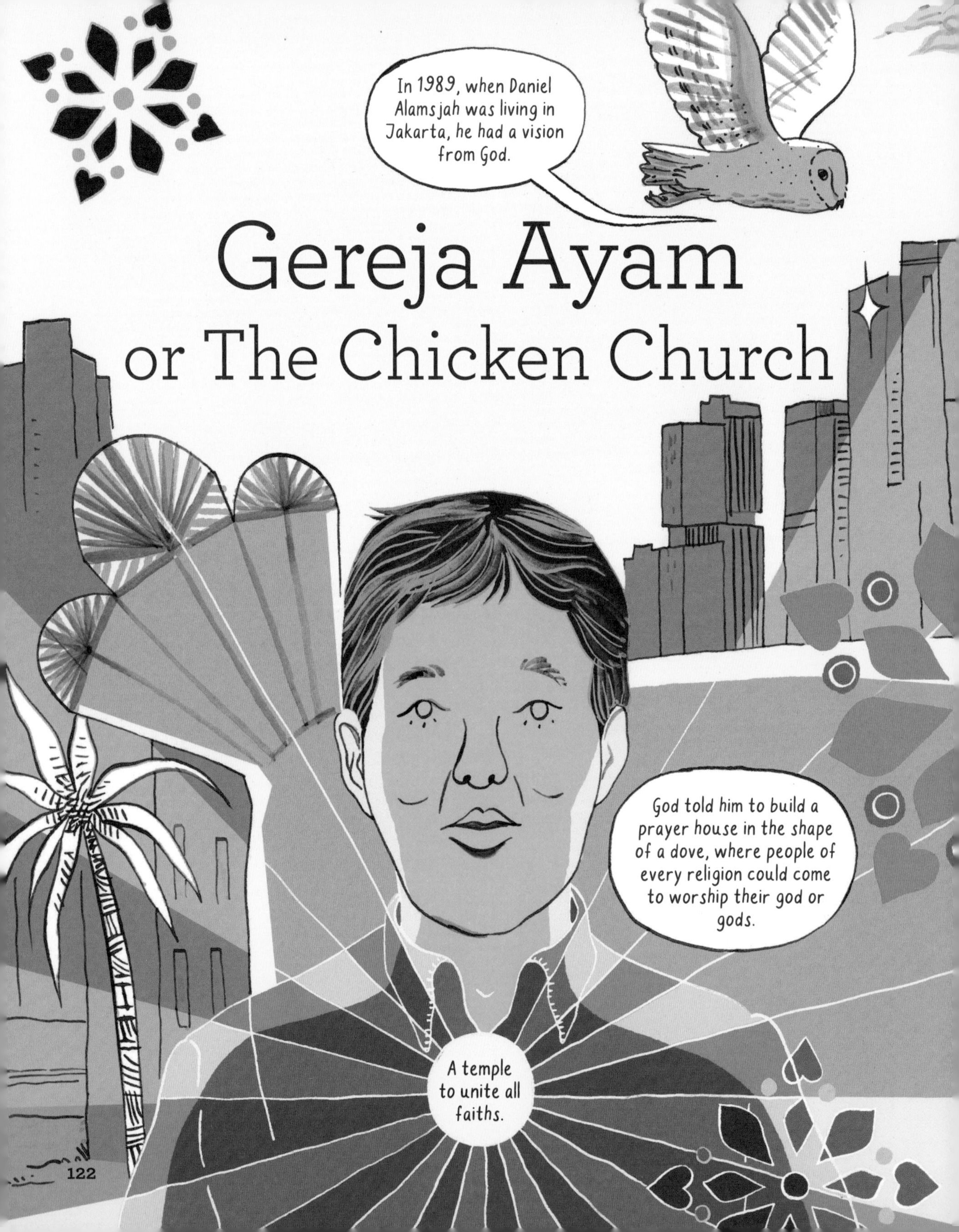
In 1989, when Daniel Alamsjah was living in Jakarta, he had a vision from God.
God told him to build a prayer house in the shape of a dove, where people of every religion could come to worship their god or gods.
A temple to unite all faiths.

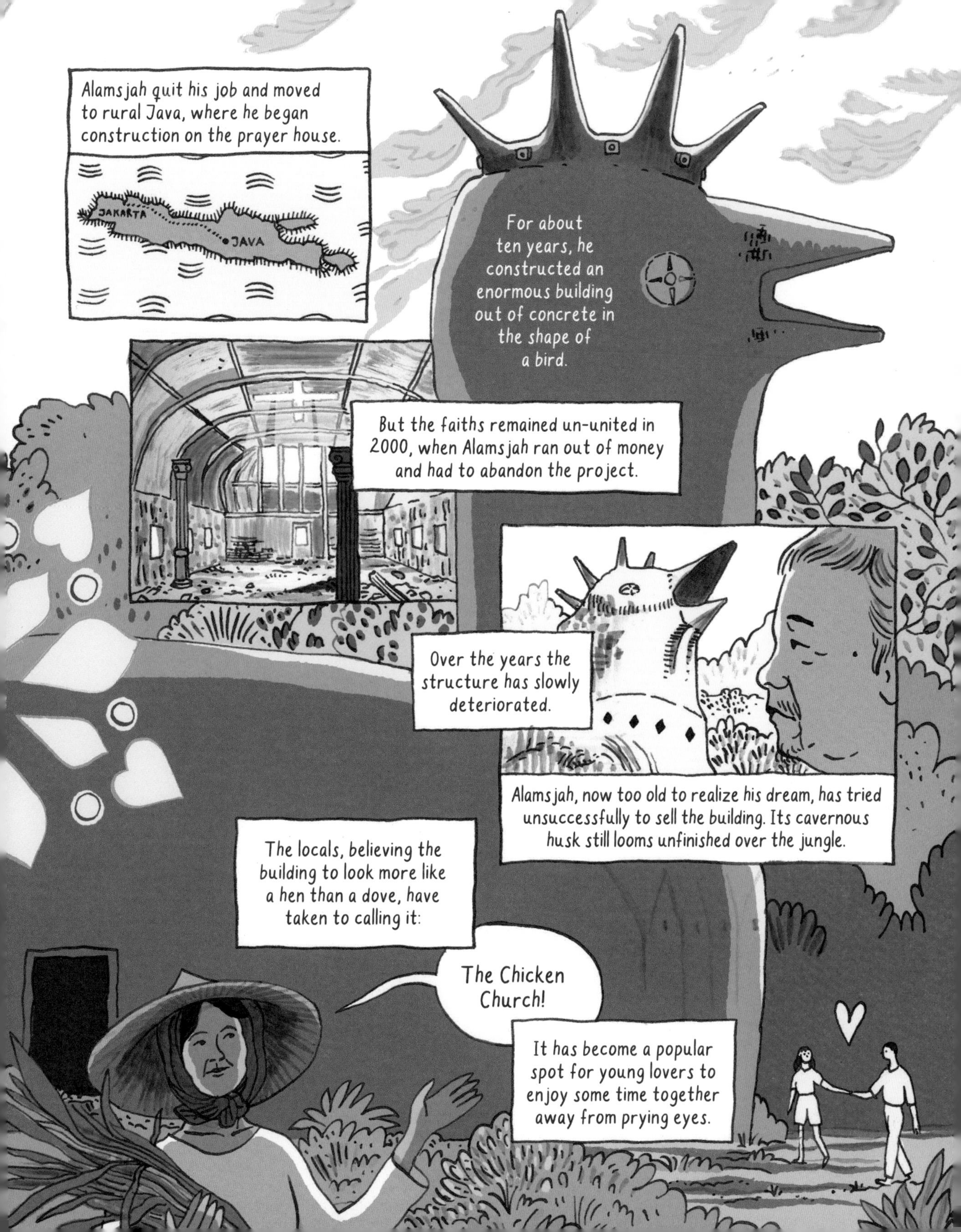
Alamsjah quit his job and moved to rural Java, where he began construction on the prayer house.
JAKARTA
JAVA
For about ten years, he constructed an enormous building out of concrete in the shape of a bird.
But the faiths remained un-united in 2000, when Alamsjah ran out of money and had to abandon the project.
Over the years the structure has slowly deteriorated.
Alamsjah, now too old to realize his dream, has tried unsuccessfully to sell the building. Its cavernous husk still looms unfinished over the jungle.
The locals, believing the building to look more like a hen than a dove, have taken to calling it:
The Chicken Church!
It has become a popular spot for young lovers to enjoy some time together away from prying eyes.

Freedom Cove

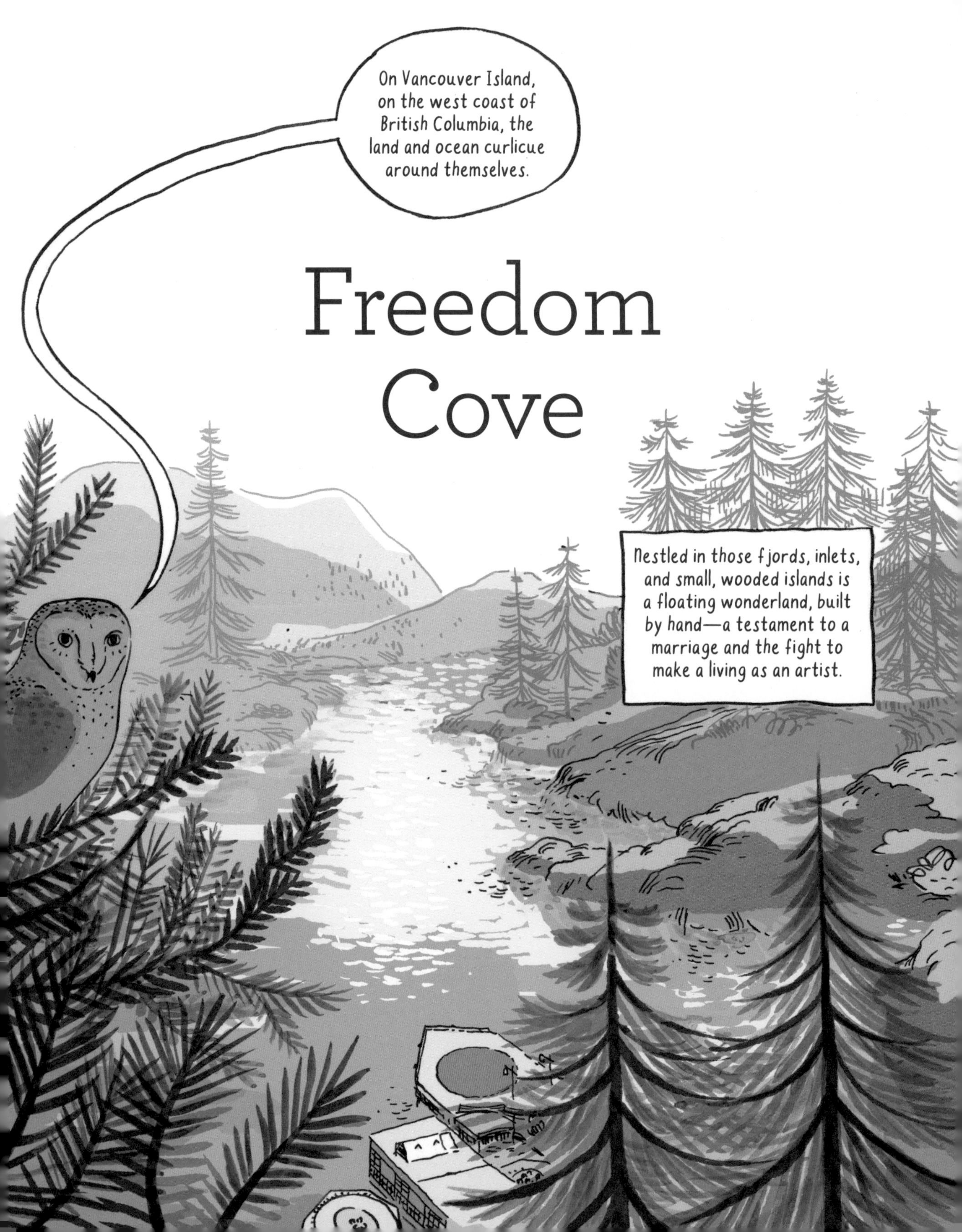
On Vancouver Island, on the west coast of British Columbia, the land and ocean curlicue around themselves.
Nestled in those fjords, inlets, and small, wooded islands is a floating wonderland, built by hand—a testament to a marriage and the fight to make a living as an artist.

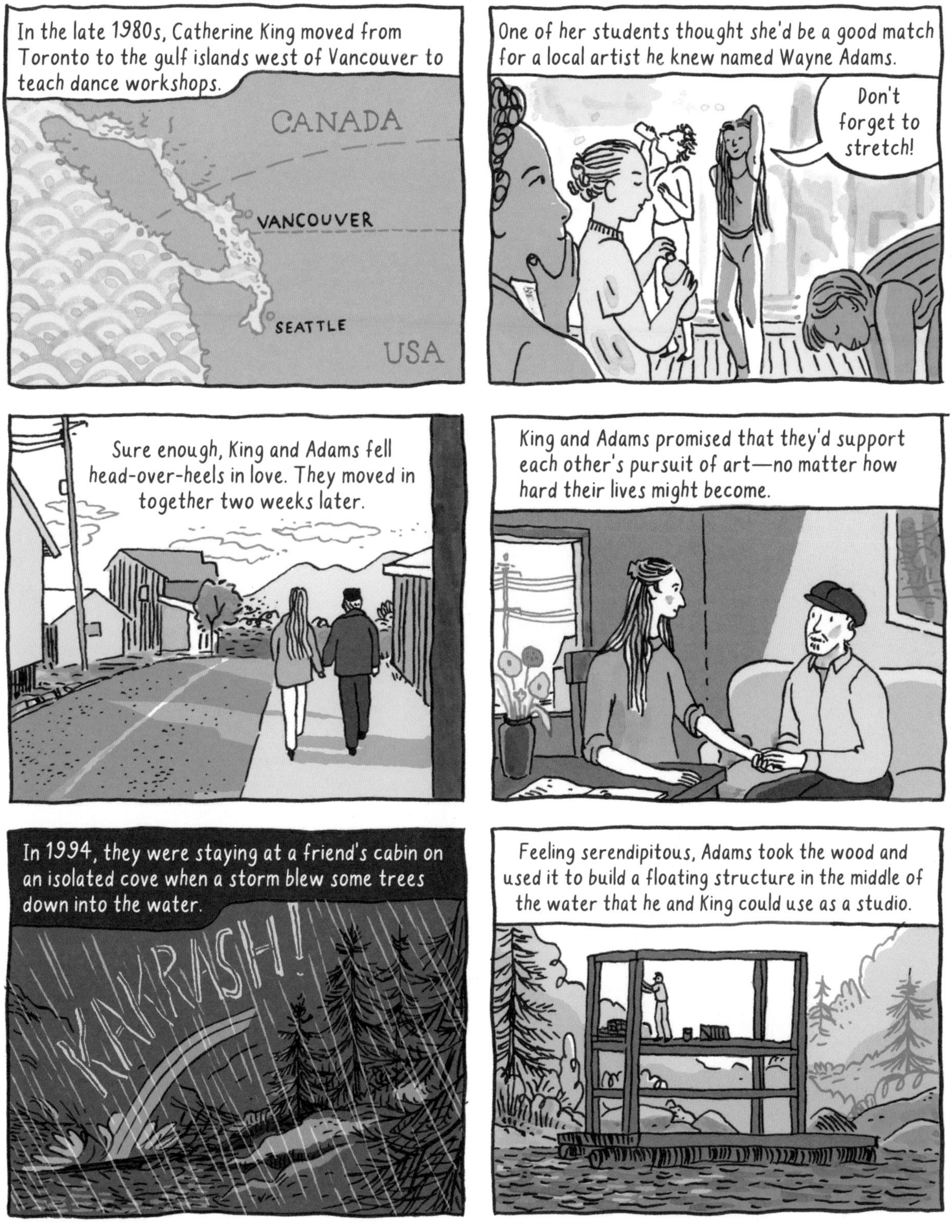
In the late 1980s, Catherine King moved from Toronto to the gulf islands west of Vancouver to teach dance workshops.
CANADA
VANCOUVER
SEATTLE
USA
One of her students thought she'd be a good match for a local artist he knew named Wayne Adams.
Don't forget to stretch!
Sure enough, King and Adams fell head-over-heels in love. They moved in together two weeks later.
King and Adams promised that they'd support each other's pursuit of art—no matter how hard their lives might become.
In 1994, they were staying at a friend's cabin on an isolated cove when a storm blew some trees down into the water.
KAKRASH!
Feeling serendipitous, Adams took the wood and used it to build a floating structure in the middle of the water that he and King could use as a studio.

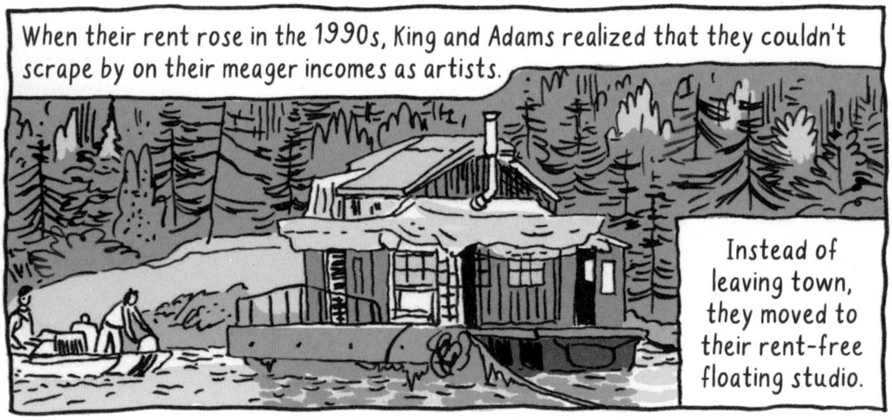

When their rent rose in the 1990s, King and Adams realized that they couldn't scrape by on their meager incomes as artists.
Instead of leaving town, they moved to their rent-free floating studio.

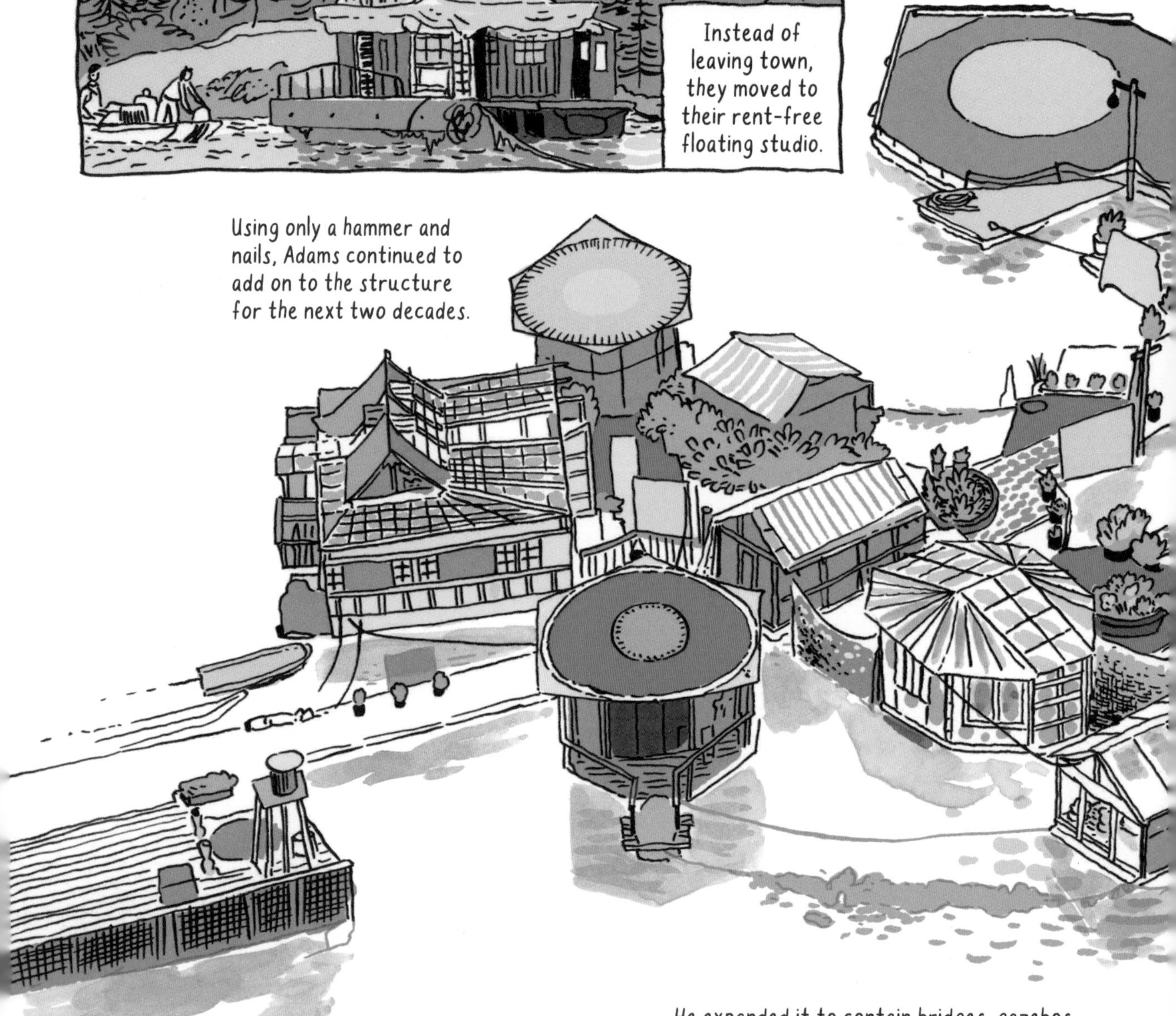

Using only a hammer and nails, Adams continued to add on to the structure for the next two decades.
He expanded it to contain bridges, gazebos, sleeping chambers, docks, an art gallery, four greenhouses, a lighthouse, and a dance floor for King.

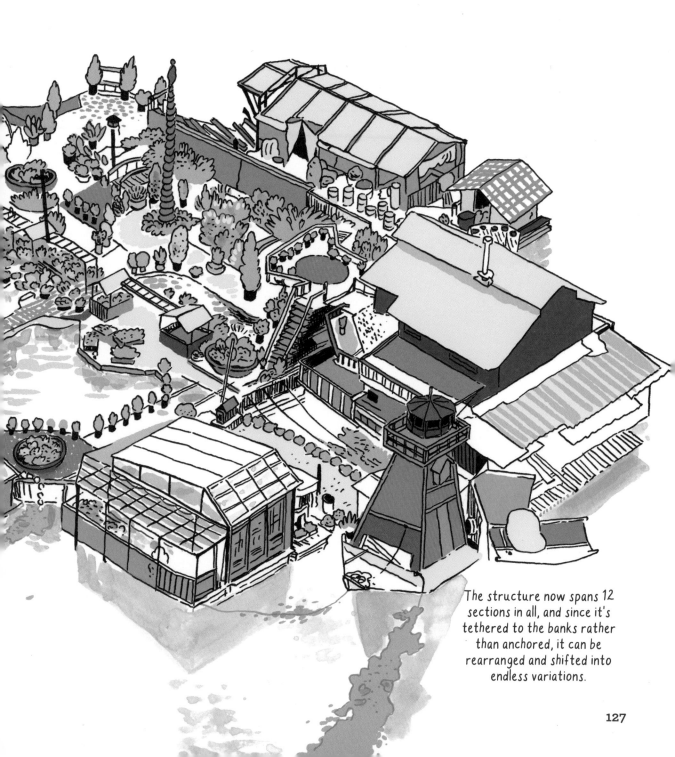

The structure now spans 12 sections in all, and since it's tethered to the banks rather than anchored, it can be rearranged and shifted into endless variations.

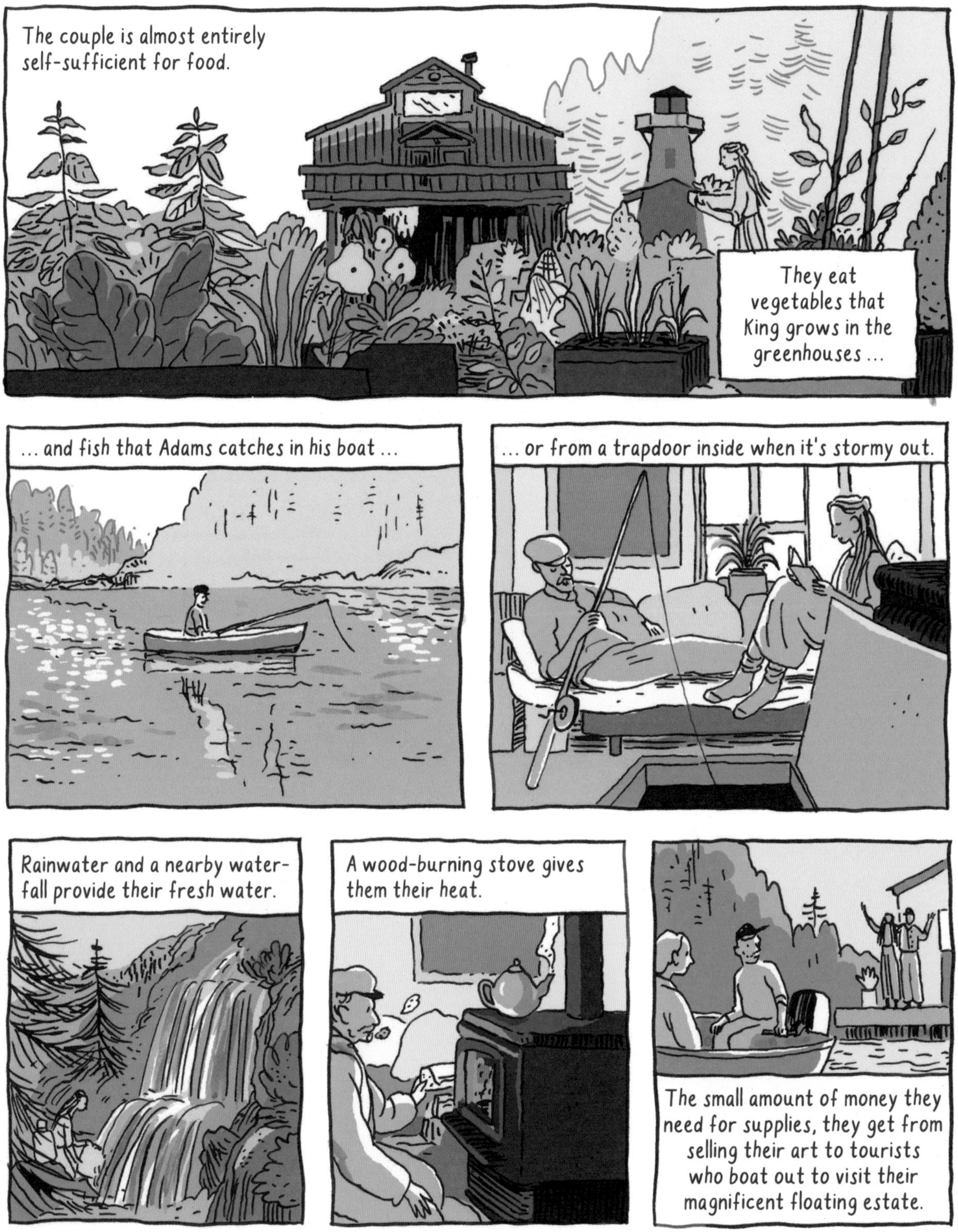
The couple is almost entirely self-sufficient for food.
They eat vegetables that King grows in the greenhouses ...
... and fish that Adams catches in his boat ...
... or from a trapdoor inside when it's stormy out.
Rainwater and a nearby waterfall provide their fresh water.
A wood-burning stove gives them their heat.
The small amount of money they need for supplies, they get from selling their art to tourists who boat out to visit their magnificent floating estate.

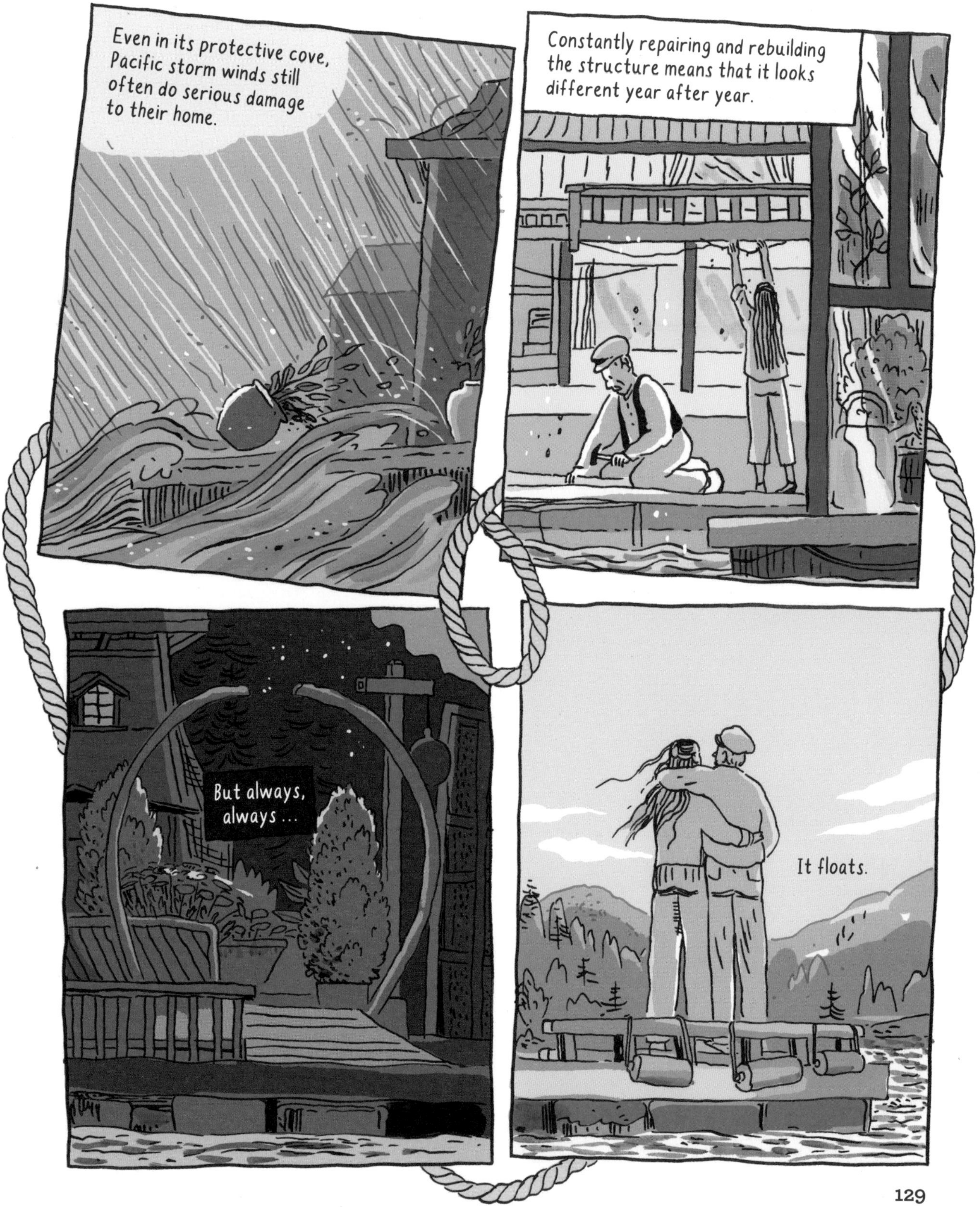
Even in its protective cove, Pacific storm winds still often do serious damage to their home.
Constantly repairing and rebuilding the structure means that it looks different year after year.
But always, always . . .
It floats.

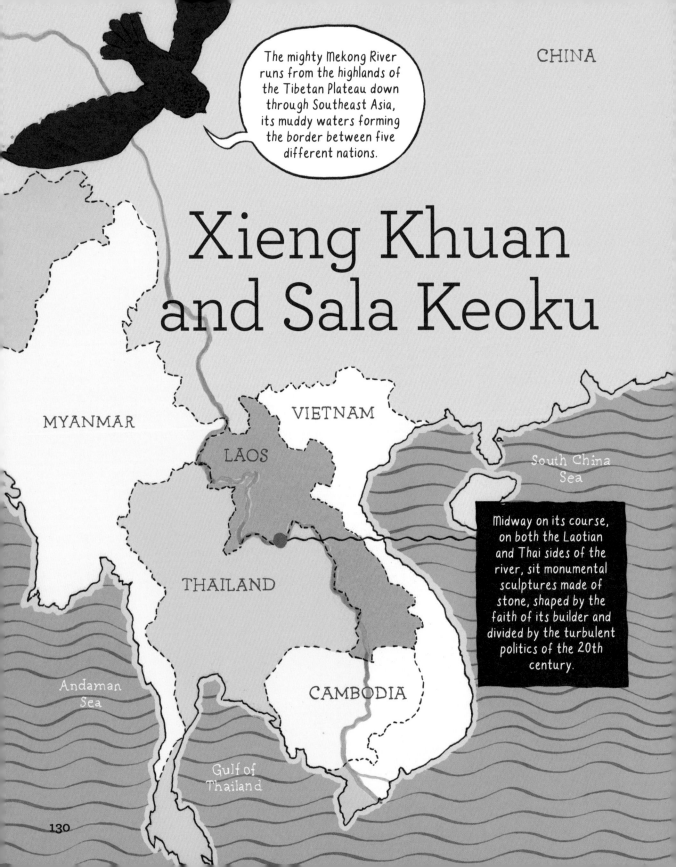

The mighty Mekong River runs from the highlands of the Tibetan Plateau down through Southeast Asia, its muddy waters forming the border between five different nations.

CHINA

Xieng Khuan and Sala Keoku

MYANMAR

VIETNAM

LAOS

South China Sea

THAILAND

Midway on its course, on both the Laotian and Thai sides of the river, sit monumental sculptures made of stone, shaped by the faith of its builder and divided by the turbulent politics of the 20th century.

Andaman Sea

CAMBODIA

Gulf of Thailand

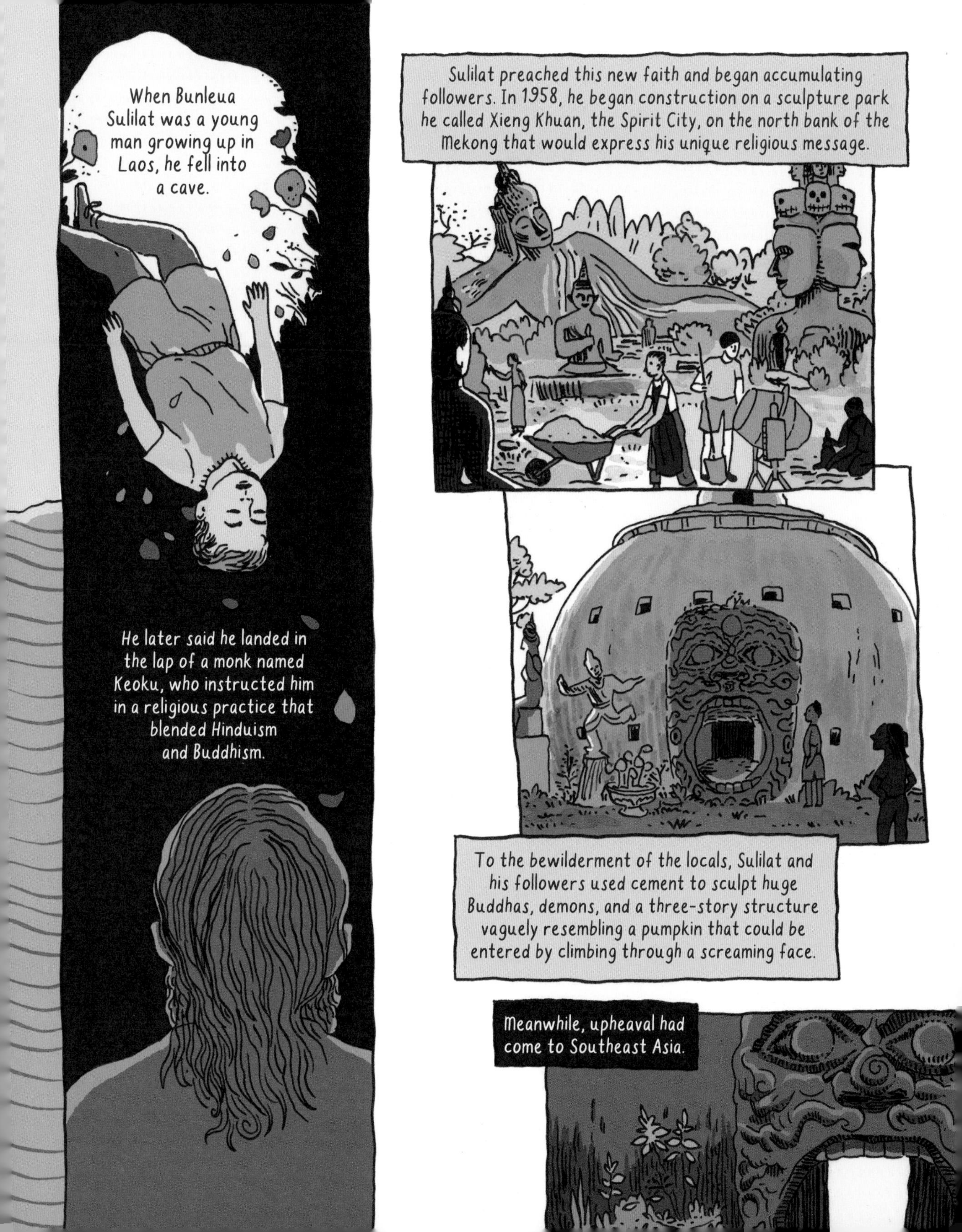
When Bunleua Sulilat was a young man growing up in Laos, he fell into a cave.
He later said he landed in the lap of a monk named Keoku, who instructed him in a religious practice that blended Hinduism and Buddhism.
Sulilat preached this new faith and began accumulating followers. In 1958, he began construction on a sculpture park he called Xieng Khuan, the Spirit City, on the north bank of the Mekong that would express his unique religious message.
To the bewilderment of the locals, Sulilat and his followers used cement to sculpt huge Buddhas, demons, and a three-story structure vaguely resembling a pumpkin that could be entered by climbing through a screaming face.
Meanwhile, upheaval had come to Southeast Asia.

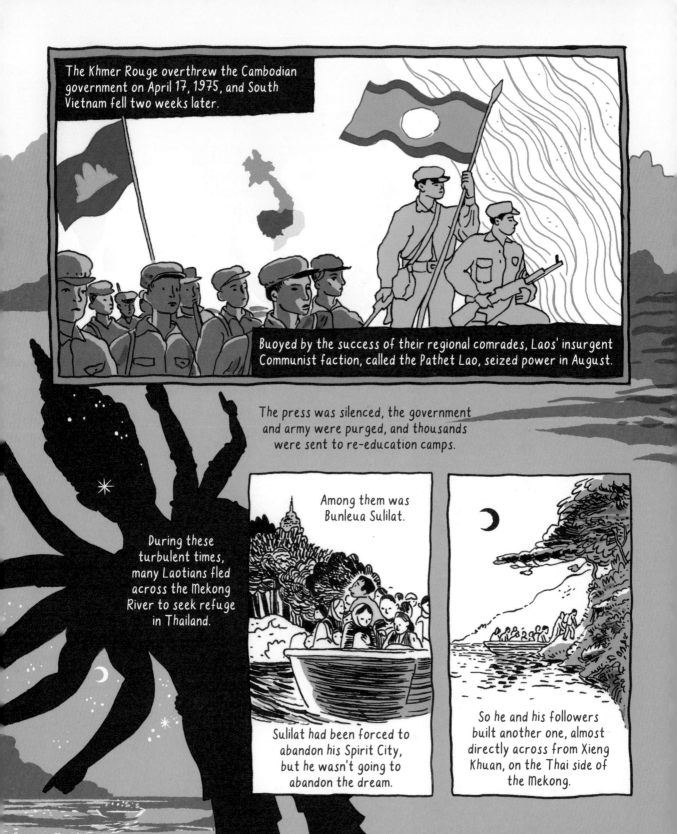

The Khmer Rouge overthrew the Cambodian government on April 17, 1975, and South Vietnam fell two weeks later.

Buoyed by the success of their regional comrades, Laos' insurgent Communist faction, called the Pathet Lao, seized power in August.

The press was silenced, the government and army were purged, and thousands were sent to re-education camps.

During these turbulent times, many Laotians fled across the Mekong River to seek refuge in Thailand.

Among them was Bunleua Sulilat.

Sulilat had been forced to abandon his Spirit City, but he wasn't going to abandon the dream.

So he and his followers built another one, almost directly across from Xieng Khuan, on the Thai side of the Mekong.

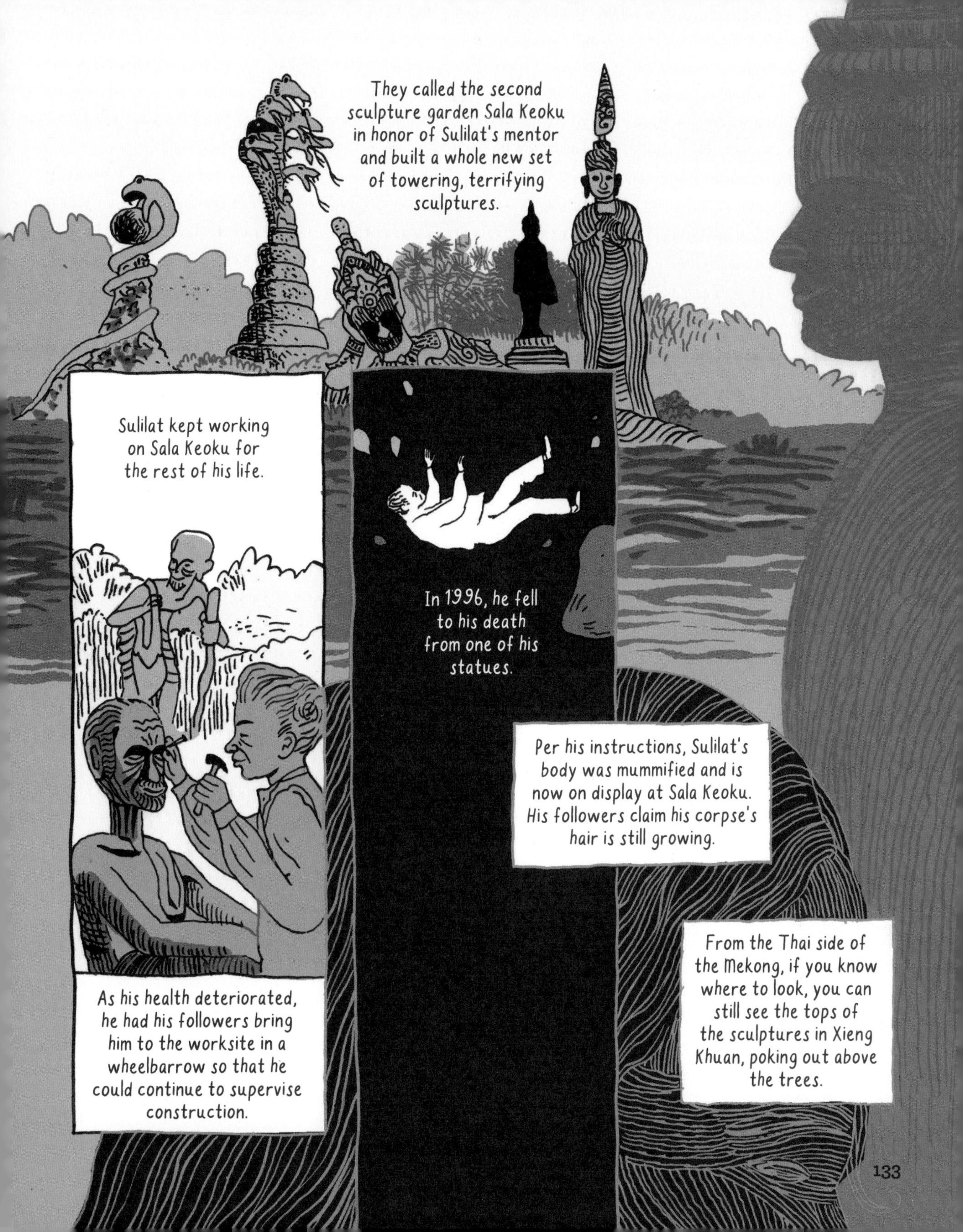
They called the second sculpture garden Sala Keoku in honor of Sulilat's mentor and built a whole new set of towering, terrifying sculptures.
Sulilat kept working on Sala Keoku for the rest of his life.
As his health deteriorated, he had his followers bring him to the worksite in a wheelbarrow so that he could continue to supervise construction.
In 1996, he fell to his death from one of his statues.
Per his instructions, Sulilat's body was mummified and is now on display at Sala Keoku. His followers claim his corpse's hair is still growing.
From the Thai side of the Mekong, if you know where to look, you can still see the tops of the sculptures in Xieng Khuan, poking out above the trees.

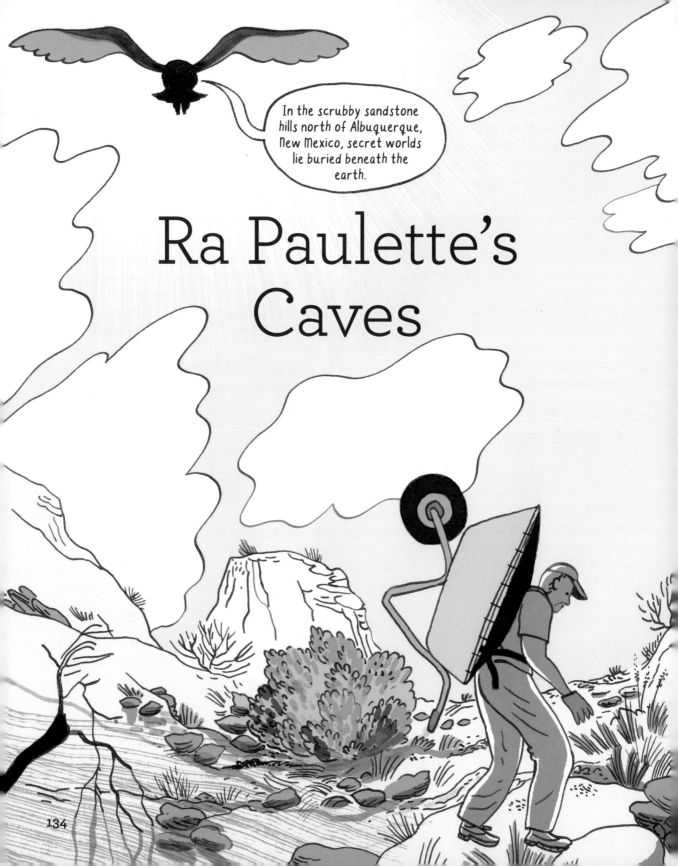

Ra Paulette's Caves

In the scrubby sandstone hills north of Albuquerque, New Mexico, secret worlds lie buried beneath the earth.

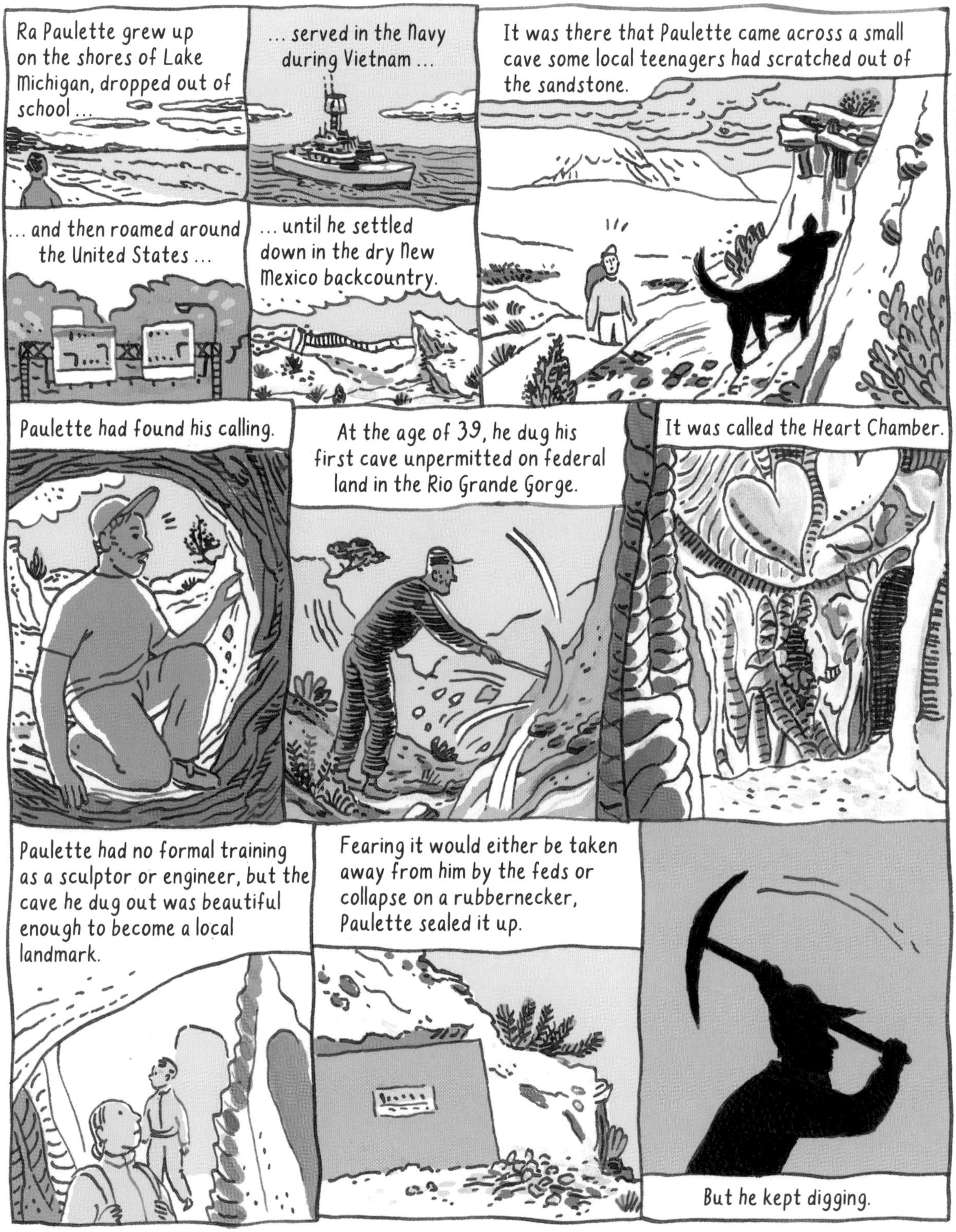
Ra Paulette grew up on the shores of Lake Michigan, dropped out of school ...
... served in the Navy during Vietnam ...
It was there that Paulette came across a small cave some local teenagers had scratched out of the sandstone.
... and then roamed around the United States ...
... until he settled down in the dry New Mexico backcountry.
Paulette had found his calling.
At the age of 39, he dug his first cave unpermitted on federal land in the Rio Grande Gorge.
It was called the Heart Chamber.
Paulette had no formal training as a sculptor or engineer, but the cave he dug out was beautiful enough to become a local landmark.
Fearing it would either be taken away from him by the feds or collapse on a rubbernecker, Paulette sealed it up.
But he kept digging.

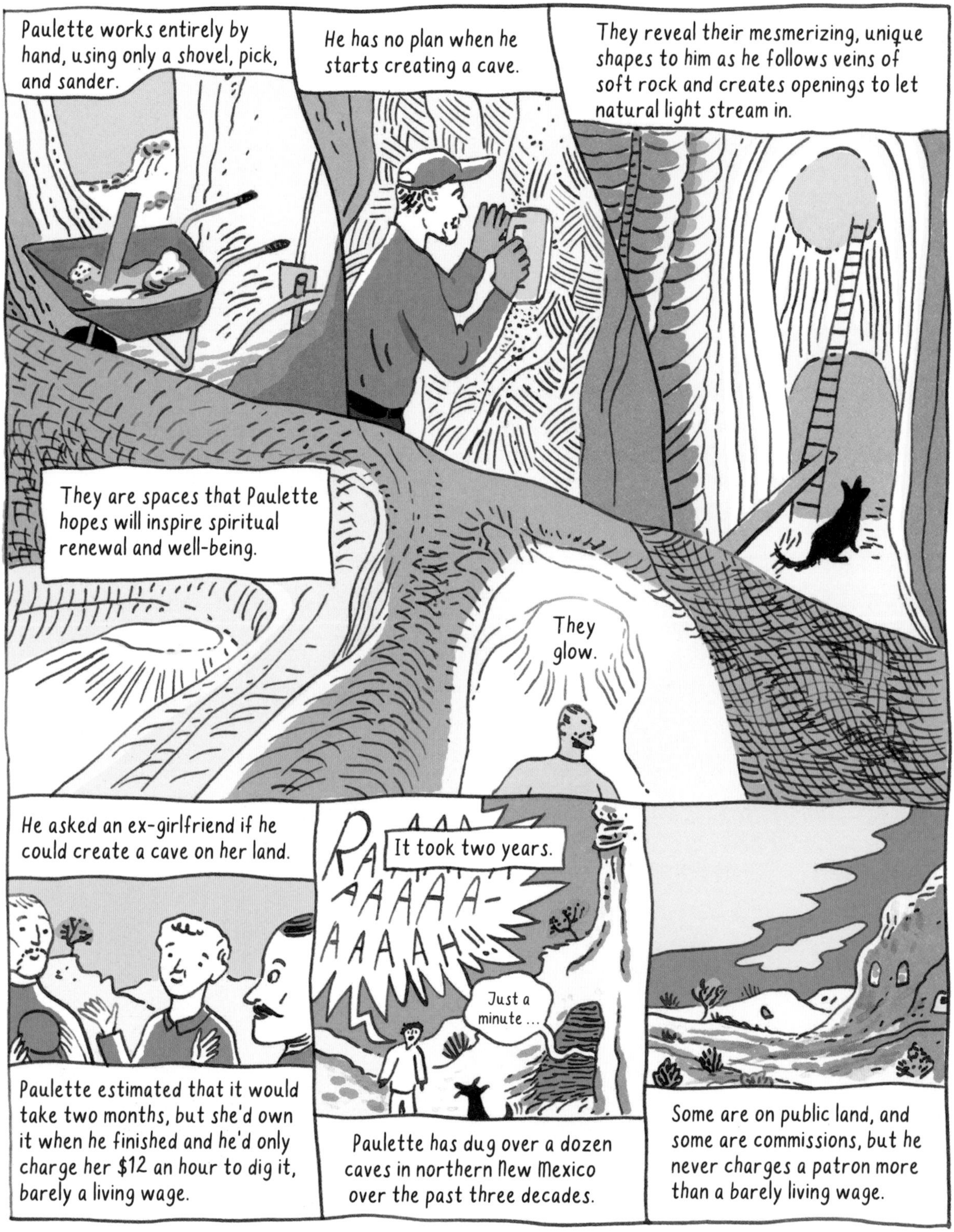
Paulette works entirely by hand, using only a shovel, pick, and sander.
He has no plan when he starts creating a cave.
They reveal their mesmerizing, unique shapes to him as he follows veins of soft rock and creates openings to let natural light stream in.
They are spaces that Paulette hopes will inspire spiritual renewal and well-being.
They glow.
He asked an ex-girlfriend if he could create a cave on her land.
Paulette estimated that it would take two months, but she'd own it when he finished and he'd only charge her $12 an hour to dig it, barely a living wage.
RAAAAAAAAA-AAAAAH!!
It took two years.
Just a minute ...
Paulette has dug over a dozen caves in northern New Mexico over the past three decades.
Some are on public land, and some are commissions, but he never charges a patron more than a barely living wage.

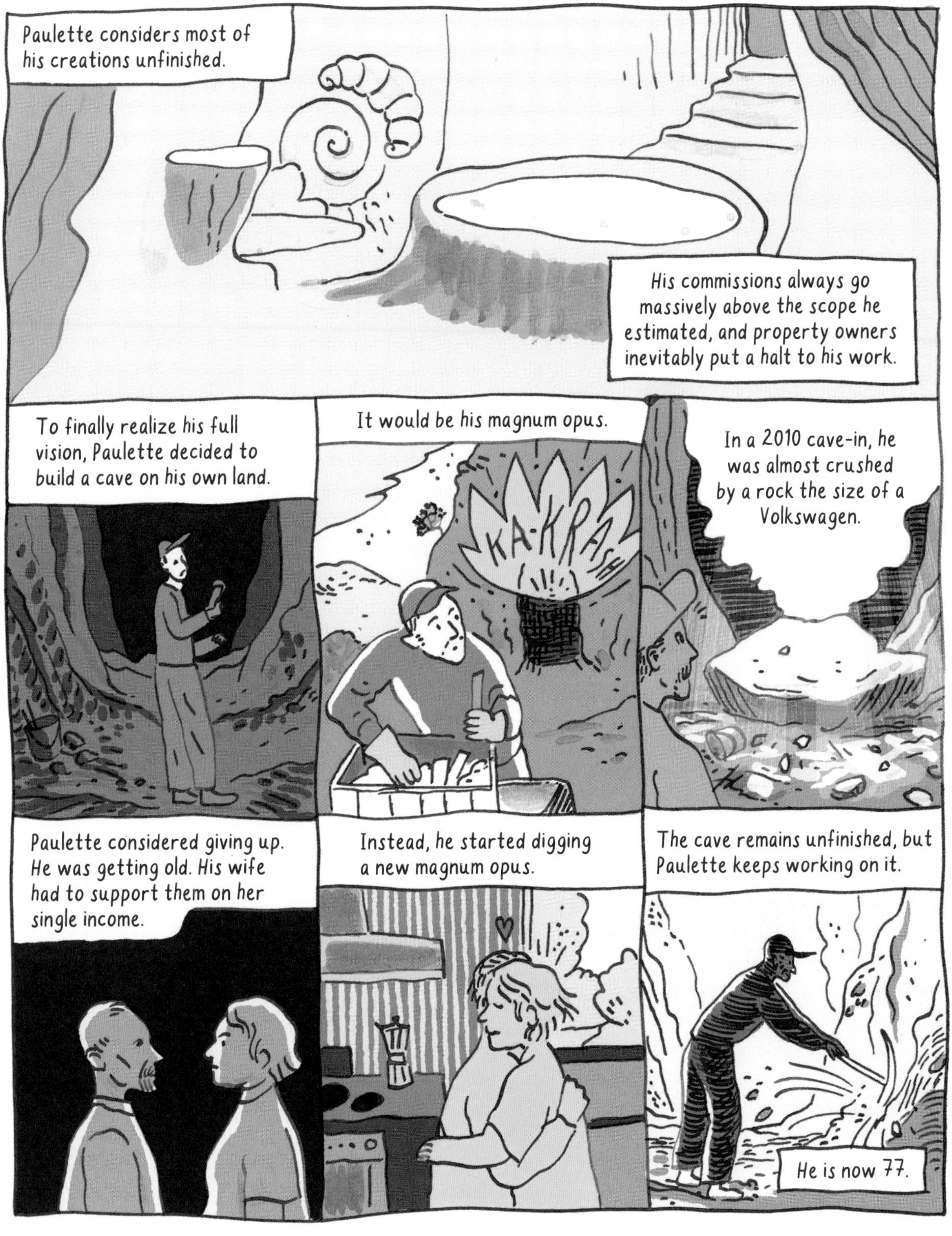
Paulette considers most of his creations unfinished.
His commissions always go massively above the scope he estimated, and property owners inevitably put a halt to his work.
To finally realize his full vision, Paulette decided to build a cave on his own land.
It would be his magnum opus.
KA-KRASH
In a 2010 cave-in, he was almost crushed by a rock the size of a Volkswagen.
Paulette considered giving up. He was getting old. His wife had to support them on her single income.
Instead, he started digging a new magnum opus.
The cave remains unfinished, but Paulette keeps working on it.
He is now 77.

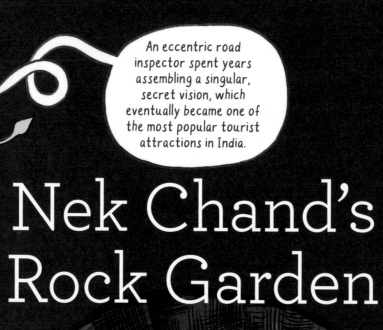

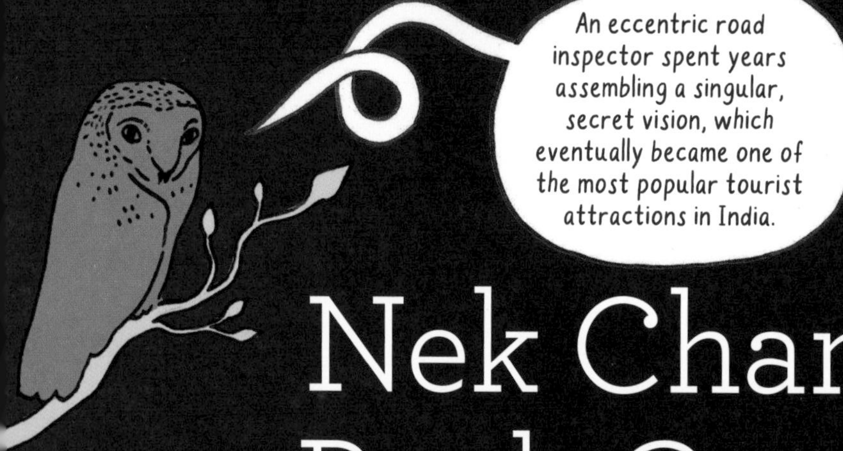
An eccentric road inspector spent years assembling a singular, secret vision, which eventually became one of the most popular tourist attractions in India.

Nek Chand's Rock Garden

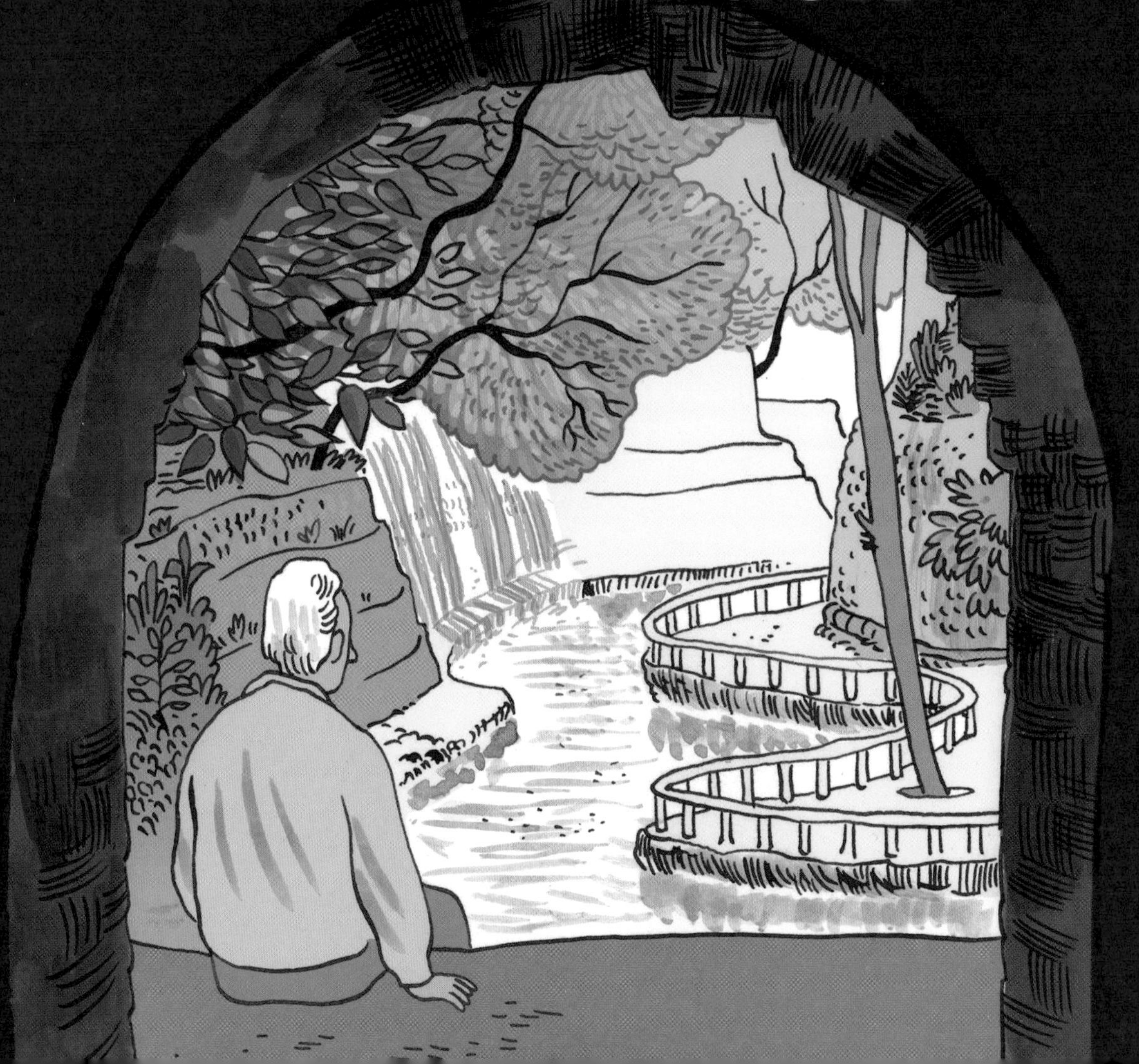

Nek Chand was born in what is now Pakistan, but he and his family fled as refugees to India during the partition in 1947.

He worked as a road inspector in Punjab's new capital city, Chandigarh.

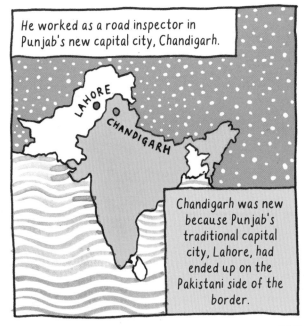

Chandigarh was new because Punjab's traditional capital city, Lahore, had ended up on the Pakistani side of the border.

The city was designed by the pioneer of modern architecture, Swiss French master Le Corbusier. His sleekly austere buildings and sweeping, carefully laid-out parks were gorgeous.

But building a whole city generates a lot of garbage and scrap. Starting in the late 1950s, Nek Chand began collecting those cast-off tiles, pipes, rocks, and bottles.

In a neglected gorge on the outskirts of the city, he used the cast-offs to build a strange and hidden place he called the "Divine Kingdom of Sukrani."

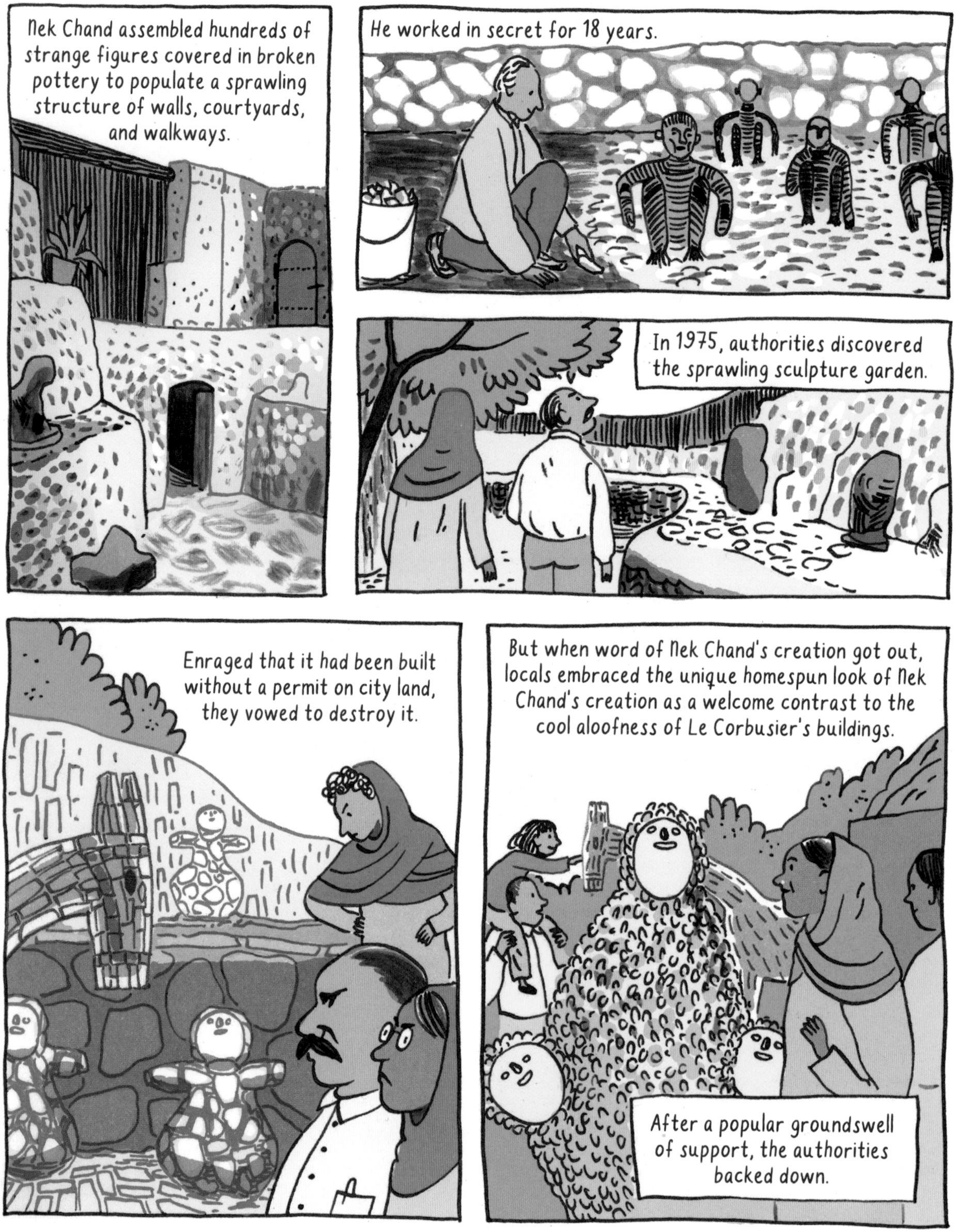
Nek Chand assembled hundreds of strange figures covered in broken pottery to populate a sprawling structure of walls, courtyards, and walkways.
He worked in secret for 18 years.
In 1975, authorities discovered the sprawling sculpture garden.
Enraged that it had been built without a permit on city land, they vowed to destroy it.
But when word of Nek Chand's creation got out, locals embraced the unique homespun look of Nek Chand's creation as a welcome contrast to the cool aloofness of Le Corbusier's buildings.
After a popular groundswell of support, the authorities backed down.

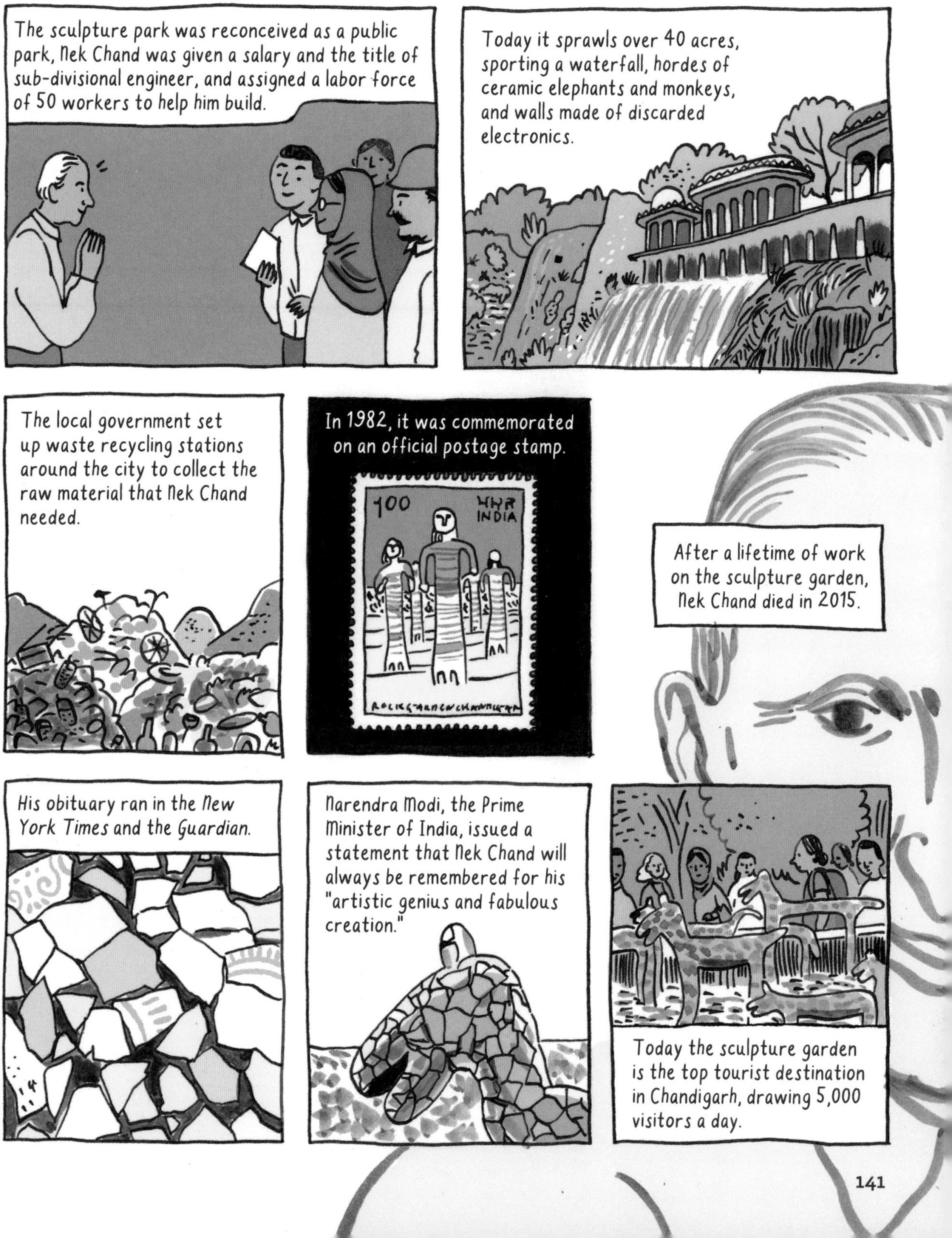

The sculpture park was reconceived as a public park, Nek Chand was given a salary and the title of sub-divisional engineer, and assigned a labor force of 50 workers to help him build.

Today it sprawls over 40 acres, sporting a waterfall, hordes of ceramic elephants and monkeys, and walls made of discarded electronics.

The local government set up waste recycling stations around the city to collect the raw material that Nek Chand needed.

In 1982, it was commemorated on an official postage stamp.

After a lifetime of work on the sculpture garden, Nek Chand died in 2015.

His obituary ran in the New York Times and the Guardian.

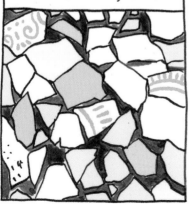

Narendra Modi, the Prime Minister of India, issued a statement that Nek Chand will always be remembered for his "artistic genius and fabulous creation."

Today the sculpture garden is the top tourist destination in Chandigarh, drawing 5,000 visitors a day.

141

V

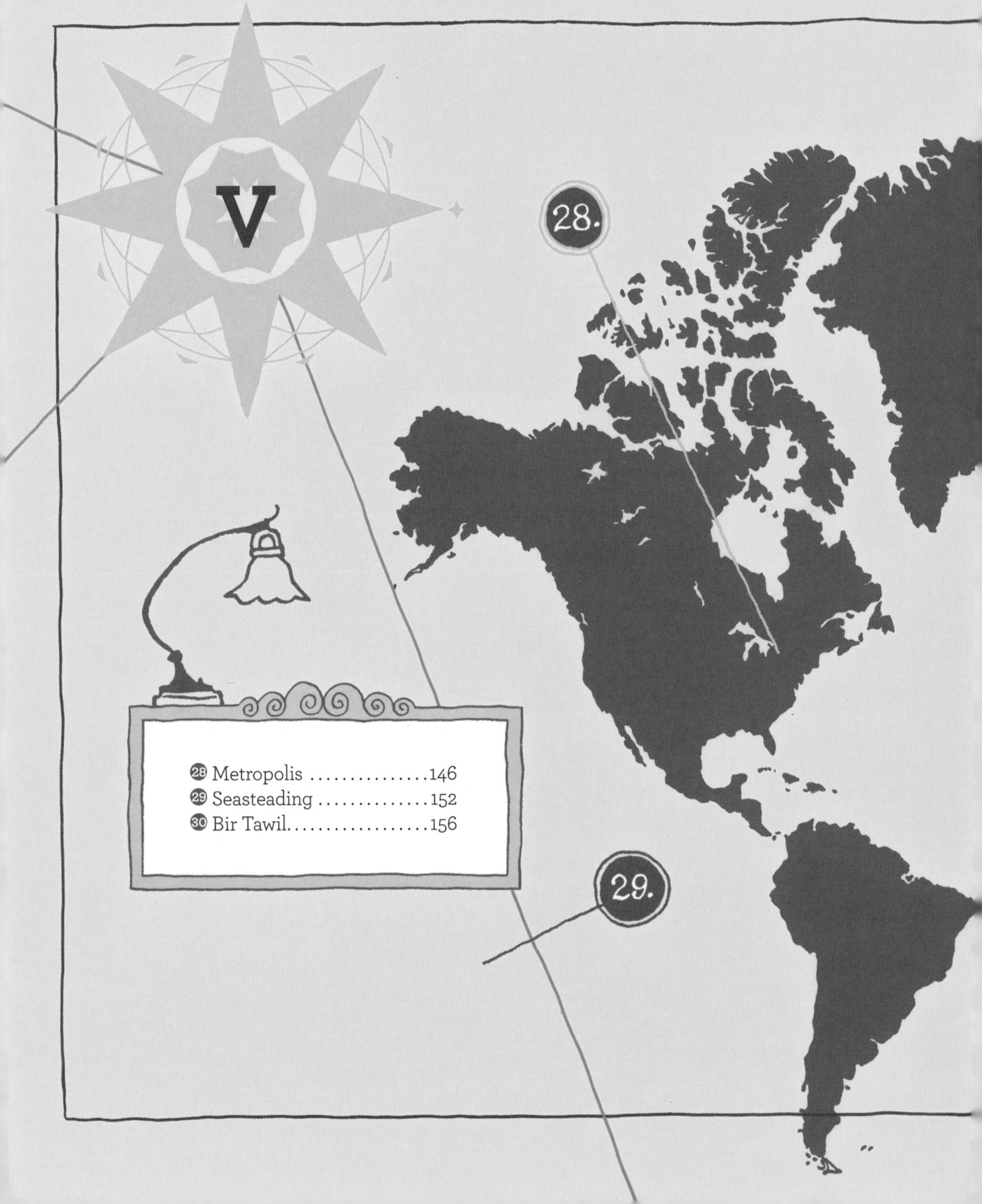
28.
29.

Strange Dreams

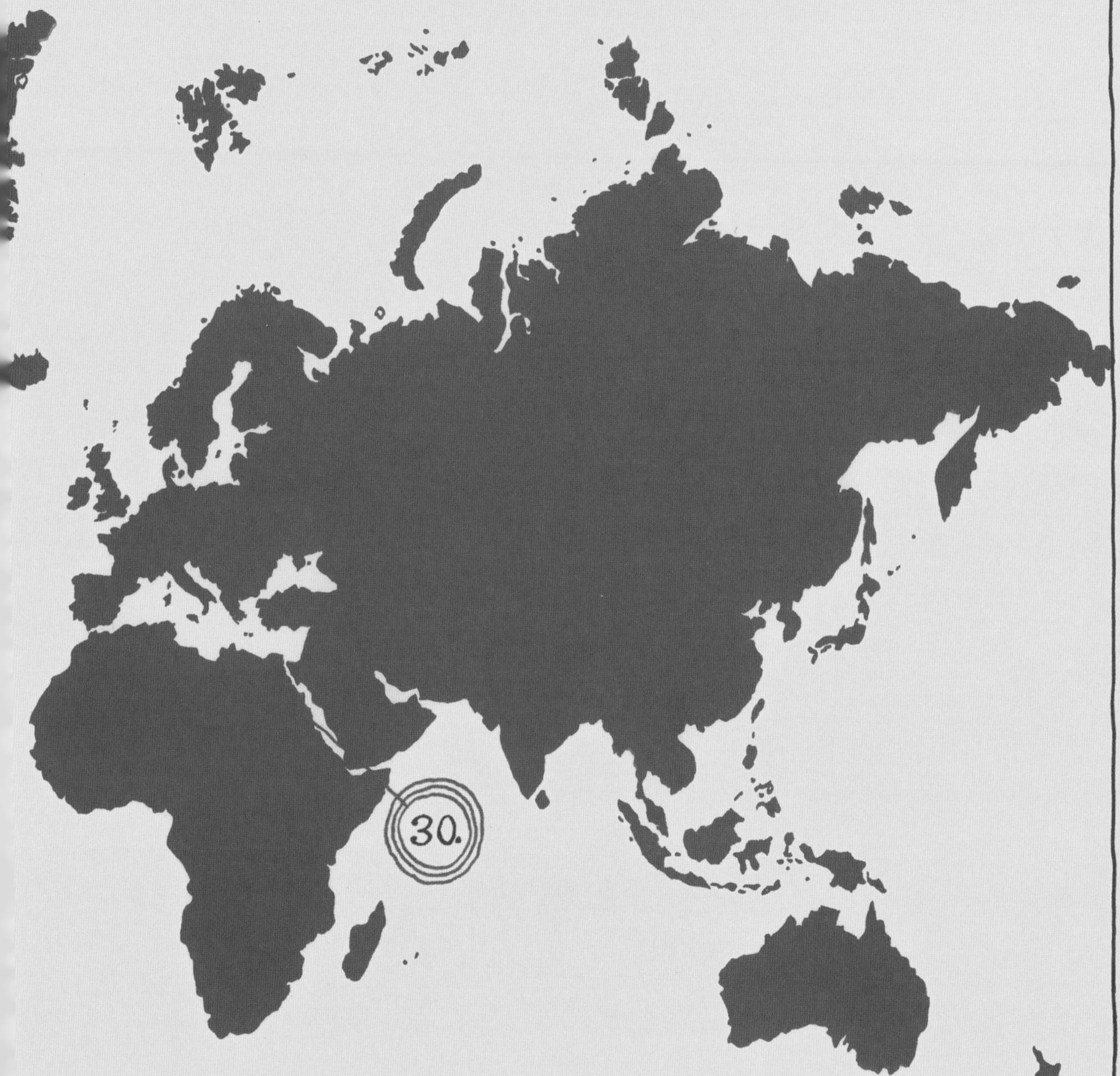
30.

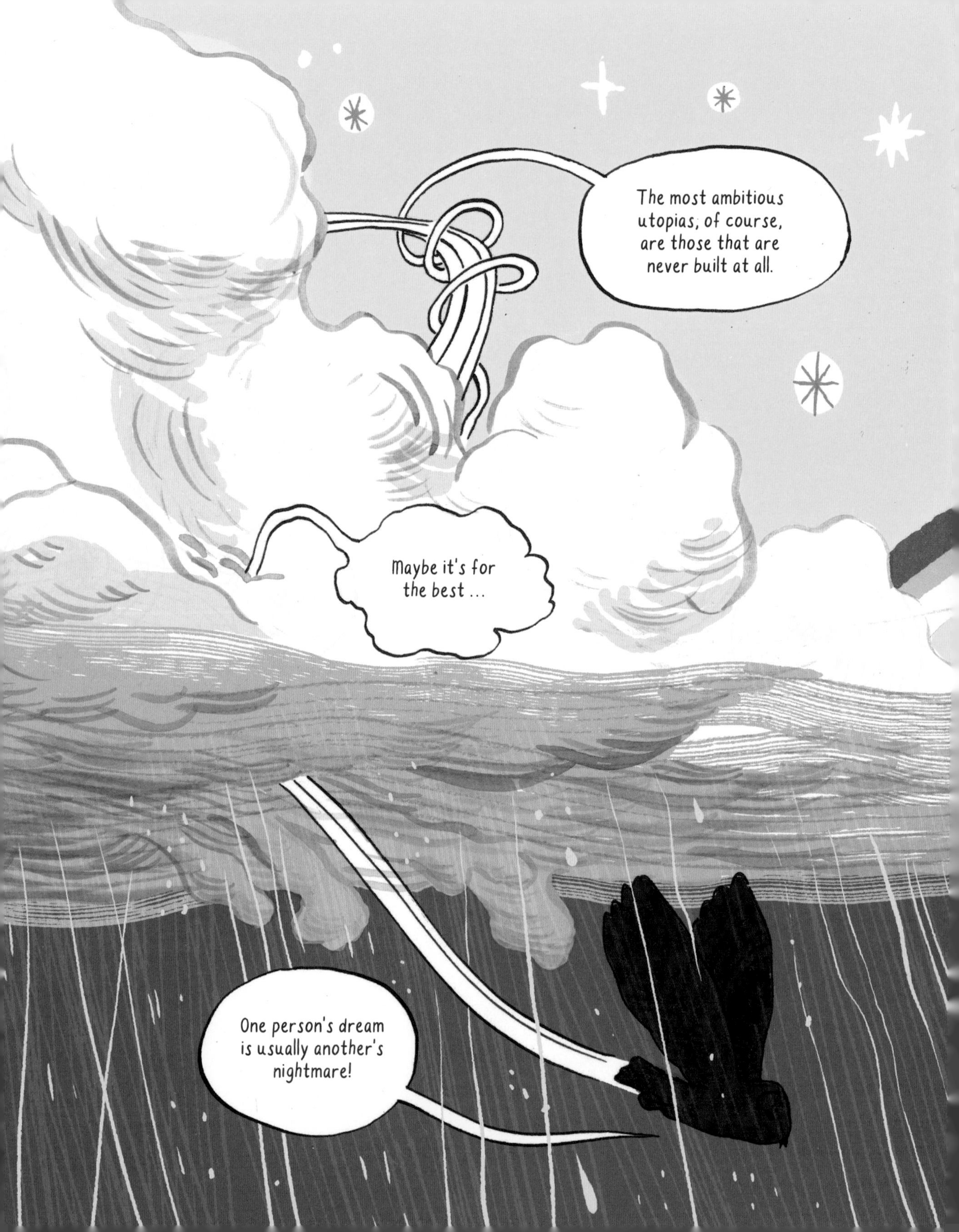
The most ambitious utopias, of course, are those that are never built at all.
Maybe it's for the best ...
One person's dream is usually another's nightmare!

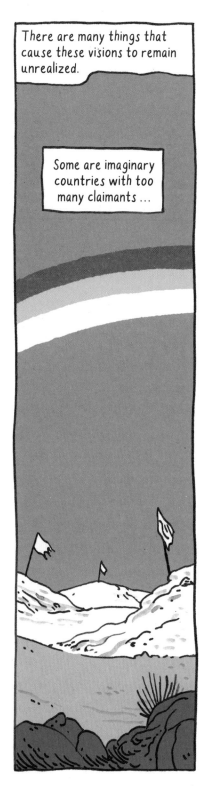

There are many things that cause these visions to remain unrealized.

Some are imaginary countries with too many claimants ...

... while others reach so high that they transcend reality itself ...

The ambition that underpins each one shimmers ...

... but ultimately it is a mirage.

Metropolis

A fortune made from safety razors at the turn of the 20th century was not enough to make a radical vision of a better future come true.
BLUE
Gillette
BLADES
King C Gillette
Patented Nov. 15, 1804

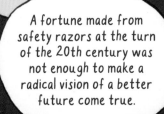

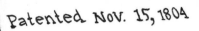

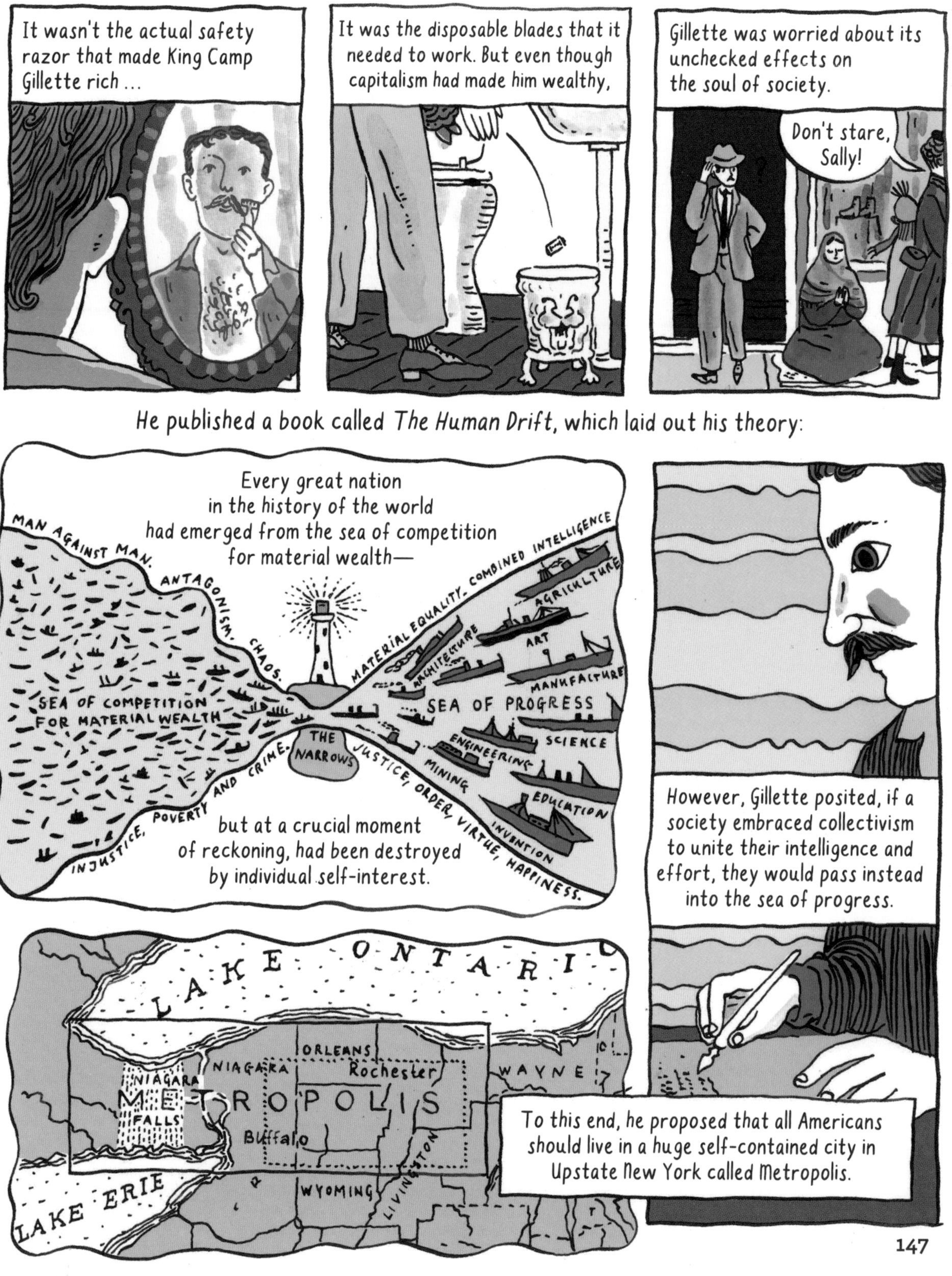
It wasn't the actual safety razor that made King Camp Gillette rich ...
It was the disposable blades that it needed to work. But even though capitalism had made him wealthy,
Gillette was worried about its unchecked effects on the soul of society.
Don't stare, Sally!
He published a book called *The Human Drift*, which laid out his theory:
Every great nation in the history of the world had emerged from the sea of competition for material wealth—
MAN AGAINST MAN. ANTAGONISM. CHAOS.
SEA OF COMPETITION FOR MATERIAL WEALTH
INJUSTICE, POVERTY AND CRIME.
THE NARROWS
MATERIAL EQUALITY. COMBINED INTELLIGENCE
AGRICULTURE
ARCHITECTURE
ART
MANUFACTURE
SEA OF PROGRESS
SCIENCE
ENGINEERING
MINING
EDUCATION
INVENTION
JUSTICE, ORDER, VIRTUE, HAPPINESS.
but at a crucial moment of reckoning, had been destroyed by individual self-interest.
However, Gillette posited, if a society embraced collectivism to unite their intelligence and effort, they would pass instead into the sea of progress.
LAKE ONTARI
ORLEANS
NIAGARA
Rochester
WAYNE
NIAGARA
METROPOLIS
FALLS
Buffalo
LIVINGSTON
WYOMING
LAKE ERIE
To this end, he proposed that all Americans should live in a huge self-contained city in Upstate New York called Metropolis.

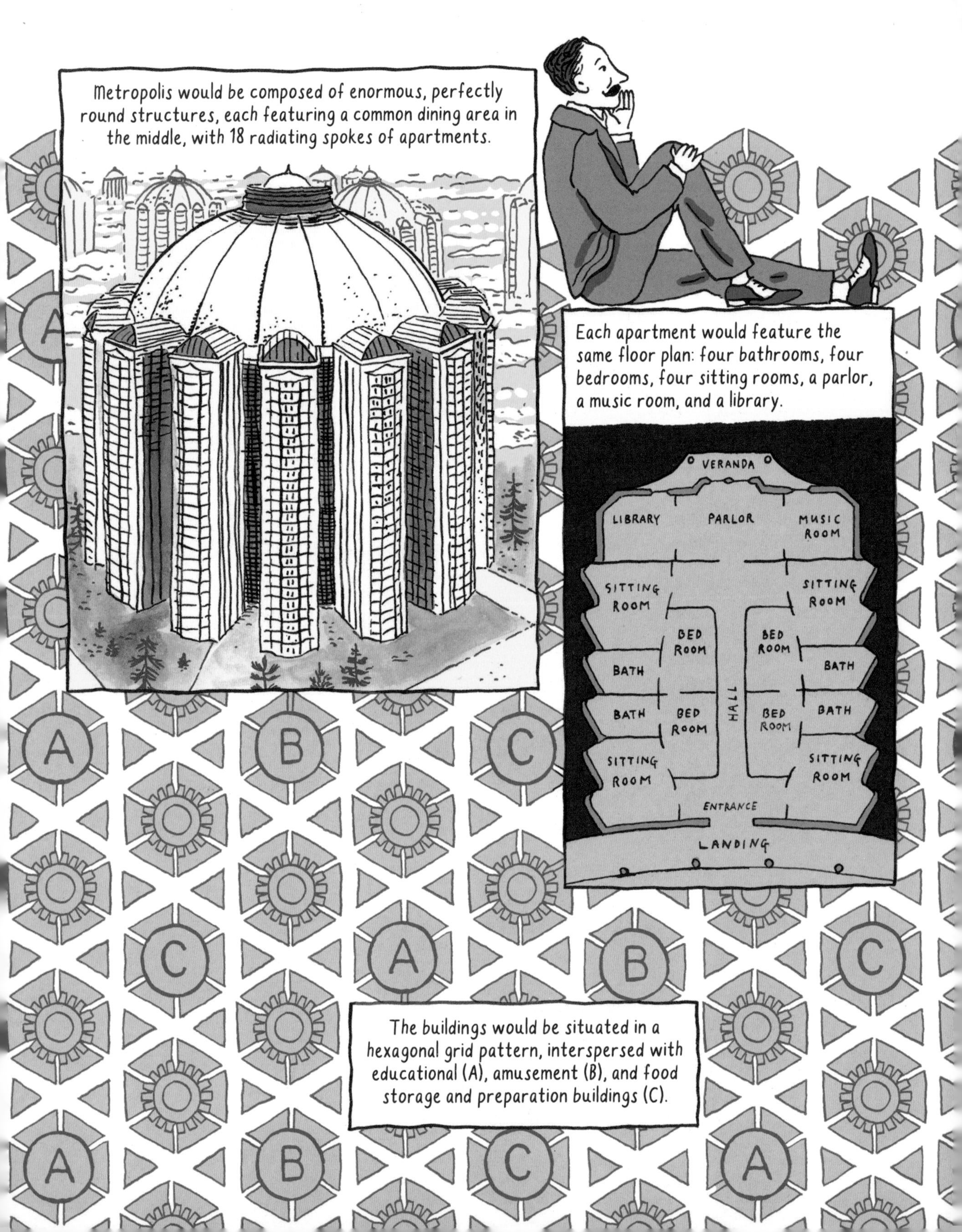
Metropolis would be composed of enormous, perfectly round structures, each featuring a common dining area in the middle, with 18 radiating spokes of apartments.
Each apartment would feature the same floor plan: four bathrooms, four bedrooms, four sitting rooms, a parlor, a music room, and a library.
VERANDA
LIBRARY
PARLOR
MUSIC ROOM
SITTING ROOM
SITTING ROOM
BED ROOM
BED ROOM
BATH
BATH
BATH
BATH
HALL
BED ROOM
BED ROOM
SITTING ROOM
SITTING ROOM
ENTRANCE
LANDING
The buildings would be situated in a hexagonal grid pattern, interspersed with educational (A), amusement (B), and food storage and preparation buildings (C).

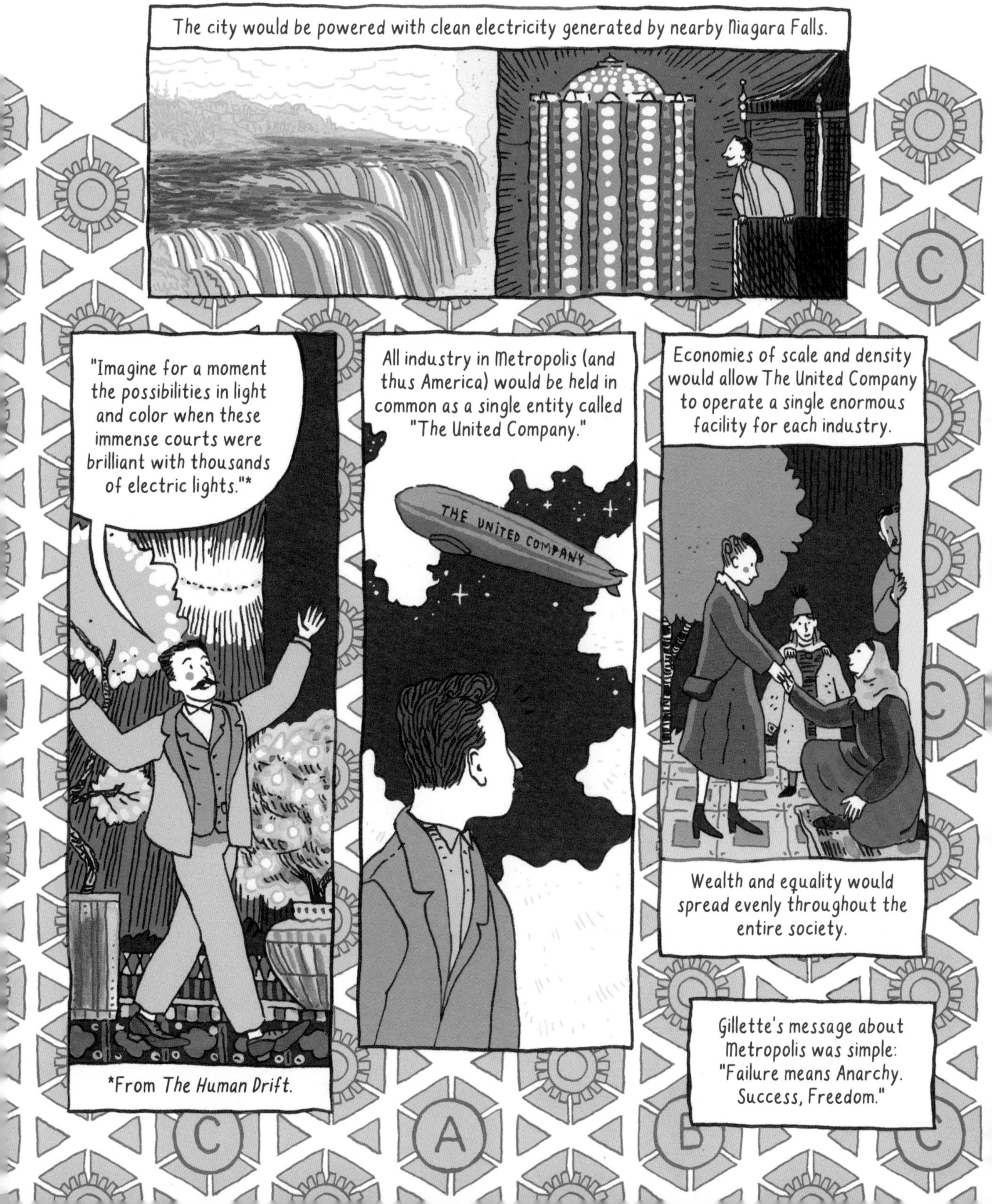
The city would be powered with clean electricity generated by nearby Niagara Falls.
"Imagine for a moment the possibilities in light and color when these immense courts were brilliant with thousands of electric lights."*
*From *The Human Drift*.
All industry in Metropolis (and thus America) would be held in common as a single entity called "The United Company."
THE UNITED COMPANY
Economies of scale and density would allow The United Company to operate a single enormous facility for each industry.
Wealth and equality would spread evenly throughout the entire society.
Gillette's message about Metropolis was simple: "Failure means Anarchy. Success, Freedom."

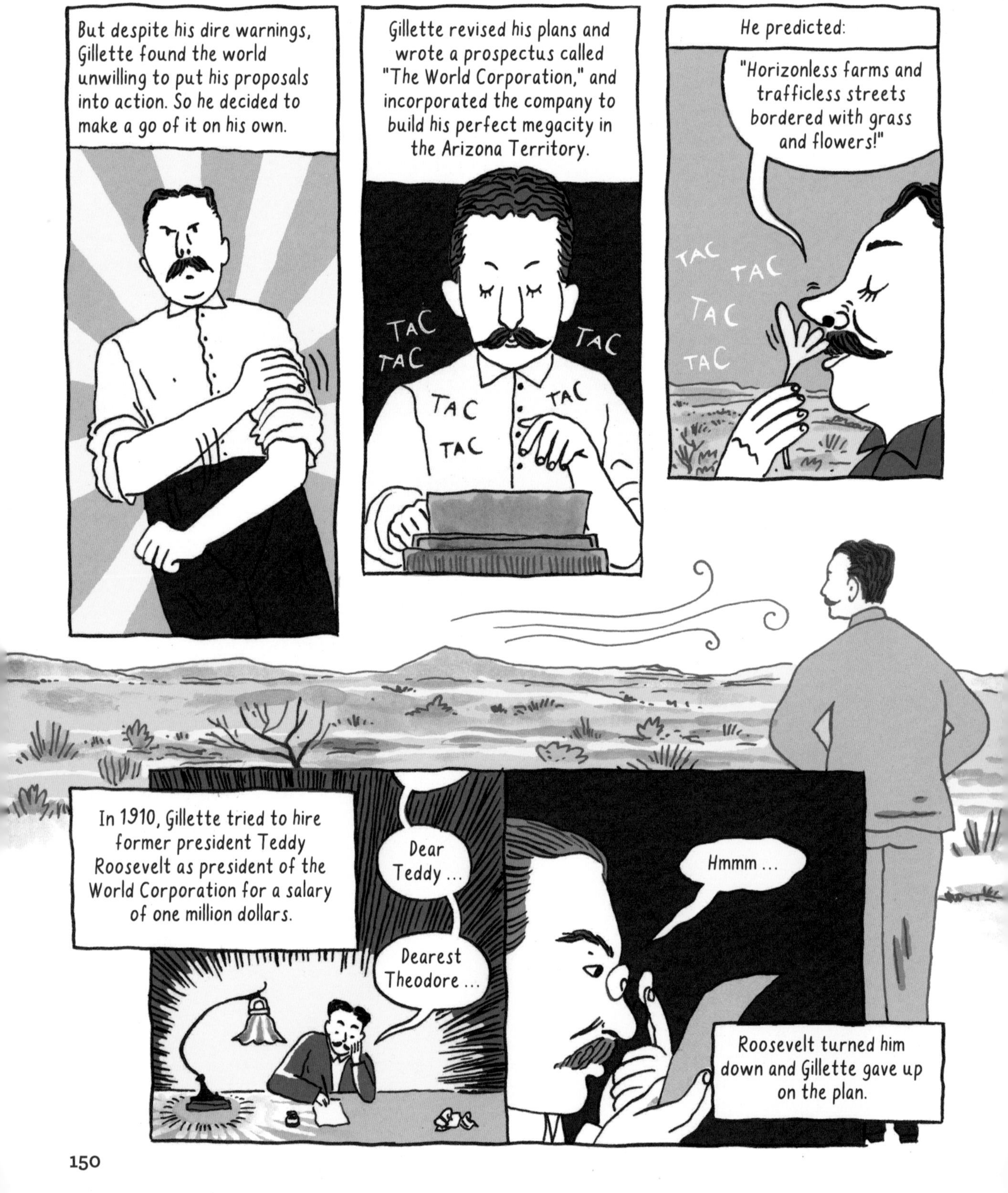
But despite his dire warnings, Gillette found the world unwilling to put his proposals into action. So he decided to make a go of it on his own.
Gillette revised his plans and wrote a prospectus called "The World Corporation," and incorporated the company to build his perfect megacity in the Arizona Territory.
TAC
TAC
TAC
TAC
TAC
TAC
He predicted:
"Horizonless farms and trafficless streets bordered with grass and flowers!"
TAC
TAC
TAC
TAC
In 1910, Gillette tried to hire former president Teddy Roosevelt as president of the World Corporation for a salary of one million dollars.
Dear Teddy ...
Dearest Theodore ...
Hmmm ...
Roosevelt turned him down and Gillette gave up on the plan.

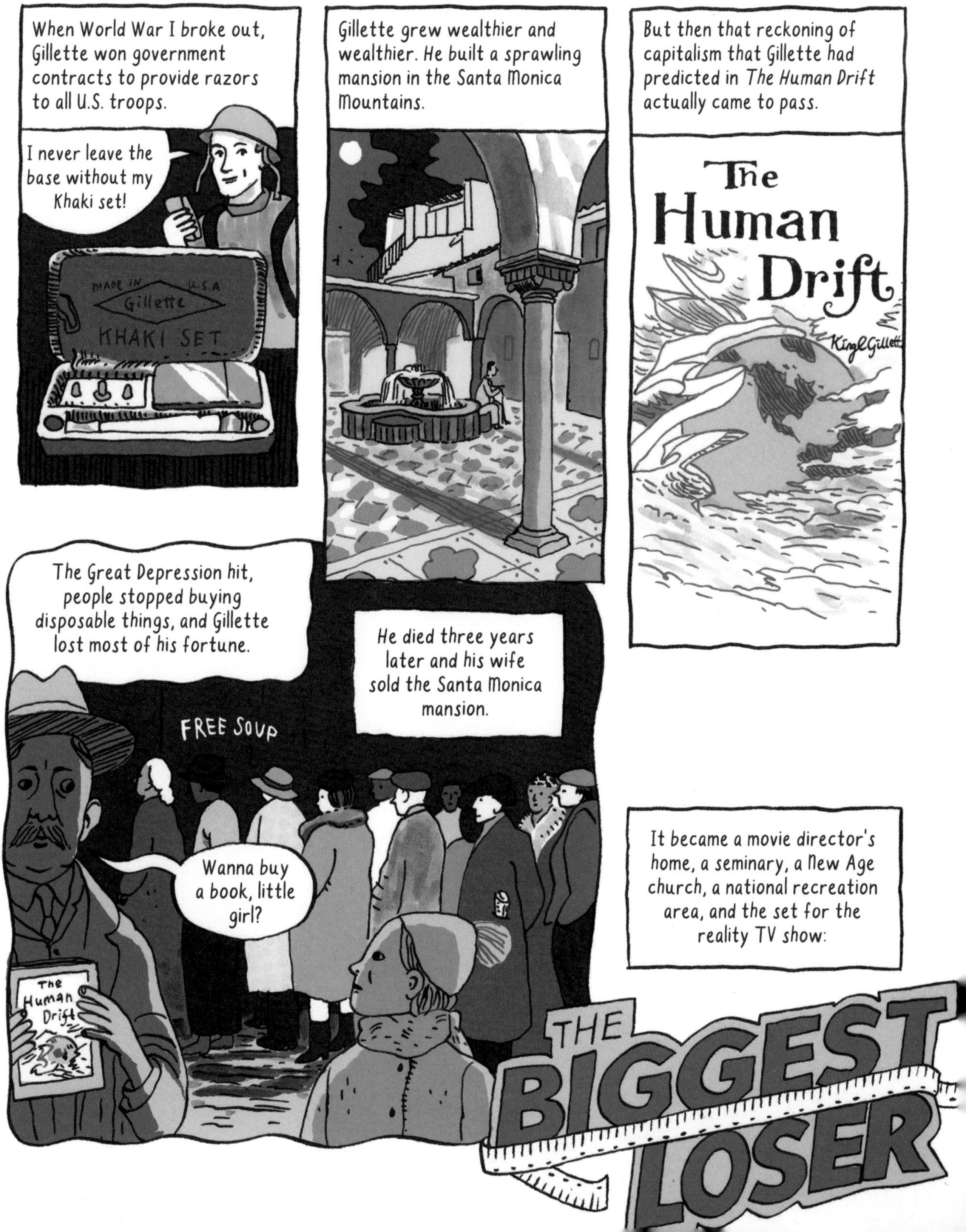

When World War I broke out, Gillette won government contracts to provide razors to all U.S. troops.
I never leave the base without my Khaki set!
MADE IN U.S.A Gillette KHAKI SET
Gillette grew wealthier and wealthier. He built a sprawling mansion in the Santa Monica Mountains.
But then that reckoning of capitalism that Gillette had predicted in *The Human Drift* actually came to pass.
The Human Drift
The Great Depression hit, people stopped buying disposable things, and Gillette lost most of his fortune.
He died three years later and his wife sold the Santa Monica mansion.
FREE SOUP
Wanna buy a book, little girl?
The Human Drift
It became a movie director's home, a seminary, a New Age church, a national recreation area, and the set for the reality TV show:
THE BIGGEST LOSER

Seasteading

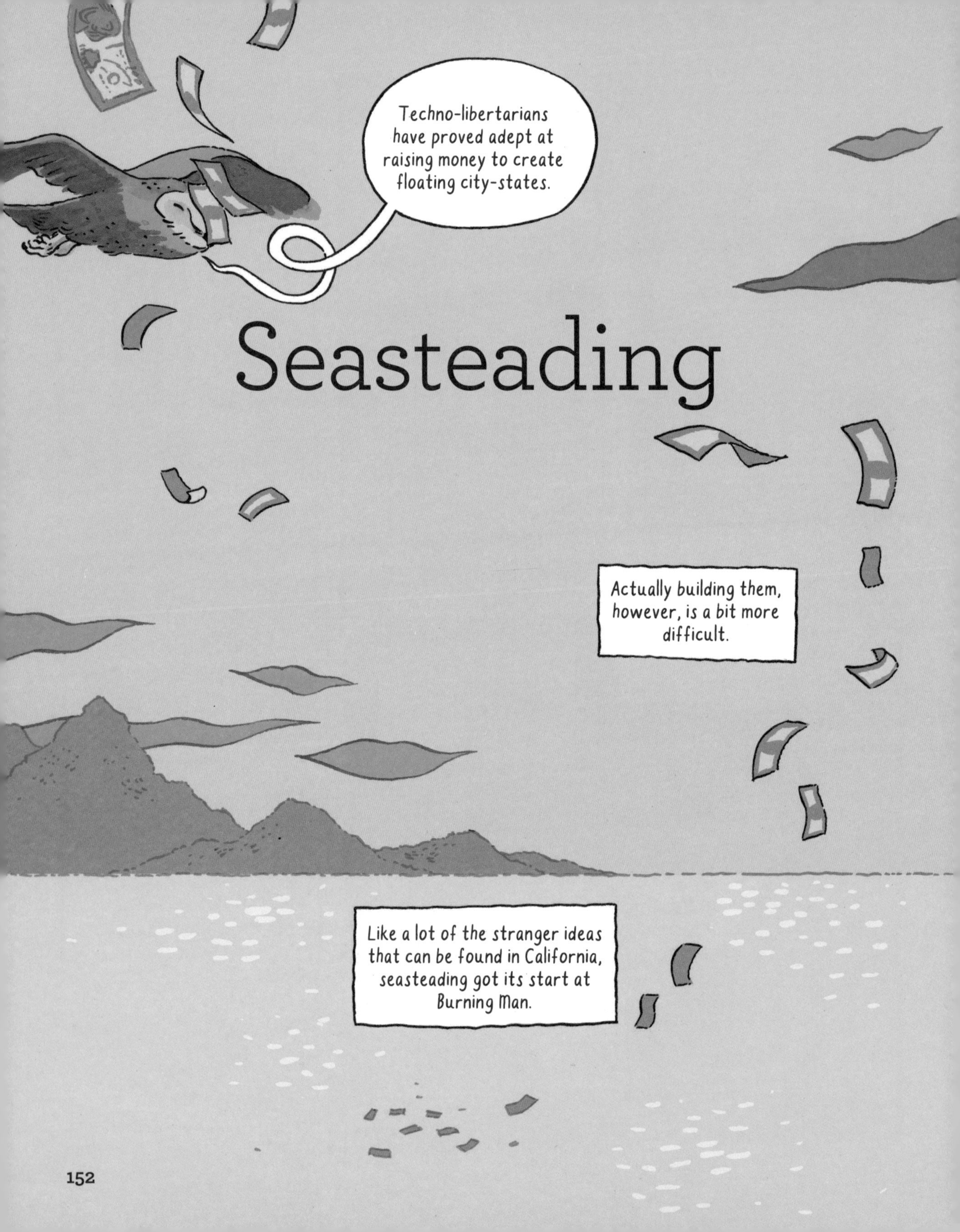
Techno-libertarians have proved adept at raising money to create floating city-states.
Actually building them, however, is a bit more difficult.
Like a lot of the stranger ideas that can be found in California, seasteading got its start at Burning Man.

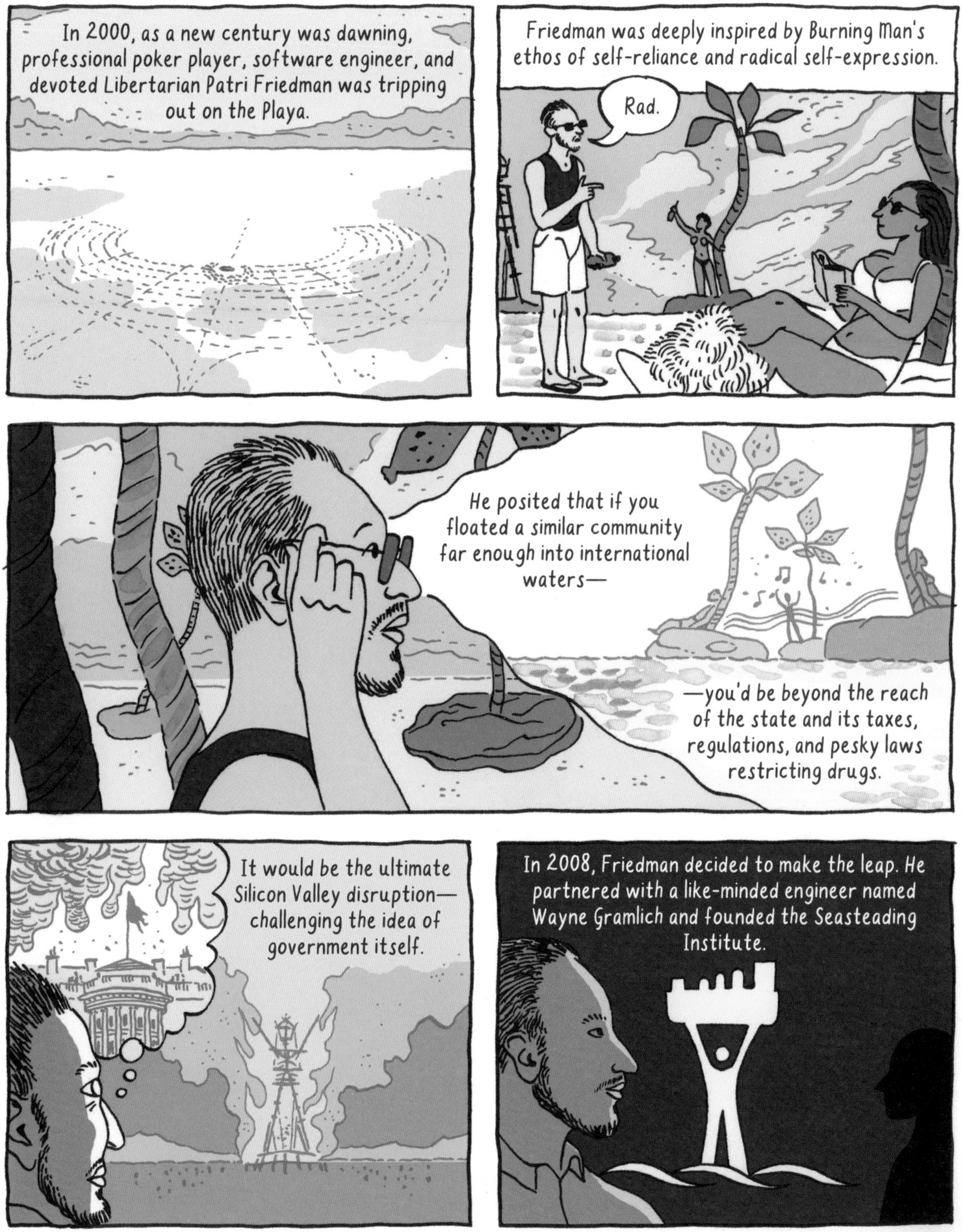
In 2000, as a new century was dawning, professional poker player, software engineer, and devoted Libertarian Patri Friedman was tripping out on the Playa.
Friedman was deeply inspired by Burning Man's ethos of self-reliance and radical self-expression.
Rad.
He posited that if you floated a similar community far enough into international waters—
—you'd be beyond the reach of the state and its taxes, regulations, and pesky laws restricting drugs.
It would be the ultimate Silicon Valley disruption—challenging the idea of government itself.
In 2008, Friedman decided to make the leap. He partnered with a like-minded engineer named Wayne Gramlich and founded the Seasteading Institute.

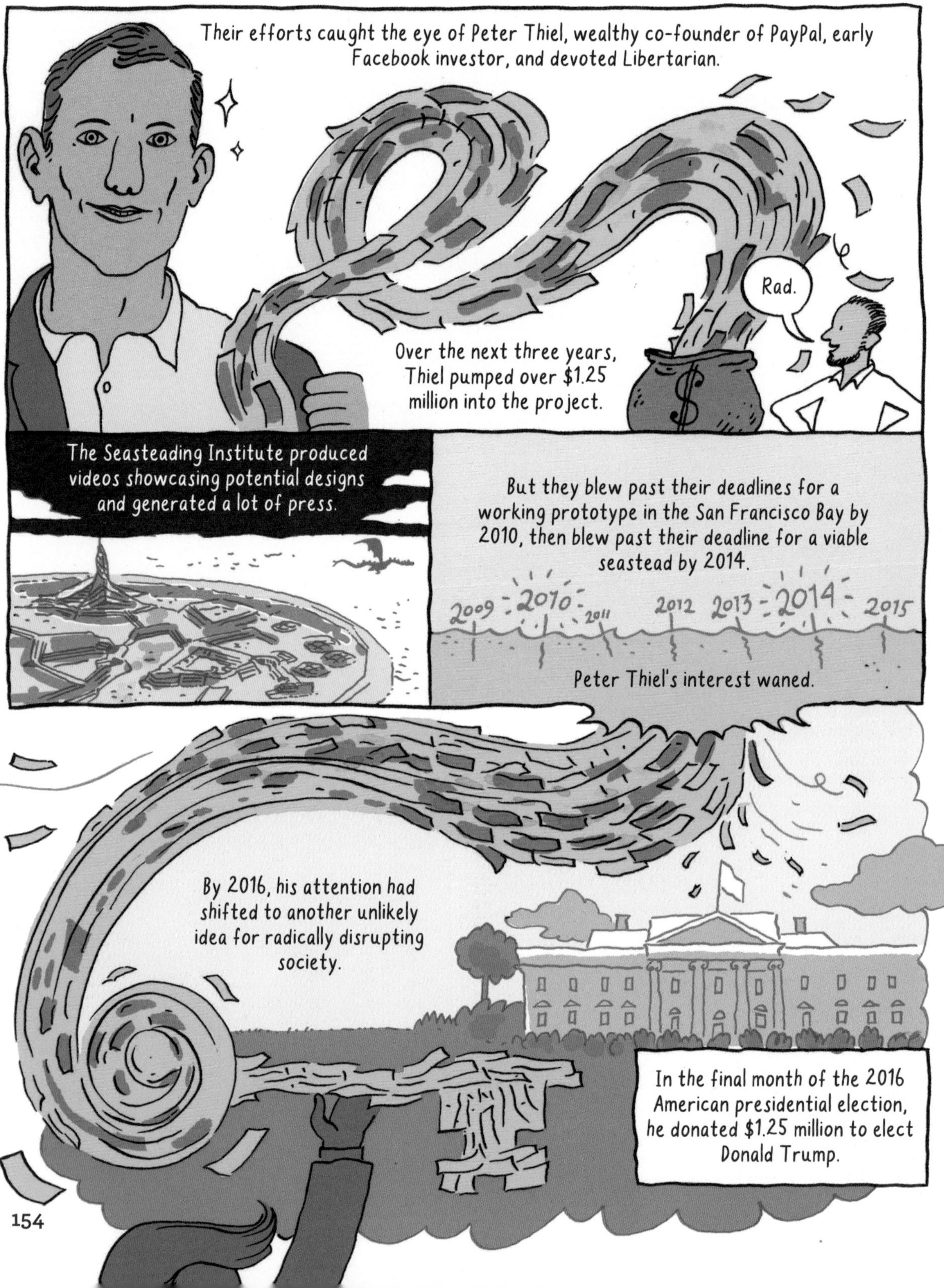
Their efforts caught the eye of Peter Thiel, wealthy co-founder of PayPal, early Facebook investor, and devoted Libertarian.
Rad.
Over the next three years, Thiel pumped over $1.25 million into the project.
The Seasteading Institute produced videos showcasing potential designs and generated a lot of press.
But they blew past their deadlines for a working prototype in the San Francisco Bay by 2010, then blew past their deadline for a viable seastead by 2014.
2009 2010 2011 2012 2013 2014 2015
Peter Thiel's interest waned.
By 2016, his attention had shifted to another unlikely idea for radically disrupting society.
In the final month of the 2016 American presidential election, he donated $1.25 million to elect Donald Trump.

Shrugging off the abandonment of their deep-pocketed benefactor, the Seasteading Institute continued their work.

UNTS UNTS UNTS UNTS UNTS

They founded an annual festival in the Sacramento Delta named Ephemerisle, which has been described as "Burning Man on the water."

In 2017, the Seasteading Institute struck a deal with the government of French Polynesia to establish a pilot model in a lagoon near Tahiti.

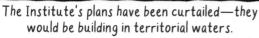

The Institute's plans have been curtailed—they would be building in territorial waters.

But French Polynesia has granted the seastead the status of:

INNOVATIVE SPECIAL ECONOMIC ZONE

The legal meaning of this is unclear.

They plan to build only a few dozen residences on a floating platform.

Cost estimates range between $10 and $50 million. It is currently unclear where the funding will come from.

Bir Tawil

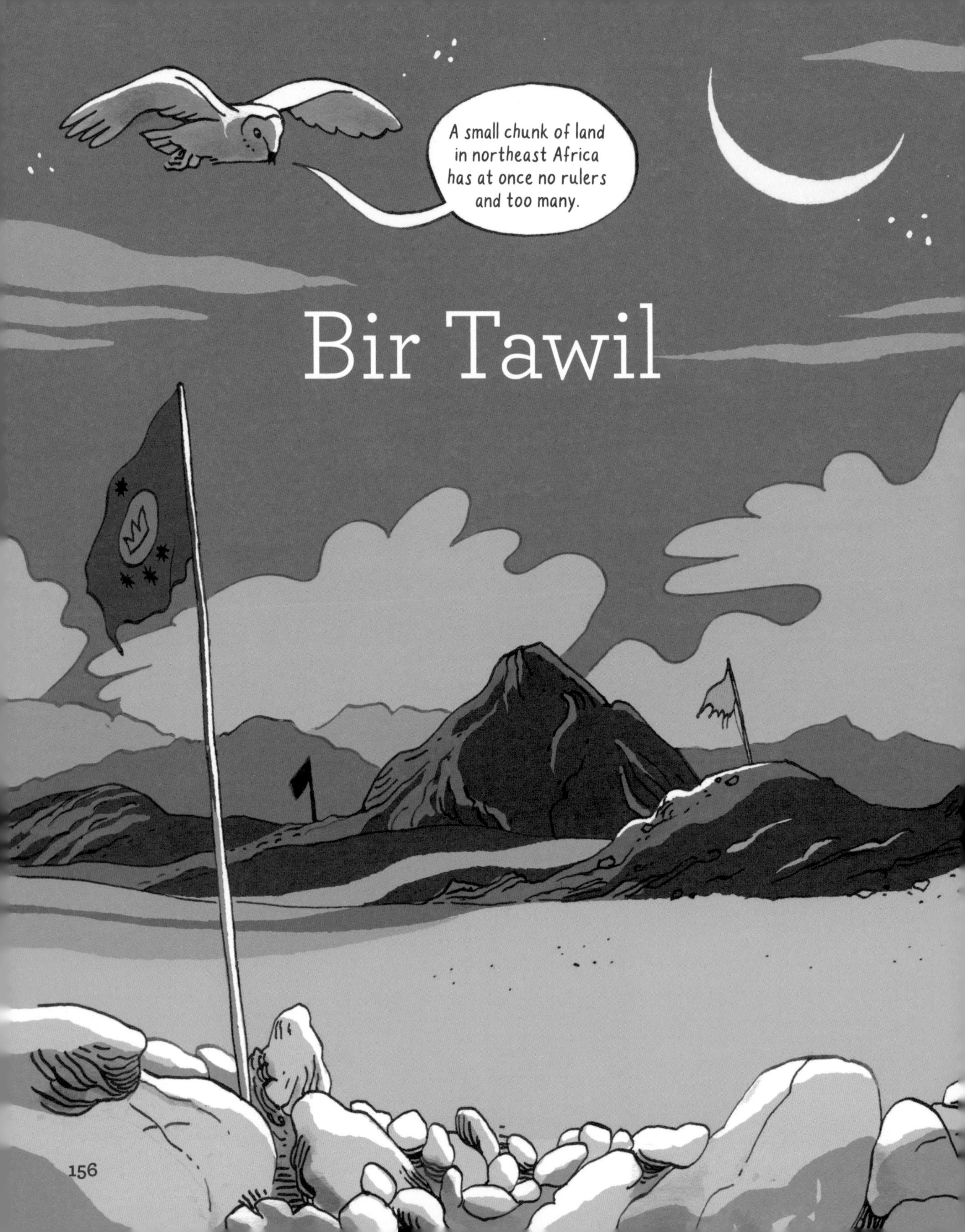
A small chunk of land in northeast Africa has at once no rulers and too many.

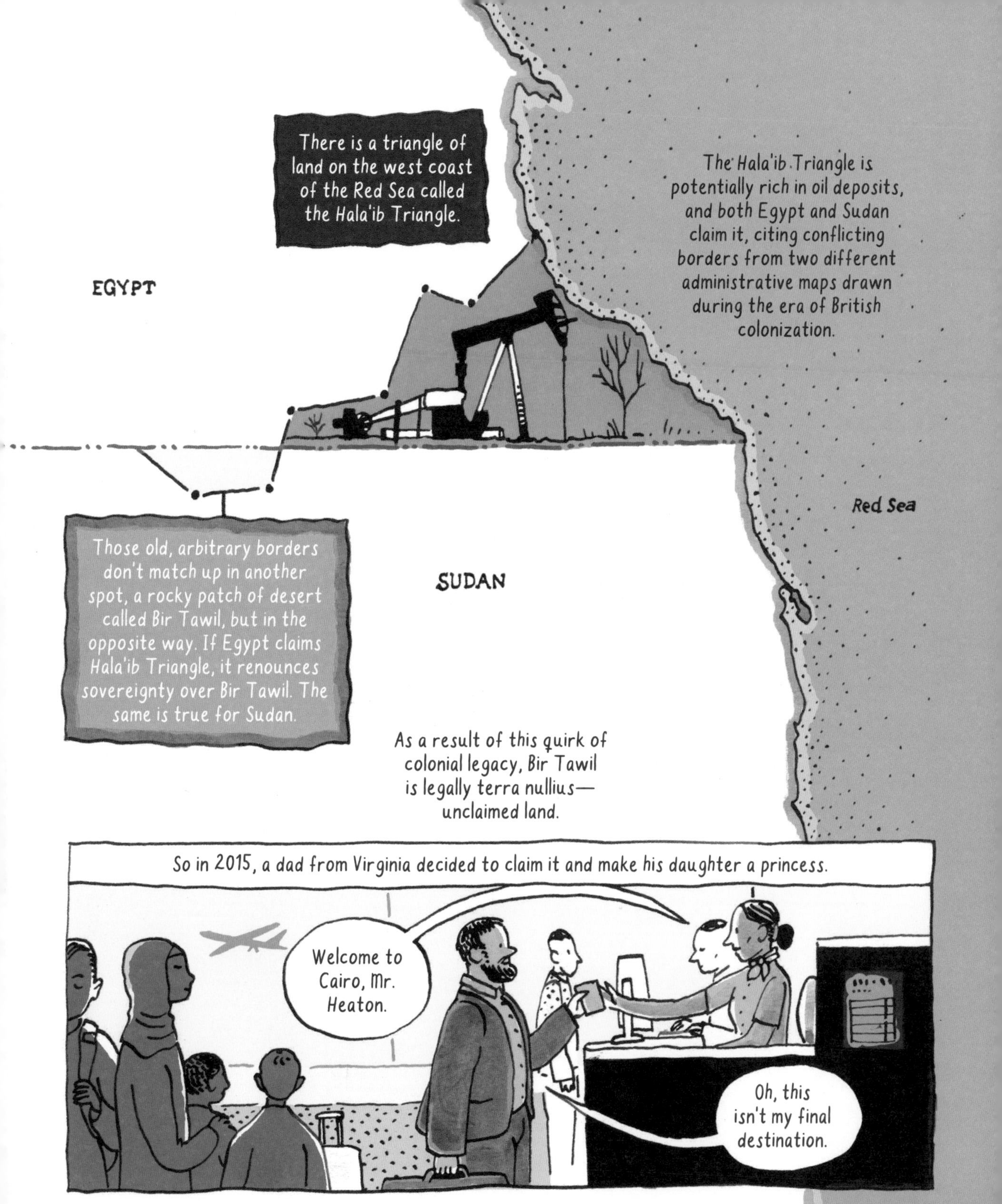
There is a triangle of land on the west coast of the Red Sea called the Hala'ib Triangle.
The Hala'ib Triangle is potentially rich in oil deposits, and both Egypt and Sudan claim it, citing conflicting borders from two different administrative maps drawn during the era of British colonization.
EGYPT
Those old, arbitrary borders don't match up in another spot, a rocky patch of desert called Bir Tawil, but in the opposite way. If Egypt claims Hala'ib Triangle, it renounces sovereignty over Bir Tawil. The same is true for Sudan.
SUDAN
Red Sea
As a result of this quirk of colonial legacy, Bir Tawil is legally terra nullius—unclaimed land.
So in 2015, a dad from Virginia decided to claim it and make his daughter a princess.
Welcome to Cairo, Mr. Heaton.
Oh, this isn't my final destination.

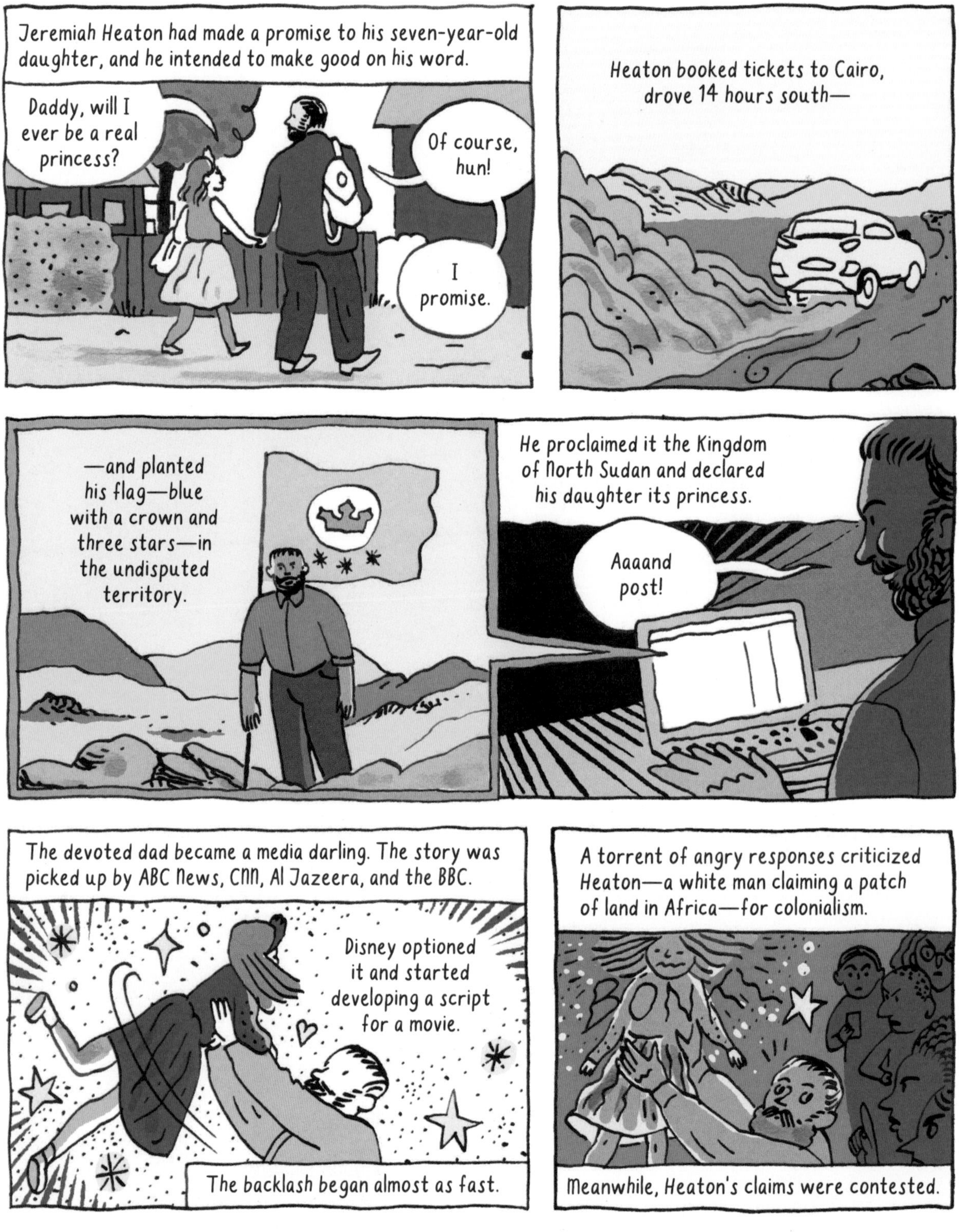
Jeremiah Heaton had made a promise to his seven-year-old daughter, and he intended to make good on his word.
Daddy, will I ever be a real princess?
Of course, hun!
I promise.
Heaton booked tickets to Cairo, drove 14 hours south—
—and planted his flag—blue with a crown and three stars—in the undisputed territory.
He proclaimed it the Kingdom of North Sudan and declared his daughter its princess.
Aaaand post!
The devoted dad became a media darling. The story was picked up by ABC News, CNN, Al Jazeera, and the BBC.
Disney optioned it and started developing a script for a movie.
The backlash began almost as fast.
A torrent of angry responses criticized Heaton—a white man claiming a patch of land in Africa—for colonialism.
BOO
Meanwhile, Heaton's claims were contested.

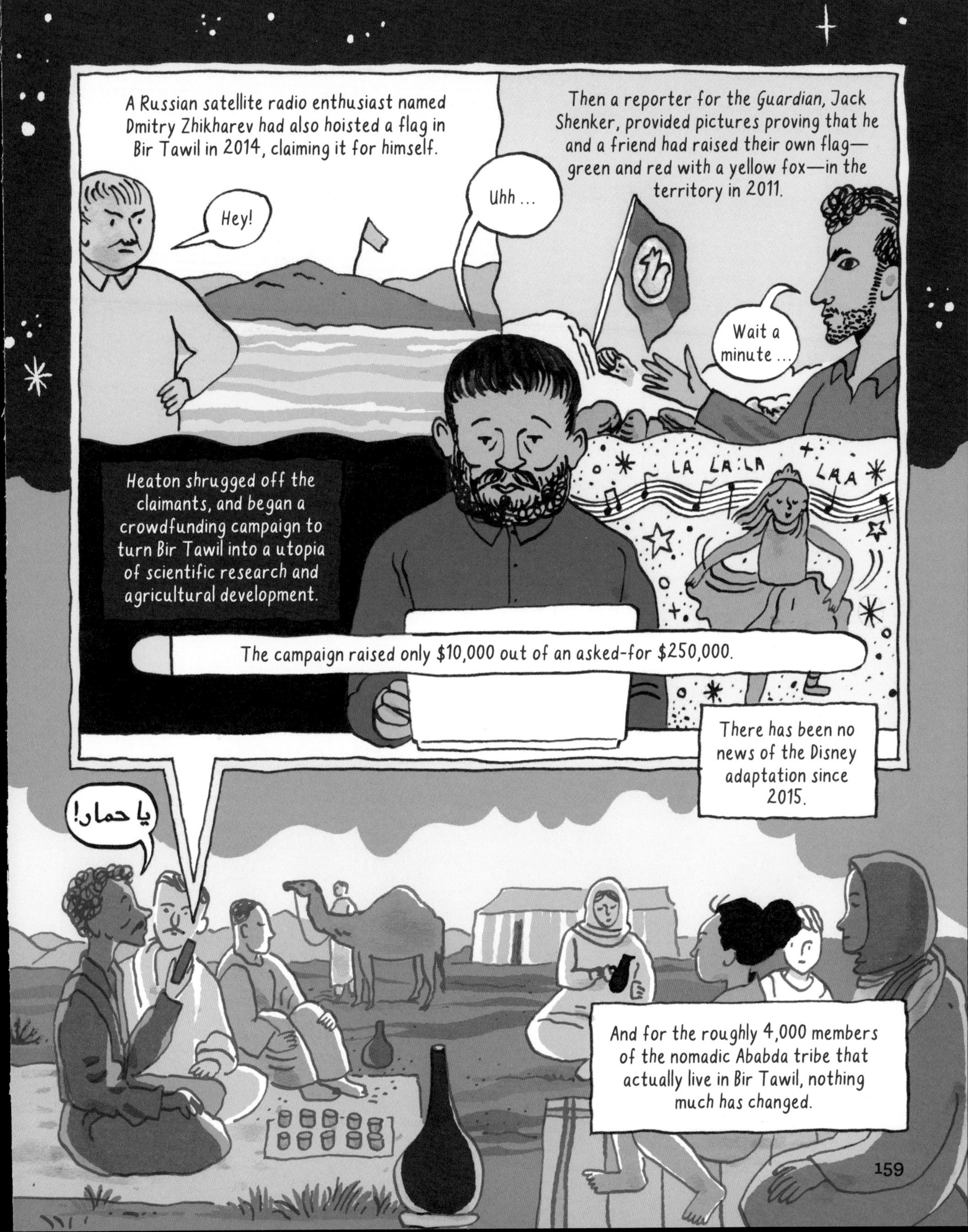
A Russian satellite radio enthusiast named Dmitry Zhikharev had also hoisted a flag in Bir Tawil in 2014, claiming it for himself.
Hey!
Uhh …
Then a reporter for the *Guardian*, Jack Shenker, provided pictures proving that he and a friend had raised their own flag—green and red with a yellow fox—in the territory in 2011.
Wait a minute …
Heaton shrugged off the claimants, and began a crowdfunding campaign to turn Bir Tawil into a utopia of scientific research and agricultural development.
LA LA LA LAA
The campaign raised only $10,000 out of an asked-for $250,000.
There has been no news of the Disney adaptation since 2015.
!يا حمار
And for the roughly 4,000 members of the nomadic Ababda tribe that actually live in Bir Tawil, nothing much has changed.

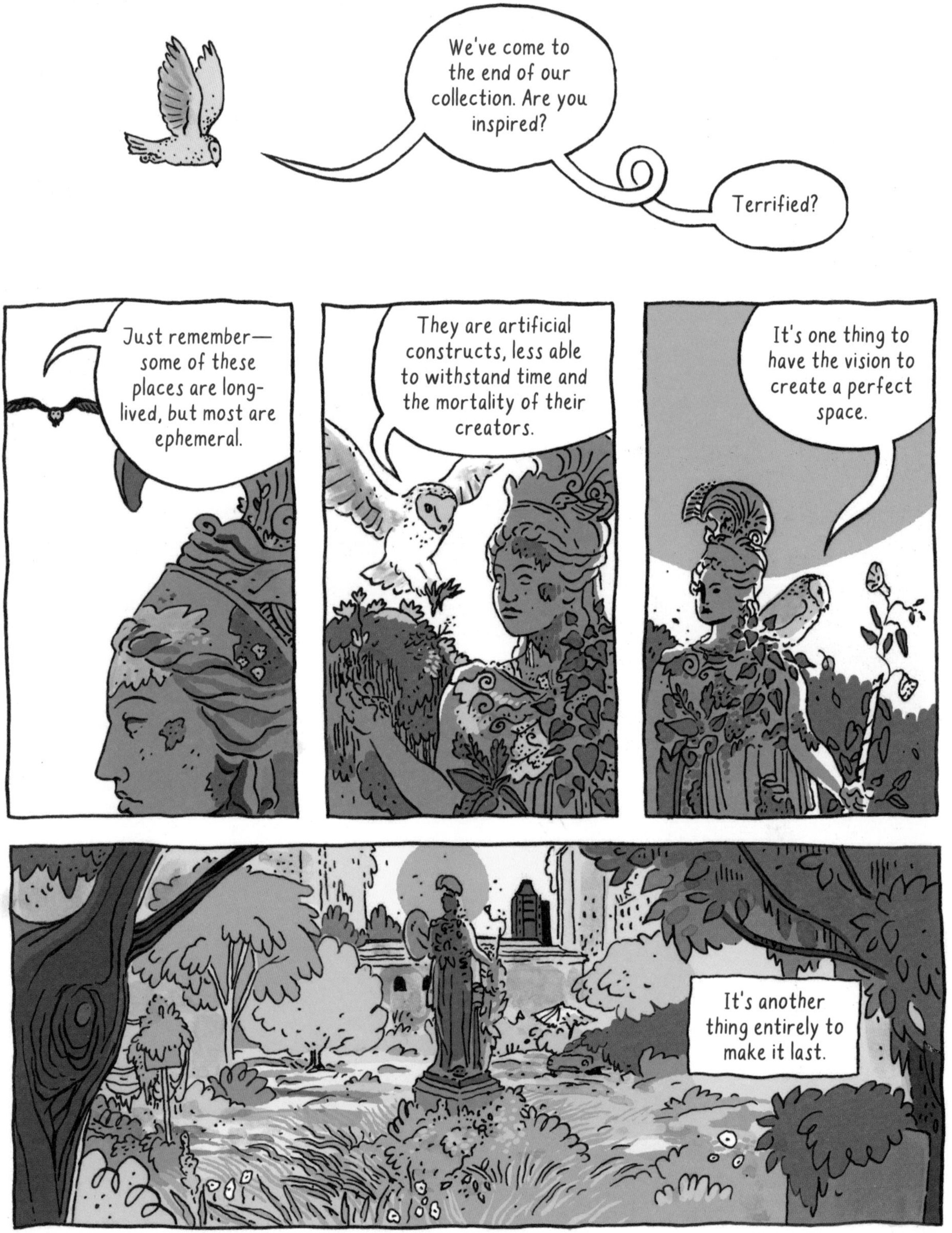
We've come to the end of our collection. Are you inspired?
Terrified?
Just remember—some of these places are long-lived, but most are ephemeral.
They are artificial constructs, less able to withstand time and the mortality of their creators.
It's one thing to have the vision to create a perfect space.
It's another thing entirely to make it last.